D1140576

THE EVOLUTION OF POLITICAL PROTEST
AND THE WORKINGMEN'S PARTY
OF CALIFORNIA

The Evolution of Political Protest and the Workingmen's Party of California

·—·

NEIL LARRY SHUMSKY

Ohio State University Press

COLUMBUS

JK
2391
,W73
S267
1991

Library of Congress Cataloging-in-Publication Data

Shumsky, Neil L., 1944–
    The evolution of political protest and the Workingmen's Party of
California / Neil Larry Shumsky.
        p.   cm.
    Includes bibliographical references and index.
    ISBN 0–8142–0551–8 (alk. paper)
    1. Workingmen's Party of California—History—19th century.
2. San Francisco (Calif.)—Politics and government.   3. Riots—
California—San Francisco—History—19th century.   4. Crowds.
I. Title.
JK2391.W73S267   1991
324.2794'07—dc20   91–17096
                                                                  CIP

Text and jacket design by Jim Mennick.
Type set in Goudy Old Style by G&S Typesetters, Austin, TX.
Printed by Cushing-Malloy, Ann Arbor, MI.

Printed in the U.S.A.

9 8 7 6 5 4 3 2 1

To Marcia
—Who has taught me more
and who has given me more
than all the others

Contents

Tables

Acknowledgments

Every historian piles up debts that can never be adequately repaid, and I am no exception. I hope that everyone who has helped me will accept my thanks and realize how much I appreciate what they have done.

There are a few individuals and institutions whose assistance deserves special recognition, and to whom I feel especially grateful. At the University of California, I received financial assistance from the History Department, the Institute for International Studies, and the Chancellor's Patent Fund. At Virginia Polytechnic Institute and State University, I have had support from the History Department and the College of Arts and Sciences. Without their generosity and support over the years, I could never have written this book.

No one except other historians can understand the extent of our dependence on librarians, and mine has been greater than most. The staffs at the California State Library in Sacramento, the San Francisco Public Library, Syracuse University Library, Stanford University Library, Huntington Library, and California Historical Society Library have all given of themselves beyond any reasonable expectations. Everyone at the Newman Library at VPI & SU has given me the benefit of his or her knowledge and ability without reservation, and I would especially like to thank the Humanities Division and the Interlibrary Loan service. There is no way for me to express my feelings about the entire staff of the Bancroft Library at the University of California. Over the years, they have increased the pleasures of doing research and reduced the drudgeries. To Vivian Fisher, Suzanne Gallup, Peter Hanff, Pat Howard, Irene Moran, Bill Roberts, and especially the late J. B. Tompkins, I can't possibly express my appreciation.

A number of friends, colleagues, and teachers have encouraged me at every step of this project and have given me their time, effort, knowledge, and support to a much greater degree than I had any right to ask. I hope that I have expressed my feelings to each of them personally and in a way that lets them know how much I value them. Linda Arnold spent hours teaching me the joys (?) of modern technology, and the process of writing, revising, and rewriting would have been infinitely more tedious without her help. Tom Dunlap, Louise Hoffman, Susan Miller, Bill Ochsenwald, and Peter Wallenstein have read various drafts of the manuscript, commented incisively on it, and improved it beyond measure. But I am most grateful for their friendship and affection. David Lux not only criticized the manuscript's contents and interpretations but also its style and writing. More than anyone else, he has persuaded me that the placement of a single word, the structure of a single sentence, can dramatically alter the effect of a thought or idea. Cyndy Bouton increased my knowledge and understanding of the "crowd," and the hours we spent discussing that phenomenon took my historical understanding to an entirely new level. Over the years, Milton Cantor has provided constant encouragement, and he frequently interrupted his own busy schedule to respond to another draft or new idea. He is the model of an eminent historian who is willing to give of himself to help a colleague. My discussions and interactions with each of these people have transformed the writing of history into a collective rather than a solitary enterprise, and I have gained tremendously from each of them, both personally and professionally.

For Gunther Barth, I have only the greatest respect, admiration, and affection. From my first day in graduate school, he has tried to help me develop into the best possible historian, and I hope that this book lives up to his expectations and justifies the time and teaching that he has given me.

To Harold Livesay I have tried to express my thanks in more personal ways, but I would like to say, once again, "Thanks for everything."

Next to last, but certainly not least, is my gratitude to Alex Holzman and the entire staff at the Ohio State University Press. Every author has heard horror stories about publishers and editors, and unfortunately some of them are true. Alex, Lynne Bonenberger, and Charlotte Dihoff have given me a different experience—doing everything possible to produce this book in a timely way that satisfies all of us, and especially me. Alex in particular has been committed to this book in a way that I will always remember and appreciate.

Finally, and most important, I want to thank my wife, Marcia, and my sons, Michael and Eric, for putting up with me. They have enriched my life in ways that transcend comment. To them, I offer not only gratitude but love.

Introduction

During the past thirty years, historians have proposed increasingly sophisticated theories to account for crowds and crowd behavior. Of necessity, the great pioneers of crowd history had to define the subject, demonstrate its significance, and rescue it from identification with the mob (and all that that identity implied). But as their colleagues accepted the concept of the crowd, those who study the history of crowds became able to ask other, more precise questions—the most important being the evolution and changing nature of the crowd. Today, the explication of crowd evolution has itself become so intricate that that question can be unraveled and its separate strands revealed. Three are especially crucial—the history of a single crowd, the development of a recurrent crowd over time, and the evolution of the crowd per se. Clearly, none of these issues is isolated, and they bear heavily on one another. In particular, the last cannot be studied without prior attention to the first two. For analytical purposes, these three issues require recognition as distinct historical questions, although they have frequently been conflated, and sometimes confused.

Studying the history of a single crowd involves asking how a particular crowd behaved and developed during its (relatively) brief existence. The task includes asking how the crowd formed and was mobilized, who joined it, who led it, and the ways its members behaved. Also, histories of a single crowd frequently treat that crowd's disappearance. When it disbanded, under what circumstances and after what achievements? If it evolved into a full-scale revolutionary movement, what conditions produced the change, and was the revolution successful?

Analyzing a recurring crowd presents a different historical problem. It means analyzing a crowd that formed and broke up more than once; the crowd always existed but was not always activated. Studying this problem forces the historian to ask related and overlapping, but nevertheless different, questions. Under what circumstances was the crowd reactivated? Did it behave differently during reincarnations than in its first appearance? How did crowd members behave between the phases of overt action? Did crowd membership and leadership differ in subsequent phases, or did the same generals command the same soldiers? How did the crowd disband after each phase, and did its denouement differ from intermediate breakups?

The last problem—the evolution of the crowd as a historical phenomenon—poses the most complex historical question, involving the attempt to formulate a general theory of crowd development. Most commonly, historians who study this problem want to know what happened to the crowd and why it disappeared. These questions presuppose the historical existence of the crowd as a normative form of behavior; crowds were a typical way of expressing opinions and making demands. But now, to a large extent, the crowd has vanished. At the very least, it no longer receives the same societal acceptance it once did. Historians frequently approach this issue within the framework of a particular model—industrialization killed the crowd. Crowds were a function of preindustrial society, and within that society, distinct kinds of crowds characterized different kinds and stages of social and economic development. By the end of the preindustrial period, the importance of the crowd had significantly declined.

This book considers all three issues—the history of a single crowd, the development of a recurring crowd, and the evolution of the crowd as a historical phenomenon. It offers insights into crowd history by analyzing a series of events that began in San Francisco in July 1877, continued into the fall of that same year, and lasted for about three years. The book proposes a new framework for understanding the evolution of crowds, the disappearance of the crowd, and the rise of democratic political institutions in nineteenth-century America.

It is possible to develop these insights only within a clear historical context. Nearly fifty years ago, Oscar Handlin used a phrase of Emile

Durkheim's to explain the structure of *Boston's Immigrants*, and the advice of these two masters is still relevant.

> The origins of a social process of any importance must be sought "in the internal constitution of the social milieu." The character of the environment—the community in its broadest sense—is particularly important in the study of the contact of dissimilar cultures. It is the field where unfamiliar groups meet, discover each other, and join in a hard relationship that results in either acculturation or conflict. As such, the qualities of the environment subtly condition all the forces involved and often exercise a determining influence upon their evolution. [1]

Therefore, this study of crowds and crowd behavior centers on specific events and grounds itself within a particular geographic, social, political, and economic milieu: San Francisco in 1877. The narrative begins with the July riots—three nights of violence at the end of the month—in which a crowd destroyed a substantial amount of property and in which a number of casualties occurred. After three nights, violence ceased, and that particular crowd disbanded, never again to re-form.

But social ferment continued to boil. Less than two months later, Denis Kearney, an Irish drayman, established the Workingmen's Party of California (WPC), a protest movement strongly critical of California's social, political, and economic institutions, and especially censorious of its richest people and Chinese immigrants. A great deal of evidence shows that the same sorts of men who had rioted in July joined the party in September. Furthermore, many, but not all, of the WPC's subsequent activities resembled those of the traditional crowd.

The juxtaposition of these two protest movements (the crowd and the party), separated by only six weeks and embracing the same kinds of members, raises two fundamental questions. And these two questions bear directly on the history of the crowd in general. Why had people become dissatisfied? Why did they express their dissatisfaction as they did? In order to understand any individual crowd—and especially to understand the crowd in general—we need to answer both questions. The mere fact of discontent did not necessarily predetermine the form of response, and a particular behavior did not inevitably develop from a particular kind of dissatisfaction. We cannot simply assume a lockstep relationship between unhappiness and riot, as the case of San Francisco's Workingmen reveals.

San Franciscans became discontented because it seemed to them that they could not accomplish their goals. Tens of thousands of citizens, especially protesters, were European (primarily Irish) immigrants. They were blue-collar workers, unskilled laborers who had only recently come to the city. They had journeyed across the Atlantic and then across the continent to create better lives, an aspiration that no longer seemed obtainable. Although widespread social mobility had occurred in the past, it no longer seemed likely. Economic transformation, economic depression, and the increased maldistribution of wealth—all seemed to block the road to success. And people worried not only about the gains they had already made but also about the expectations that now seemed frustrated.

The transformation of California's economy ushered in a new era, seemingly characterized by less opportunity. The capital requirements of the technology that revolutionized mining obliterated the role of the individual placer miner. International trade transformed agriculture, and the need for specialized knowledge and skills limited the chances of yeomen farmers. The completion of the transcontinental railroad tied San Francisco to the national market, and competition with eastern traders diminished the profits of local merchants. The construction of capital-intensive factories changed the nature of manufacturing, and mass production and specialization of labor decreased the well-being of craftsmen and artisans. In every sector of the economy, growth and change seemed to threaten opportunity.

In the 1870s, depression compounded the problem, and every sector of the economy suffered. The transcontinental railroad precipitated a commercial panic, and recurrent drought plagued agriculture. Several factors brought on a financial collapse—most notably stock speculation and a resultant market crash; the destruction of Virginia City, Nevada, by fire; and the failure of the Bank of California. Competition with eastern manufacturers forced California industries to lower prices, and so they cut wages; others couldn't compete, so they cut employment. Hard times blackened the present and seemed to presage a baleful future.

But not everyone suffered. Some benefited from the new economy.

Charles Crocker and Leland Stanford, Mark Hopkins and Collis P. Huntington built the transcontinental railroad and became millionaires. John Mackay and William S. O'Brien, James G. Fair and James C. Flood uncapped the heart of the Comstock lode and became multimillionaires. With their great wealth, they established a new style of life in San Francisco. They mimicked the English aristocracy and tried to define a new relationship between themselves and the rest of society. They believed that their wealth entitled them to respect, status, prestige, and honor, and they used their money to create a new social world, the world of Nob Hill.

This new world vividly revealed the maldistribution of wealth in the city and threw South of Market and its poverty into sharp relief. Here the masses of the city lived in substandard housing, experienced deteriorating family relationships, and despaired over their lives. They worried about money, they hungered for food, and they occasionally gave up altogether, deciding that life was unbearable.

By 1877, San Francisco's masses felt cheated and angry. They didn't understand economic transformation or the causes of depression. They recognized only their own poverty, contrasted to the wealth of Nob Hill, which was starkly disclosed by the great mansions looming over the city. It seemed to them that a conspiracy had developed, a conspiracy to monopolize wealth and end opportunity, and they decided to unmask the plot and destroy it.

In 1877, their feelings of anger, resentment, and hostility erupted—first in the July riots and then in the Workingmen's Party of California. But neither the riots nor the party was foreordained. Anger and frustration did not necessarily portend violence or political action. To understand why people raged does not explain why they expressed their ire in a particular way. Asking why they rioted, why they stopped rioting, and why they formed a political party in the aftermath of the riots are separate and distinct questions.

San Franciscans rioted because riot was a typical form of political behavior for the disenfranchised European and American masses. Earlier crowd historians have demonstrated that the crowd enabled people lacking access to formal political institutions to express political opinions and make political demands. And statistical analysis of the membership of the Workingmen's Party of California reveals that they were recent immigrants to the state—especially from Europe, most especially from Ireland (where the crowd still prevailed)—and came from those segments of society that populated the crowd.

But if crowd members rioted for historical reasons, we cannot avoid wondering why they abandoned their crowd after three nights, never to form it again. Answer: the full weight of authority—municipal, state, and federal—combined forces to crush the crowd. And yet this answer itself presses a central new question upon us. Why did constituted authority not just change but completely reverse its traditional response to the crowd? Crowd historians have clearly demonstrated that constituted authority historically recognized the legitimacy of the crowd, especially during its heyday. Officials negotiated with crowd leaders to end riots and generally satisfied many of their demands. Why then did San Francisco, California, and United States officials prove unwilling to conduct business as usual in San Francisco in 1877?

The officials themselves told the crowd why not. To them, riot had become unacceptable because other modes of political action had become available. In formal statements and resolutions, newspaper editorials, and ministerial edicts, civic leaders told the populace that they had the right to meet, pass resolutions, submit petitions, and vote. But they could not riot. These leaders expected men to cast ballots, not bullets.

At this point, the history of the July riots and San Francisco's crowd begins to provide a new structure for understanding and interpreting the disappearance of the crowd. As politics in San Francisco became democratized, and as citizens obtained access to formal political institutions, they were denied access to other institutions, particularly the crowd. When they acquired the right to hold political meetings, express political opinions in a formal context, create and participate in political parties, and even vote, they lost the right to riot, to rebel, and to revolt. If the case of San Francisco can tell us anything about the history of the crowd, it demonstrates that the crowd disappeared as part of the democratization of politics in the nineteenth century. Increased access to political institutions not only allowed people to behave in a new way, but it also prevented them from behaving in an old one.

This insight suggests strong links between two phenomena that historians rarely associate with each other—crowds and political parties. Social historians, particularly those of preindustrial society, most especially those of preindustrial Europe and America, study crowds. Considering crowds to be social movements, they interpret them as manifestations of larger social contexts. Political historians, particularly those of modern society, most especially those of nineteenth- and twentieth-century Europe and America, study political parties. Considering parties to be political action, they interpret them as manifestations of the larger political context.

The experience of San Francisco in 1877 suggests that crowds and parties were closely related to each other. Like political parties, the crowd was a form of political action, whether its overt objectives were political, social, or economic. Prior to the democratization of politics in the nineteenth century, different sorts of people behaved in different ways politically. Some, the upper crust, had access to formal political institutions and used them to accomplish their purposes; they had no need to traffic with the crowd. Others, the rabble, had no access to those institutions; they relied on the crowd to accomplish their purposes. The crushing of San Francisco's crowd in 1877 strongly suggests that all that changed with the democratization of politics; as a democratic ideology developed, the same sort of political activity came to be expected of all citizens. Consequently, as access to formal political institutions broadened, people abandoned the barricade for the voting booth. And, if that is so, historians need to demolish the barrier that separates the history of the crowd from the history of the political party, even, at least in this instance, to tear down the barrier that divides social from political history.

But events in San Francisco did not conclude with the crushing of the crowd, or even with the formation of the Workingmen's Party of California. No sooner had the political machinery quashed the July riots than a flock of new parties sprang up to compete for support from San Francisco's rioters. The crowd now had to make a crucial decision: which party to join. Most crowd members embraced the Workingmen's Party of California, and the reasons for their choice suggest even more about the metamorphosis of crowd into party.

Previous historians have argued that the WPC's political theories and policies, particularly its hostility to Chinese immigrants and its opposition to Chinese immigration, attracted the allegiance of San Francisco's workingmen in 1877. But in fact, several other parties also expressed anti-Chinese sentiments, at least one of them even more vehemently than the WPC. Therefore, something else must have attracted workingmen to the WPC. In terms of policy and program, the WPC's broader worldview distinguished it from other parties also seeking support. The WPC argued that social and economic problems in San Francisco resulted from a monstrous conspiracy between the city's economic elite and the Chinese immigrants. The WPC and its leaders claimed that the city's wealthiest people were plotting to overthrow the American republic, destroy freedom, and replace white American workingmen with Oriental slaves. The WPC meant to stem this perfidy and renew the republic.

But the reasons for the WPC's appeal transcended formal policies, programs, plans, and theories. The central difference between the WPC and other parties lay in its mode of action and style of behavior. In some ways, the WPC behaved like the traditional crowd, in others like a political party. The best way to resolve this paradox is by recognizing that the WPC was neither a crowd nor a party; it bridged the crowd and the party. The WPC introduced those who traditionally expressed political opinions through the crowd to the ways of the party. It eased its members out of the crowd and into the voting booth. It taught them how to abandon bullets and how to use ballots.

Thus, an analysis of the July riots and the Workingmen's Party of California not only produces a reevaluation of those events and a new way of understanding the disappearance of the crowd, but also reveals a previously unrecognized political phenomenon—the transition between crowd and party. Although historians have long recognized the democratization of politics and the increased base of political participation in the nineteenth century, they have rarely asked how the formerly disenfranchised masses learned to use the new forms of political expression and behavior that had become available. They have simply assumed that citizens knew what to do when they received new political opportunities, that formal political participation came naturally.

The events in San Francisco in the summer and fall of 1877 suggest a different hypothesis: that people needed to be taught and to learn to use the new (at least to them) political techniques. They needed to be led out of the crowd and into the party. In 1877, the WPC educated

San Francisco's masses, revealing both what happened to the crowd and also how people learned to use the new modes of political behavior. The members of the crowd were expected to use modern means of political expression, but they didn't know how. The WPC taught them. Similarly, it teaches us a great deal about the disappearance of the crowd and the creation of modern political institutions.

The day that I wrote this introduction, a remarkable serendipity reinforced my own faith in its conclusions. I was discussing it with several colleagues, Tom Dunlap, Burt Kaufman, and Peter Wallenstein, and I wondered about the broader implications of this book and its arguments. In particular, I pondered the existence of a similar relationship between the end of civil rights demonstrations in the early 1970s and the passage of the Voting Rights acts of 1965, 1970, and 1975. Peter, a mine of bibliographic knowledge, suggested that I consult two books by Steven F. Lawson, *Black Ballots: Voting Rights in the South, 1944–1969*, and *In Pursuit of Power: Southern Blacks and Electoral Politics, 1965–1982*. In *Black Ballots*, I read the following:

> Of all the measures proposed by the civil-rights advocates, franchise expansion commanded the greatest appeal to the nation and its lawmakers. There was a conservative side to expansion of voting rights that attracted Northern politicians, who preferred to see the efforts of the civil-rights troops channeled into "quiet" registration drives rather than into the more provocative freedom rides and mass marches.[2]

Statements in Lawson's second book bear an even more remarkable similarity to my interpretation of events in San Francisco a century before.

> The right to vote has commanded widespread appeal because conservatives as well as liberals recognize it as a cardinal principle of our democratic faith. Furthermore, it has been perceived to be the preferable option for producing social change. In fact, as Southern blacks have acquired and used the ballot, they have been less inclined toward adopting disruptive tactics, such as mass demonstrations, that were so crucial to the civil rights movement during the era of disfranchisement.[3]

Later, Lawson demonstrates that when they were

> caught in the crossfire between rising black militancy and escalating white opposition, Johnson strategists sought safer ground on which to maintain

their moral commitment to the civil rights movement without demolishing the broad-based political coalition which had supported the Great Society. The Voting Rights Act played a key role in their overall thinking, especially after the proliferation of riots. They counted on enfranchisement and the exercise of the ballot to provide a legitimate alternative to violence, to offer blacks a political stake in the system, and to reduce racial tensions. In 1966, a year before a fierce riot erupted in Newark, President Johnson had admonished a Democratic party rally in that troubled city: "Remember this: There is more power in the ballot than there is in the bullet, and it lasts longer."[4]

Did a desire to crush the crowd actually contribute to the democratization of formal institutional politics in the nineteenth century, as Lawson shows it did in the twentieth? In fact, was democratization a way of crushing (or at least neutralizing) the crowd? The events in San Francisco in 1877 don't answer this question, but it is hard to avoid wondering, especially when we remember not only the events of the 1960s and 1970s but also the events of the 1910s and 1920s, when passage of the Nineteenth Amendment contributed to the temporary demise of the women's movement. In any event, the relationship between the end of the riot and the expansion of suffrage in twentieth-century America confirms my own conviction that in the nineteenth century the democratization of formal politics rendered the crowd unacceptable and brought crowd members into the formal political process.

I

MEMBERSHIP

Prologue: July Rioters

Rioting erupted on the night of July 23, 1877. As so often happens, the violence originated with a peaceful demonstration, a protest meeting called by the Workingmen's Party of the United States (WPUS). This socialist organization had roots in the Marxian International Workingmen's Association and later fed into the Socialist Labor Party of the United States. That night it urged San Franciscans to express sympathy for striking eastern railroad workers, and the demonstrators adopted resolutions declaring solidarity with the strikers, attacking the evils of watered stock, and opposing subsidies and franchises for private persons and organizations. The protesters also criticized the encroachment of capital on the rights of the people and demanded immediate governmental action to institute reforms.[1]

Shortly after nine o'clock, someone on the fringe of the crowd yelled, "On to Chinatown!" and a rush began. The crowd abandoned its original meeting place on the sandlots across from San Francisco's City Hall and raced up the street. An attack on a Chinese laundry commenced the initial night of violence. When policemen tried to choke the tumult, the crowd dispersed, only to reassemble in front of another laundry, which they also demolished. A nearby liquor store met the same fate, and then the rioters tore off for Chinatown. When a broken lamp accidentally set one building ablaze, the rioters cut fire hoses and disrupted the firemen's work however they could. By the end of the evening, the crowd had destroyed about twenty laundries and ransacked a plumbing store that they had mistaken for a laundry. Rioters had also pelted the Chinese Methodist Mission with rocks. Before the police could restore order, the crowd had destroyed about $20,000 worth of property.[2]

More rioting broke out the next night. The crowd gathered in front of the United States mint and resisted all police attempts at dispersal. After a while, part of the mob headed for the Mission Woolen Mills and threatened to burn them because of their large Chinese labor force. Because the militia had been forewarned, the factory was well-defended, and the crowd could do little more than wreck some wash-houses close by.[3] Thus ended the second night of disruption.

The worst violence occurred on the third night, July 25. During the day, rumors had spread that an attack on the docks of the Pacific Mail Steamship Company was impending, and the authorities gathered forces to protect them. When the crowd discovered the stratagem, it torched a nearby lumberyard and retreated to neighboring Rincon Hill to watch the flames. From this vantage, the crowd again attacked fire fighters and impeded their work. Succeeding events were predictable. The police charged the hill. Someone began shooting. Only after a strenuous battle did the crowd disperse, leaving in its wake four men dead, another fourteen wounded, and $500,000 worth of property in ruins. The Battle of Rincon Hill was the culmination of serious violence; calm slowly returned to a frightened city.[4]

No one has ever determined who rioted in San Francisco at the end of July 1877, and none of the remaining documents answers the question with any certainty. No identifiable leaders captained the crowd. No mass arrests suggest its social composition, and the violence appeared to occur spontaneously with neither planning nor formal organization.

Nevertheless, contemporaries speculated about the crowd's composition. They especially wondered if the city's working class precipitated and actively participated in the July riots. Most contemporaries said no and specifically denied the involvement of organized labor and the working class. Governor William Irwin attributed the trouble to three groups: hoodlums bent on mere destruction, thieves desirous of plundering the city, and "a small sprinkling of Communists or Internationalists" hoping to "usher in the millennium by a judicious use of the torch." Irwin thought the city lucky that laboring men had refused to participate in these nefarious schemes.[5]

Other observers agreed. William T. Coleman, leader of the extra-legal Committee of Safety formed to protect the city, rejected any no-tion that the working class had caused the trouble. Henry George, the social critic who was then a San Francisco journalist, took essentially the same position. He assigned no direct responsibility for the riots and merely commented that "gangs of boys" had raided Chinese laun-dries in remote parts of the city. Lucy Senger, whose house faced the route taken by the crowd on the first night of rioting, described the events in a long letter, and she agreed with more prominent San Franciscans. She referred simply to "hoodlums" as she characterized that part of the crowd that interfered with the firemen.[6]

Newspapers unanimously echoed these assessments. Every major daily in the city pinned the blame on unidentified troublemakers. Ac-cording to the *Alta*, "an aggregation of the hoodlum element" was re-sponsible. The *Bulletin* blamed "a class of overgrown boys—hoodlums with a mixture of overgrown criminals." The *Call* thought that "idle and unruly lads" were "at the bottom of the mischief," while the *Chronicle* referred to "a class of idle, bumming, thieving loafers known as hoodlums."[7]

More than that, every newspaper in the city specifically denied that the working class was a party to the riots. According to the *Alta*, "none of those who participated" in the meeting of July 23, "either as speakers or listeners," shared in the subsequent events. The *Bulletin* forcefully asserted that the working classes were "not involved at all." The *Call* claimed that "workingmen, employed or unemployed, have nothing to do with the depredations." And the *Chronicle* informed its readers that "no men who are in the habit of earning a living by work were in the mobs." San Franciscans rejected the idea that the city's working class might consider riot an acceptable and useful means of political expression.[8]

In the century since the riots, historians too have wondered about the role that workingmen and the working class played. Unlike con-temporaries, they have conceded, sometimes implicitly, that working-men were almost certainly involved. Although some overtly deny workingmen's participation, even they subtly ascribe a role to the work-ing class. In *Popular Tribunals*, Hubert Howe Bancroft maintained (like Governor Irwin) that "hoodlums, thieves, and extreme commu-

nists . . . composed the rioters." He also reported that many workingmen's associations had denied involvement. And yet he described
the riots in a chapter entitled "The Labor Agitation of 1877–8."
Bancroft also assigned labor at least indirect responsibility when he
wrote that its sympathy for striking railroad workers in the East provided "indirect encouragement" to the rioters.[9]

In his *History of California*, Bancroft's interpretation of working
class involvement was less ambiguous. Once again, he described the
riots in a chapter concerned with labor, "Chinese, the Labor Agitation, and Politics." In addition, he claimed that many workingmen
took part, although he stopped short of assigning them general responsibility. He claimed that an "anti-coolie club" incited a "portion of the
workingmen" to riot and that they destroyed some laundries during
the trouble, but he carefully avoided implying involvement by the entire working class. As he put it, the "acts of the lower communistic
element of the workingmen's association were repudiated by the more
intelligent."[10]

Later historians, especially those sympathetic to labor, have expressed ambiguities similar to Bancroft's. Both Lucile Eaves, in her
History of California Labor Legislation, and Ira B. Cross, in his *History
of the Labor Movement in California*, described the July riots in the context of the labor movement during the late 1870s; but both also
claimed that some group other than labor was responsible for the violence and property damage. According to Eaves, the July riots were
fomented by hoodlums, "a class of rough and lawless youth" who
liked, as one of their "chief forms of diversion," to "torment . . . in-
offensive Chinamen." They were responsible for the attacks.[11]

Cross also included the July riots in his treatment of labor in the
1870s. He, too, claimed that a "gang of hoodlums" proposed the attacks on Chinatown and was responsible for the destruction. Nevertheless, his terminology suggests that he harbored some doubt. In one
telling phrase, he referred to "hoodlums and the unemployed" in the
same breath. Their "escapades" on the first night gave them confidence, and "it was difficult to surmise to what lengths they would go."
In analyzing events of the second night, Cross mentioned a gathering
of "a thousand hoodlums and unemployed" before he described the

rioting itself. These phrases at least suggest an unconscious belief that members of the working class joined the so-called hoodlums.[12]

Alexander Saxton, one of the most recent historians to consider the July riots, openly asked if labor and the working class incited the riots, and he concluded that they almost certainly played a part. In view of the massive character of the rioting and the degree of distress and unemployment in San Francisco that summer, he deduced that "involvement must have cut deeper than any drifting contingent of 'hoodlums' and transients could quite account for."[13]

Michael Kazin, the latest historian to study the July riots, tried to determine who participated by studying arrest reports and inferring membership from the list of those apprehended. He ran into a blank wall. Of the fifty San Franciscans picked up and charged with riot-related offenses, Kazin could identify only twenty-one in the City Directory and/or Register of Voters. As a result, he could only report that "61.9% of the [21] men lived in the South of Market Street neighborhood, the center of the unskilled white working class in late nineteenth century San Francisco."[14]

The lack of direct primary evidence about who participated in the July riots has rendered historians unable to do more than infer that workingmen and the working class took part in the violence. An indirect approach, however, allows us to determine the composition of the crowd with a high degree of confidence. By studying subsequent events in San Francisco and their participants, we can deduce a great deal about the social and economic composition of the July crowd.

In September 1877, less than three months after the riots had subsided, Denis Kearney, a drayman and Irish immigrant, formed the Workingmen's Party of California. For the next two years, that organization was the most powerful force in San Francisco politics. The sudden appearance of the WPC in the weeks after the July riots, its extraordinary growth in the next few months, the similarity of its name (though not its ideology) to the WPUS (which had called the initial meeting on July 23), and the frequent use of the term *sand lot riots* as a synonym for the WPC all suggest that the July riots and the WPC were related to each other and that both events had similar participants.

One crucial contemporary document strongly supports the existence of a relationship between the July riots and the WPC, and the belief that many July rioters later joined the party. That document is the *Report* of the Joint Committee on Labor Investigation appointed by the California legislature in 1878. Ordered to look into the trouble in San Francisco, the five members of this committee could not agree upon a single report and reached three separate conclusions. Two of the three reports strongly suggested a similarity between the July rioters and the Workingmen.[15] The chairman of the committee and one member concluded that the events of July constituted "the initial point of labor agitation in San Francisco" although they could find no evidence that the leaders of the Workingmen's Party "and the great body of their followers" participated in the riots. A third member of the committee claimed a clearer connection. Although he granted that the WPC itself was not responsible for, or even connected with the July riots (since it had not yet been formed, it could hardly have been), he pointed out that "it had its incipiency soon after, and followed close upon its heels, leaving the presumption strong that the parties responsible for the terrible scenes of riot and incendiarism in July are incorporated with the present movement."[16]

If these conclusions are correct, the best way of determining the composition of the July crowd is to determine the membership of the WPC. After all, it hardly seems credible that these two movements—occurring so close in time, having such similar names, and both receiving contemporary description as "riots"—were not directed at and did not appeal to the same groups of San Franciscans.

1. Workingmen

Denis Kearney was the most notable of San Francisco's Workingmen. Indeed he is generally credited with, or blamed for, organizing the WPC. Actually, he did not conduct the meeting at which the party was born. That honor belonged to J. G. Day, a Canadian carpenter of Irish ancestry.[1]

On September 12, 1877, about six weeks after the July riots, Day presided over a meeting called by the Workingmen's Trade and Labor Union of San Francisco, a short-lived organization he and Kearney had created in the aftermath of the violence. The meeting recommended nothing more radical than establishing soup kitchens to feed the hungry and also resolved that "workingmen sever all affiliations with existing political parties." Instead, they should organize a new party to be called the Workingmen's Party of California. The new organization's program was unexceptional and proposed nothing remarkable in the context of the times. It called for abolishing assessments on candidates for public office, holding state and local officials accountable for their acts, creating a bureau of labor statistics, and immediately reducing the hours of labor. Out of this preliminary meeting, however, arose an organization that terrorized San Francisco, provided the cartoonist Thomas Nast with images for his wildest fantasies, and even attracted the attention of Lord James Bryce as he analyzed the American political system.[2]

The next step in the formation of the Workingmen's Party of California came about a week later. On September 21, Kearney delivered a speech that attracted great public attention. At a meeting to determine ways of helping the city's unemployed, Kearney appeared to urge every workingman in San Francisco to shoulder a musket. He also seemed to argue that a little judicious hanging of the city's capitalists would not be out of order—was in fact required. He predicted that twenty thousand San Franciscans would be armed within a year, organized, and prepared to take whatever they desired, regardless of constituted authority. In the climate of fear pervading San Francisco after the July riots, his bold rhetoric elicited denunciations from several newspapers, attention the party would certainly not have gotten otherwise.[3]

Perhaps because he enjoyed his newfound notoriety, perhaps because he was serious, perhaps because someone else put words in his mouth, Kearney delivered an even more inflammatory speech a few nights later. At a meeting to choose permanent officers for the new party, seven hundred men appeared, probably attracted by the publicity given Kearney's earlier speech. After this throng elected Day president and Kearney treasurer of the WPC, Kearney addressed them. He proclaimed that bullets were not wanting, that San Francisco would meet the fate of Moscow if the Chinese were not driven from the city, and that the plight of workingmen must be alleviated. From that night on, his clarion call, "The Chinese Must Go!" became the rallying cry of the party.[4]

Apparently horrified by the escalation of Kearney's rhetoric, Day interrupted and announced that he would not conduct a meeting where such speeches were tolerated. But Kearney had become the crowd's darling. He had become its leader, in fact if not in title. The crowd hooted Day from the stage and cheered Kearney. Less than two weeks later, the WPC modified its leadership. Kearney became president, Day, vice-president, and H. L. Knight, secretary.[5]

The men attending this meeting also adopted a statement of principles that Knight had written. It called for a new political party to unite all poor and working men against the "encroachments of capital." Specifically, it promised to "wrest the government from the hands of the rich and place it in those of the people where it properly belongs." Other goals included ridding the country of cheap Chinese labor, destroying land monopoly in California, and creating a system of taxation that would make great wealth impossible. The WPC also announced its intention of providing properly for the poor, unfortunate, weak, helpless, and young because the country was "rich enough to do so, and religion, humanity, and patriotism demand" it. Finally, the party would elect only competent workingmen and their friends to public office.[6]

Then the organization of San Francisco's masses began in earnest. A branch materialized in every ward. These units met monthly to conduct local business, and anyone "willing to work for a living" could join. Every member paid the twenty-five-cent initiation fee and ten cents a week dues. After a branch had enrolled fifty members, it could split in two according to residence. Any member could attend the monthly business meetings and "take a full equal part in the government of the party."[7]

San Franciscans enrolled in droves. Indeed, the response was so great that secretaries "found it almost impossible to accommodate the large number of signatories." During the weeks after its initial organization, the WPC met nightly. Within a month, branches had sprung up in each of the city's twelve wards, and members had set regular meeting times and places. In less than four months, eleven branches had emerged in the Eleventh Ward alone. Special ethnic and occupation groups flourished: German, French, Italian, and Scandinavian clubs; shoemakers', cooks and waiters', carpenters', and cabinet-makers' auxiliaries. The party attempted to organize San Francisco's blacks and also to set up a branch for youth.[8]

Today, more than a hundred years later, ascertaining who joined the Workingmen's Party of California, who followed the lead of Denis Kearney, and who rioted in July challenges us. The party kept membership lists, but not surprisingly they have vanished. The "mass of important testimony" taken by California's Joint Committee on Labor Investigation has also disappeared. These documents might have fingered the members of the party, and their absence makes identification difficult.[9]

Without these documents, one can resort to the many contemporary characterizations of WPC membership, but the inconsistencies and contradictions among them make conclusions problematical. The party itself made several statements about its supporters that appeared in pamphlets and brochures meant to describe the party and explain its principles. One tract defined the Workingmen in social, occupational, moral, and intellectual terms. Workingmen, it proclaimed, were not "stupid peasants." They were "scholars, skilled artisans, soldiers" who knew "how to live and how to die." They realized that they were being squeezed "between the aristocrat and the Chinaman" and they would "scatter both like chaff before the wind."[10]

This characterization, and the use of such terms as *scholars* and *skilled artisans* implies a somewhat higher social status than the term *workingmen* suggests, and yet it is corroborated by a participant. According to Frank Roney, an active member and president of the Eighth Ward club, the

> staunchest members of the Workingmen's Party were the small property holders. . . . The party developed as being specially designed for their salvation. . . . The fellow without property was not considered, nor did he seem to want consideration. His hope was to be a small property holder at some time in the near future; consequently, his sympathies were with the class to which he later hoped to belong.[11]

Roney's case seems overstated, but it jibes with the party statements already quoted and also with advertisements in the party's semi-official history. Six shoe stores, five boarding houses, four grocers, three brewers, two jewelers, two cigarmakers, two photographers, two printers, a butcher, a shirtmaker, a hatter, and a corsetmaker—all these small businesses purchased ads. Over and above them, four attorneys, an accountant, a business college, and a real estate agent publicized themselves. It is impossible to determine whether these advertisers themselves supported the WPC or whether their clientele (real or anticipated) favored the party. In either case, the ads suggest that Roney's interpretation of party membership and support has merit.[12]

Nevertheless, this construction of the Workingmen as artisans, craftsmen, and property owners would have surprised many contemporaries. To journalists of the day, the question of party membership primarily concerned unemployment. Did San Francisco's unemployed compose the WPC? Some said yes while others denied the existence of substantial joblessness in the city. The *Alta*, mouthpiece for the city's business community, completely repudiated the idea of massive unemployment in San Francisco, denied that the Workingmen were unemployed laborers, and claimed that there was "not a city on earth" where more people owned their own homes and were independent."[13] Generally speaking, the *Alta* portrayed the Workingmen in the same terms it had used to depict the July rioters—criminals, ruffians, and hoodlums.

Other newspapers accepted the existence of unemployment, implying a relationship between unemployment and the Workingmen—but they did not consider joblessness an adequate justification for discontent and protest. The *Bulletin* believed that there were about twenty-five thousand men out of work by April 1878, but it also claimed that unemployment was an inadequate reason for destitution and deprivation. No healthy San Franciscan need be without food and lodging. The "evil at base" was "improvidence and waste." Thousands of workingmen never saved a dollar. Had they put aside what they spent on tobacco and whiskey, no problem would have existed. "At the bottom of this evil" was "the lack of right education, which secures habits of industry, frugality, temperance and thrift." The *Bulletin* complained that modern civilization had "multiplied human wants. Fifty years ago, workingmen rarely made journeys of hundreds of miles. The parlor did not contain a costly carpet, and very few books were within reach of the household. The wages of labor are much greater now. But the dollar . . . is used for the procurement of a hundred things which were not within reach fifty years ago."[14] This newspaper thus characterized Workingmen as unemployed spendthrifts, a very different interpretation from the *Alta*'s.

Like its major newspapers, San Francisco's two most important weeklies, the *Argonaut* and the *Wasp*, disagreed about the membership of the WPC. In fact, they never quite decided who the Workingmen were. Sometimes the *Argonaut* accepted the aforementioned unemployment theory even as it bemoaned the extent of joblessness in San Francisco and criticized government and business for not providing enough work. "Better for San Francisco to pay one dollar per day for men to carry sand in baskets to the ocean than to let them associate with starvation and desperation." Other times, the magazine combined poverty and jealousy to define the Workingmen. The depression had made laborers realize their poverty for the first time, and lack of work gave them leisure to contemplate "the profuse elegance" of their rich neighbors. For the rich who would "herald their wealth in brazen monograms along the streets on their horses' bridles and upon their carriage doors; for those who have imported liveried lackies from abroad to assist my dainty lady from her carriage," they had only contempt. Such scenes caused them to "loathe and despise society."[15] On still other occasions, the *Argonaut* trotted out the criminal, ruffian, hoodlum theory.

> The men who compose labor mobs, and participate in bread riots in San Francisco, are lazy hounds—criminals who mean plunder. There can be no such thing as real suffering in California. If it exists, it is the result of improvidence, laziness, sickness, misfortune, or crime. If a man is sick, let him go to the hospital. If he is criminal, let him go to prison. If he is lazy, let him go to the devil.[16]

Clearly, the *Argonaut* had no coherent editorial policy on who the Workingmen were, or about the composition of the WPC.

Neither did the *Wasp*, its major competitor. This weekly admitted the existence of want and deprivation in the city but also proved unable to develop a reasonable understanding of that fact. To its editors, the key problems were overeducation and a basic unwillingness to perform manual labor, particularly farming. Too much education had socialized the children of farmers, mechanics, and laborers into dissatisfaction with their "humble but independent lot." No sooner did these children leave school than they rushed to the city "to engage in posting ledgers or measuring tape; or in default of such employment they degenerated into book peddlers or insurance agents." As a result, the urban labor force increased beyond the city's needs. This development had caused unprecedented distress in San Francisco. Because farm and manual labor were becoming distasteful, because the children of the working class thought that they could dress well, keep their hands clean, go to the theater, and enjoy life in the city, the economy had collapsed. "There can be but one result where such a condition of things obtains—social and political disaster."[17]

The muddle, contradiction, and disarray among contemporary observers have shown up in the works of later historians. Clio's devotees have had no more success in defining the members of the Workingmen's Party than earlier analysts. One of the first, Hubert Howe Bancroft, stressed class and ethnicity. He claimed that the Workingmen were foreigners, "almost to a man," rarely of much intelligence, and "neither able nor inclined" to discuss the relations between labor and capital. Later, he espoused the jealousy theory, asserting that the principles of the WPC

> found ready acceptance among a class who envied the aristocrat rolling in wealth which their hands had gathered, who hated the encroaching Chinaman, and who detested the politician as a betrayer and parasite. They were dazzled by the glittering prospects which arose like a mirage before them, picturing shady groves and cooling fountains to the exhausted traveller in the desert.[18]

John C. Young could hardly have differed more. Writing at the turn of the century, he viewed the Workingmen as forerunners of the Progressives. According to him, the WPC was a popular, and not a workingmen's, movement. The party was "chiefly inspired by the determination of a part of the community to bring about a reform in the management of civic affairs." He insisted that the activities in San Francisco during the late 1870s "foreshadowed the awakening of the rest of the country." San Franciscans were simply "twenty-five or thirty years in advance of the modern movement" led by Theodore Roosevelt.[19]

Alexander Saxton has used a different approach to determine the party's membership. He has focused on Denis Kearney and Frank Roney. Saxton has so clearly conceded that the Workingmen were just that (the subtitle of his study is *Labor and the Anti-Chinese Movement in California*) that he uses Kearney and Roney as exemplars of different types of nineteenth-century labor leaders. Roney represented "a labor leadership already becoming specialized, but which had not yet crossed the threshold into professionalization." Kearney "spoke for the men down under—and for himself as their tribune."[20]

All these attempts—from the *Wasp*'s to Saxton's—to determine the membership of the Workingmen's Party of California share one characteristic: they are impressionistic and based on opinion for which there is no definitive evidence. There are, however, other ways of establishing the membership of the WPC and the composition of the July crowd. The most fruitful is to use various documents that lend themselves to statistical analysis. Voting records are among the most useful of such documents, and between 1878 and 1880, the WPC nominated candidates in a number of municipal elections and took positions in others. Patterns of voting behavior derived from election returns can be correlated with data from voting registers, city directories, and manuscript census schedules to determine who supported the party.

The most important election took place in June 1878. That month, California voters elected delegates to a constitutional convention, and the WPC ran a full slate of candidates. The state legislature had tried to sponsor a constitutional convention several times in the recent past, but statewide plebiscites rejected the idea until September 1877. At that time, popular discontent generated the feeling that a new constitution might solve California's problems, and the voters agreed to a convention. State officials set the election of delegates for June 1878, and the meeting itself for the following September. The convention was to include 152 delegates, 3 from each of the state's forty senatorial districts and 32 from the state at large.[21]

After a heated campaign, election day arrived. In the end, the WPC carried San Francisco. Its candidates swept all ten of the city's senatorial districts for a total of 30 delegates, and they elected another 22 from other parts of California. Altogether, its 52 seats constituted more than one-third of the convention, and the party's delegates played a major role in writing the California Constitution of 1879.[22]

Statistical analysis of returns from this election permits a close approximation of the party's support. The first crucial document is the Great Register of the City and County of San Francisco. It lists every citizen registered to vote in 1877 and also provides that person's address, occupation, age, place of birth, and place and year of naturalization (if applicable). Additional demographic information appears in the manuscript census schedules for 1880. These provide details about family structure, type of household, and parental nativity.[23]

It must be recognized at the outset that this methodology contains an inherent bias. In 1877, neither women nor men younger than twenty-one could vote in California. Therefore, neither women nor very young men are included in the Great Register, and they are not represented in the voting statistics. Consequently, the following analysis does not pertain to them. This is unfortunate because some evidence suggests that both women and young men participated in the

WPC and its activities; they certainly marched in parades, were present at various social activities, and received consideration from the party. However, the newspapers (also biased) report their participation only minimally, and there is no evidence that either women or young men occupied leadership positions. As a result, it is extraordinarily difficult to determine how significant a role they played in the party and its activities. No previous historian has ever attributed a major influence to them, but it is impossible to determine whether that lack results from an absence of evidence, bias on the part of the historians, or an actual lack of significant involvement by either women or younger men.

Taking a one-third sample of those adult men who are listed in the Great Register provides a total sample of 12,618 individuals, enough to offer 99.7 percent confidence that the level of error is no greater than 1 percent. Every member of the sample was traced to the manuscript census schedules. Not everyone in the sample could be located because of death, emigration from the city, false voting registrations, incompetence of the census enumerators, or mobility within the city. Those who could not be located were then followed through the city directories for 1878, 1879, and 1880 using name, address, occupation, and variant spellings of names to determine if an individual had moved. In this way, many other individuals were located in the census schedules. This methodology provided two samples: a total sample selected only from the Great Register and a subsample of 6,473, who could also be found in the census and for whom a larger set of data therefore exists.

Next, these demographic data were aggregated to provide a statistical picture of each precinct in the city. The characterizations of San Francisco's 136 precincts were correlated with voting behavior (what percentage of the voters in each precinct cast ballots for the WPC candidates?) to determine the social characteristics of the WPC supporters.[24]

This statistical analysis provides a clear picture of the typical Workingman (see Appendix). He was relatively young, probably less than forty-five, and had immigrated to the United States, probably from Europe and most particularly from Ireland. In San Francisco, he probably had a blue-collar job and may well have been a common laborer. The Workingman was also someone whose ties to San Francisco were tenuous at best. In all likelihood, if he was an immigrant, he had not become a citizen until after 1870. But, whether native born or foreign born, he had probably not registered to vote before 1876. Perhaps most interesting of all, he was likely to have such a common name, or hold such a typical job, or be so transitory—in other words, to be so anonymous—that he could not be traced from the voting register to the city directories and the manuscript census schedules. He was truly obscure.

Workingmen tended to be younger than San Franciscans who voted for other political parties in 1878. Of the five-year age groups between twenty-one and forty-five, all but one correlate positively with voting for the WPC. Of the five-year age groups between forty-six and eighty, every one correlates negatively with voting for the WPC. Even more remarkably, of the twenty-three individual ages from twenty-one to forty-three, all but five correlate positively with voting for the WPC. Of the thirty-eight separate ages between forty-four and eighty-one, all but seven correlate negatively with voting for the WPC. Workingmen were significantly younger than other San Franciscans.

This age difference almost certainly derived from another important difference between Workingmen and other San Franciscans, place of birth. Foreign-born citizens supported the WPC strongly, and, since immigration is an age-specific process biased in favor of the young, it is not surprising that Workingmen were younger than their fellow citizens. The generalization that foreign-born citizens supported the WPC masks variations among regions and nations. Although nativity from every section of the globe (with the single exception of South America) correlates positively with voting for the WPC, the strongest correlation is with Europe, and European-born San Franciscans voted overwhelmingly for the party. But even this statement cloaks differences. Among Europeans, the strongest support came from Irish immigrants, and an Irishman who opposed the WPC in 1878 was rare indeed. Although the Irish supported the WPC most strongly, all but one European group (Central and Eastern Europeans),[25] including every nationality from Scandinavia, Western Europe, and the British Isles, voted for the party. Whereas Europeans generally supported the Workingmen's Party, native-born Americans voted against it just as heartily. Strong negative correlations exist between birth in every region of the United States and voting for the WPC, with the greatest opposition coming from those born in New England, the Mid-Atlantic states, and the Old Southwest. Even more astounding, positive correlations exist between voting for the WPC and only five states of the Union. In each of those cases, the correlation is extremely weak. The Workingmen's Party of California was unquestionably an immigrant movement.

The party was also a blue-collar organization, if that term can be used to describe workers of the late nineteenth century. Given the occupational structure of immigrants to the United States at the time, this is again not surprising. Craftsmen and factory operatives voted heavily for the WPC, and, as a group, common laborers could hardly have voted for it more solidly. Taken as a whole, the correlation between blue-collar occupation and voting for the party is about as high as possible. On the other hand, men with white-collar jobs or occupations voted just as heavily against the party. Those with professional, technical, managerial, or proprietary positions voted for opposition parties in great numbers. So did sales workers, although not as tenaciously. Of all the white-collar groups, however, it was clerical workers, the newly emerging lower middle class, who voted against the WPC most vigorously, even more strongly than common laborers supported the party.

The party's overwhelming support from almost every ethnic group, and almost every segment of the working class, suggests that an unusual kind of analysis must be applied in order to understand the WPC. In recent decades, historians have tended to study individual ethnic groups and parts of the working class rather than tending to study immigrants and working men. Obviously, they have discovered significant ways in which specific cultural contexts shaped the behavior of discrete portions of the social fabric. However, instances such as this suggest that there were times when different groups acted in concert, when they overcame unique cultural contexts and worked in unison for common goals. In order to understand such moments, it is necessary to focus on the ties that bound them rather than the boundaries that divided them. As a result, this study does not emphasize particularities among ethnic groups and segments of the working class and stresses instead the commonalities that enabled them to act together.

Workingmen, then, were young immigrants with blue-collar jobs. They were also men whose relationship to San Francisco was new and insubstantial. The analysis of the voting register, city directories, and manuscript census schedules provides three measures of social stability, and all three reveal that Workingmen had come to the city recently and had not yet established permanent, enduring ties to San Francisco. The first measure is the year of naturalization for immigrants. Clearly and strikingly, the more recently an immigrant had become a citizen, the more likely he was to vote for the WPC. Immigrants who had been naturalized between 1875 and 1878 had a strong tendency to support the party. So did those naturalized between 1870 and 1874, but their propensity to vote for the WPC was slightly less. The same statement holds for those who had become citizens between 1865 and 1869. For those immigrants who had become citizens before 1865, however, the tendency to vote for the WPC dropped off sharply, actually becoming very weakly negative for the few citizens naturalized prior to 1840.

The same generalizations hold for the relationship between voting behavior and year of first registration to vote. The more recently an individual had registered to vote, the more likely his vote went to the WPC. The cutoff year was 1875. People who first registered to vote between 1866 and 1875 tended very much to vote against the WPC. People who first registered to vote in 1876, 1877, or 1878 tended to vote equally strongly for the Workingmen's Party. Year of naturalization and year of registration taken together reveal that Workingmen tended to be immigrants who had only recently become citizens of the United States and even more recently become active in San Francisco politics. They were not men with a long involvement in the city and its life.

Tracing members of the sample from the voting register to city directories and manuscript census schedules substantiates this generalization. Men who can be traced and located were much more likely to vote against the party than men who could not be found. The strongest correlation exists between those men who at the time of the 1880 census no longer lived at the address given in the voting register of 1878, and whose names and/or occupations were so common that they could not be located in the directories. They tended to vote for the WPC, as did men who were not listed in the city directory or could not be found in the census even if they were in the city directory. In other words, party support came from men so anonymous that their lives could not be traced over a three-year period through basic records. On the other hand, their counterparts, those who could be traced through the various documents, tended to vote against the WPC.

The analysis of the voting register, city directories, and manuscript census schedules clearly shows that Workingmen differed from other San Franciscans. They were younger, foreign-born, blue-collar workers. Perhaps the key factor is that they tended to have lives even more difficult to document than most others. They had become citizens and registered to vote only recently, and vital public records documented their lives less fully. They were the underside of San Francisco in the late 1870s, and by 1877 they had become profoundly discontented. In July, they rioted, and six weeks later, in the aftermath of the riots, they formed the Workingmen's Party of California. The rest of this book explains the context of their dissatisfaction, how the riots evolved into the party, and why these people joined the WPC. In doing so, it explains a great deal about the transformation of political life in late nineteenth-century American cities.

II

THE CITY AND
ITS DISCONTENTS

Introduction

Two popular movements developed in San Francisco, one after the other, during the summer and fall of 1877. The first lasted only a few days, the second several years. Violence characterized the first, political organization and socioeconomic theorizing defined the second. Despite these differences, it seems likely that the same men—or the same sorts of men—animated both movements. Indeed, it is hard to believe that two broad popular movements, so closely linked in time and space, could have boasted separate populations. In fact, most historical accounts recognize a relationship between the July riots and the Workingmen's Party of California, even if occasionally grudgingly.

The timing of these movements raises several historical questions. First, how to account for a level of discontent high enough to generate not one but two popular uprisings. Second, how the later movement developed so quickly from the earlier. And third, how to explain the differences between the two movements—the first a few nights of violence, the second an organization that has figured in the history of American political parties and labor movements.

The answers to these questions comprise the remainder of this book. Part II explains the sources of discontent in San Francisco during the 1870s and places them in a particular context. More especially, it explains the timing and the specific grievances of San Francisco's protesters. After all, these riots, and this party, did not occur in New York, Philadelphia, Chicago, or Boston; they took place in San Francisco. They did not occur in 1827, 1847, or 1867; they took place in 1877. And, if we are to understand these events, we also need to understand, quoting Handlin/Durkheim once again, "the internal constitution of the social milieu." How did this city, and its history, produce these events at this time? The answer to this question emerges only after a careful examination of a world view commonly held by San Franciscans, their life experiences in the city, the depression of the 1870s, the transformation of the city's economy, and the interrelationships among these elements. In short, the events of 1877 were a web whose junctures were dream, expectation, reality, and the reasons for the disjunction among them all.

2. Dreams and Expectations

Many San Franciscans became increasingly discontented as the 1870s wore on. Dissatisfaction grew out of the widening gap between expectations and achievements. San Franciscans had come to California to better themselves, and the history of the state after 1849 had persuaded them that they truly inhabited a golden state. But, during the 1870s, economic transformation, depression, and social change had made them doubt that they could still make it. Fear that failure had become as likely as success generated discontent, discontent that welled over during the tumultuous summer of 1877.

During the late nineteenth century, San Francisco was a city of immigrants. The vast majority of residents had been born outside California, either in another state or abroad. As late as 1880, barely one-third of San Franciscans were native-born Californians (see table 2.1).[1]

Like most nineteenth-century immigrants, San Francisco's newcomers hoped to do well in their adopted home. Although most of them never expected to become rich, the fantasies of the forty-niners shaped the culture of San Francisco and made it seem like a city of guaranteed success. A few were, in fact, frustrated gold-seekers "determined to become rich, if not in the mines, then at least because of them." They considered San Francisco a depository of wealth "to be mined as vigorously as placers and veins." They had come to San Francisco "bound to the creed of getting ahead in life."[2] Of course, this same goal characterized every American city of the day, but in few places did its intensity match that in San Francisco. San Franciscans

TABLE 2.1   GROWTH OF SAN FRANCISCO'S POPULATION,
1870–80

Year	Total Population	Foreign-Born		California-Born		Other US-Born	
		No.	%	No.	%	No.	%
1870	149,473	73,719	49.3	38,491	25.8	37,263	24.9
1880	233,959	104,244	44.6	78,144	33.4	51,571	22.0

were Americans writ large. The first of them had come not just "to do well" but to find gold, and the mentality of the gold rush permeated the city for decades after 1849.

The forty-niners recorded their aspirations in letters, journals, reminiscences, and songs, and they frequently magnified the depths of their yearnings. Alonzo Delano placed himself among "that class of nomad Anglo-Saxons" who had the "modest desire of obtaining sudden wealth" by gathering "golden lumps." Charles Pancoast, a brother miner, reckoned himself "a fortune hunter" easily swayed by "wild rumors of quick fortunes." Others gleefully sang "O! California" instead of "O! Susannah." Soon they'd "be in Frisco," and there they'd "look around." When they saw "the gold lumps there," they'd "pick them off the ground." They'd "scrape the mountains clean," they'd "drain the rivers dry, a pocketful of rocks bring home, so brothers don't you cry."[3]

Some observers took these hyperbolic expressions literally. One traveler to California, I. J. Benjamin, asked what drove people to California and then answered his question simply. Nobody "hurried to California to look for a decent income," or "to find wealth as the last reward of persistent diligence: these were obtainable elsewhere." Here every man wanted "to become rich quickly." If he did not, he pouted that "fate cheated him."[4]

Tapestries portraying the desire to get ahead in San Francisco were embroidered carefully and deliberately for decades after the gold rush. Tourists to the city embellished travel accounts to sell books. Immigrant aid associations exaggerated opportunities in order to attract newcomers and increase the labor force. In fact, their tales were not without reason. The early history of the city's economy seemed to support the claim that San Francisco had a boundless future. Perhaps most important of all, the careers of men like Leland Stanford and

Charles Crocker, James G. Fair and John Mackay offered living proof that any San Franciscan could make it.

Throughout the 1850s, returning travelers predicted that San Francisco would become the great commercial metropolis on the West Coast—the Pacific Ocean's New York. As the years passed, tourists landing in San Francisco shifted from predictions of future grandeur to descriptions of present glory. "No one" could "see San Francisco without surprise." Who could have anticipated the "magnificence" of its central streets where hotels, stores, banks, and offices equaled those of Liverpool or Dublin? This city, "the wonder of wonders," had "everything that wealth and prosperity" could create. It was "without a doubt . . . the most marvelous city on the globe." Before then, "no such city of wealth, power, substantiality, and active necessity to the world, ever grew up in such a space of time." Here, in a city less than thirty years old, the bread equaled that of Vienna and the pork "would have soothed the soul of Charles Lamb." San Francisco truly offered a "paradise" for the "poor wretches starving out a miserable existence in the cellars and garrets of . . . great cities in the East."[5]

While the effusions of visitors and tourists inclined Easterners and Europeans to believe the dream, the pamphlets and speakers of immigrant associations actively encouraged them to go west. During the late 1860s, San Francisco businessmen worried increasingly about the supply of labor; therefore, they sponsored several organizations to bring immigrants to their city. In 1867 they founded the Immigrant Aid Association, in 1871 the California Immigrant Union (CIU), and a few years later the Immigration Association of California. Each of these bodies sent speakers to the East and to Europe to promote immigration. Moreover, each organization weighted its emissaries down with pamphlets and literature extolling the state's virtues. Just in 1872, for example, the California Immigrant Union sent out nearly 40,000 pamphlets praising California. That same organization also sponsored lectures in the East that attracted large audiences.[6]

The CIU's efforts, however, pale alongside those of the Immigration Association of California. In the early 1880s, this group annually circulated almost 200,000 documents meant to lure immigrants to California. Pamphlets, folders with maps, and descriptions of the public lands in the state—the CIU blanketed the East with all these forms of literature. Its agent in Council Bluffs, Iowa, obtained the names of thousands of farmers in the East and Midwest and sent propaganda to every one of them. Its representative in Europe established relations with 450 licensed immigration agents from Germany, Austria, Belgium, Switzerland, and France. Translating some 26,000 brochures into various European languages, the IAC tried to flood the continent with literature.[7]

All this propaganda had the same purpose, to convince prospective emigrants to head for California. One of the most widely disseminated tracts was John S. Hittell's *All About California*. This booklet, which appeared in twelve editions, presented California as the true paradise. For the laboring man, wages were high, and the supply of labor was "not sufficient to meet the necessities of the country." For the manufacturer, the growth of extensive mechanical industries was "inevitable." Meanwhile, California's great distance from the East would "make continued importation of many manufactured articles impossible." For the farmer, 48 million acres of land remained open for purchase, much of it "remarkably fertile, some producing more wheat, more grapes and fruit to the acre than any land in the Atlantic States or Europe." Every Californian could enjoy a climate "remarkably conducive to health and longevity." Infallibly, all these advantages, and hundreds more, would conjure a large profit for any and all who came soon. And, even if an individual's anticipations went unfulfilled, he would "still have the satisfaction of living in a country" where he could "enjoy life without painful exertion."[8]

Lectures delivered throughout the East and Midwest deviated little from the pamphlets. Charles Hall's "Illustrated Lecture on California" glorified life in the state. Winters were springlike, and every variety of crop produced prolifically. Volunteer crops of grain sometimes surpassed the original in yield, and many vegetables had two, or even three, seasons a year. The laboring classes were "the most prosperous in the world," and "a man with a good trade and economical habits" could "accumulate a little fortune in ten or fifteen years." In sum, California's "grand combination of climate, soil, mineral wealth, commercial advantages, and great extent of area" made her capable of supporting thirty million people, and offered "a brilliant future."[9]

Such publicity, such portraits, such journalistic hype—these attracted tens of thousands to the Golden State between 1849 and 1880. In all likelihood, few of them accepted the images at face value. But if these pictures were even partly realistic, a much better life could be had in California. Drawn by the roseate images, the latecomers swelled the ranks of San Franciscans already thirsty for success. On into the 1870s, tourists, visitors, and travelers noted the acquisitive nature of many San Franciscans. According to one traveler, "a characteristic feature of life in the Golden City was the emphasis on money, money, money." In San Francisco, "no serious thought of religion or of anything save what is purely temporal and transitory" intruded. San Franciscans would "drain their pockets, sell the clothes off their backs, the home that shelters them, the very land they live by, all in the race for wealth." These metropolitans were "perpetually anxious to amass more money." The "shrewdest Yankee" could not "excel them in looking after the main chance." These people thought that "the whole duty of man consists in getting money."[10]

While literary license certainly exaggerated the desire for success in San Francisco, some of the city's residents would do almost anything, take any gamble, assume any risk. Not surprisingly, they sometimes became easy marks for confidence men. The year 1872 particularly favored con artists and afflicted success hunters. That spring, a man from Portland calling himself Frederick Hendson registered at a Boston hotel. Telling people that he had discovered a fabulous gold mine, he displayed a diagram and rich specimens of gold-bearing quartz. Of course, he himself lacked capital to develop the mine, and he wanted to form a partnership of fifty men. Each would contribute $250 and agree to fight the Indians who surrounded the mine's supposed location. With the Indians dispersed and the mine opened, Hendson would receive the first $50,000 in profits. The company would share the rest. The upshot was predictable. Hendson found his fifty suckers, dumped them in San Francisco, pocketed his $12,500, and disappeared.[11]

San Francisco had more than its share of victims like Hendson's; even leading citizens and businessmen succumbed to the dream of more. "When it came to the matter of . . . quick riches, the residents' gullibility knew no bounds." Therefore, when several prospectors arrived in San Francisco peddling shares in a great diamond and ruby mine, thousands begged for the chance to invest. The *Call* quickly saw through the fraud and editorialized that California was "afflicted periodically with some such excitement which unsettles many people." The paper warned "prudent" men to "have care before embarking on this, one of the wildest, if not the most improbable of all the fortune-promising schemes that have for years been presented to dazzle the eyes of the public." But in an atmosphere in which respected men like William Ralston, president of the Bank of California, and Milton S. Latham, former governor of California, created the New York and San Francisco Mining and Commercial Company to exploit the new discoveries, how could ordinary people be expected to curb their appetites? Their money was saved only when Clarence King and other geologists located the site of the phony mines and exposed the fraud.[12]

The Hendson affair was a classic con, the Great Diamond Hoax a monumental fraud, both so well done that people put up hard cash for the chance to get rich. The perpetrators were so skillful that they avoided apprehension. But San Franciscans had developed a reputation for such gullibility and craving something for nothing that confidence men promoted schemes that made these two seem reasonable. On August 8, 1872, even while the city was caught up in the diamond hoax, a local journalist wrote with some bemusement that "all the ups and downs of stock-gambling, diamond-hunting, and treasure-seeking pale before the new receipt of 'how to get rich in a hurry.'" According to the latest scheme, a group of French settlers from Louisiana had once founded a city in New Mexico. The city grew and became wealthy until an earthquake destroyed its water supply. After struggling for some time, the citizens abandoned their homes, but before they left, they buried all their treasures, including life-size statues of saints cast in gold and silver. The people vanished, but now, centuries later, a man had arrived in San Francisco bearing a map that disclosed the "exact site" of the riches. As the *Call* put it, "tell a man the wonderful tales of the Arabian Nights are true, and he will laugh you to scorn; but still . . . shares are bought in Arizona diamond companies, and some few believe in the Deserted City. What next?"[13]

Hendson's gold mine, the Great Diamond Hoax, and the buried city reflect exaggerated distortions and perversions of the desire for success, but they also suggest the intensity of that goal among San Franciscans. Journalists noted the attitude toward money in the city and worried that this "desire to get rich suddenly, this excessive haste, this high pressure speed" might "result in ruin." The *Wasp* feared disaster because of the strong "temptation to speculation" in San Francisco. When it referred to speculators, the journal meant not only "chronic stock gamblers" but also merchants who hazarded the profits and even the very capital of legitimate business. In fact, gambling was the closest thing San Francisco had to an official sport in the 1870s, and nearly everyone played one game or another. Some bet on the turn of a card in the splendid and luxurious, vast and magnificent gambling halls. Others fancied themselves bulls and bears and wagered at the stock exchange. Still others favored more mundane kinds of chance and bought lottery tickets. Inevitably, some San Franciscans took advantage of the mania. When the Mechanics' Institute needed money for a new library, it held a lottery, and when Charlie Butterfield, an unemployed workingman, needed money for food, he tried to raffle off his ring.[14]

A few shrewd San Franciscans recognized their own natures and those of their fellow citizens. Harriet Lane Levy, herself the daughter of a prosperous merchant, was awestruck by her millionaire neighbors. Years later, she recalled them as "characters in a novel," and she never quite got over seeing huge cans of milk delivered for daily baths. She tried "to resist the argument for importance offered by the display" and was able "to retain her assurance" when she saw a victoria with a single driver. "But coachman and footman, clad in colored livery, rigid above a closed coupe, scattered" her "identity. At the approach of a plum-colored livery . . . her spirit brushed the sidewalk." To Miss Levy and others of the day, money possessed a "precedence that it never lost in computing relative values in life, making . . . it the basis of serenity and confidence." The standard of prestige for many San Franciscans was wealth. "To have money was to be somebody; to have none was to be nobody; the man who had more was better than the man who had less."[15]

Mrs. Fremont Older, the wife of California's progressive editor, also remembered the 1870s in San Francisco. To her, the people of the city comprised two classes, "millionaires and those who hoped to be millionaires." Mrs. Older claimed that San Franciscans actually seemed to believe that "the rainbow's pot of gold was found on Twin Peaks," that "Aladdin's lantern could be had for the asking," that "Jack's beanstalk had grown to the sky." In this extraordinary city, "foot passengers were warned against stubbing their toes: there was danger of falling upon Comstock quartz projecting from the ground."[16]

In this urge to succeed, San Franciscans resembled citizens from every part of the United States. One of the strongest desires among nineteenth-century Americans was getting ahead. Throughout the country and throughout the century, men on the make watched and waited for the main chance. Even ministers of the gospel succumbed to, and encouraged, American cupidity. Russell Conwell, a Philadelphia preacher and founder of Temple University, proclaimed that the "opportunity to get rich, to attain unto great wealth" was "within the reach of almost every man and woman." Americans could literally grasp "'acres of diamonds.' . . . Never in the history of the world did a poor man without capital have such an opportunity to get rich quickly," an opportunity that every man had best seize "as part of one's Christian and Godly duty."[17]

Conwell blared his message from one end of the United States to the other. He preached "Acres of Diamonds" 6,152 times to a collective audience estimated at 13 million and published it in countless magazines. Following its first separate appearance in 1888, at least eleven different editions ultimately materialized, one with dozens of illustrations and biographies of successful men and women.[18]

European travelers frequently noticed, and criticized, this aspect of the American personality. As early as 1832, the Englishwoman Frances Trollope (admittedly no great admirer of Americans) wrote that "nothing" could "exceed their activity and perseverance in all kinds of speculation, handicraft, and enterprise which promises a profitable pecuniary result." One of her countrymen, long resident in the United States, told Mrs. Trollope that he had never overheard a conversation between Americans without the word *dollar* being pronounced. And Mrs. Trollope concluded that such unity of purpose and sympathy of feeling could be found "nowhere else, except, perhaps, in an ant's nest." Charles Dickens agreed with the lady tourist. In *Martin*

Chuzzlewit, he observed that all of the Americans' "cares, hopes, joys, affections, virtues, and associations seemed to be melted down into dollars. . . . Men were weighed by their dollars, measures gauged by their dollars; life was auctioneered, appraised, put up, and knocked down for its dollars. The next respectable thing to dollars was any venture having their attainment for its end." Americans would "do anything for dollars!" [19]

American novelists also recognized the avarice of their fellow citizens. William Dean Howells described the effects of greed in *The Rise of Silas Lapham* and *A Hazard of New Fortunes*. Cupidity dominated Frank Norris's *The Pit* and *McTeague* (a novel of San Francisco that became the basis for Erich von Stroheim's classic movie entitled *Greed*). Mark Twain and Charles Dudley Warner satirized the American quest for wealth and provided an epithet for the entire era in *The Gilded Age*. Earlier in the century, James Fenimore Cooper had castigated the United States for being a country in which "money has got to be so completely the end of life that few think of it as a means." The "malign influence" dominated the entire nation and "swallowed up" all principles "in the absorbing desire for gain." As one of his characters put it, "The tulip mania of Holland was trifling compared to this!" [20]

The national context of economic desire, along with the phenomenon of the gold rush, partly explains the search for success in San Francisco. But the strength of the quest in that city had another dimension. For about twenty years, the actual existence of widespread opportunity persuaded people that a better life was possible there. During the two decades after the gold rush, California was isolated and thousands of miles away from sources of supply. Major sectors of the economy remained undeveloped with no distinct channels of trade, no old established firms, and no accumulated capital. For varying numbers of years, mining, commerce, agriculture, and manufacturing depended on individuals working alone, not in organized units. Moreover, success or failure often resulted from luck rather than particular skills or technical knowledge. In this regard, California's economy resembled any other American frontier region—the Atlantic Coast in the seventeenth century, the trans-Appalachian West after the Revolution, or the Pacific Northwest in the late nineteenth century. As a result, during the 1850s, California's economy was open, fluid, and did offer great opportunities.

The first sector of the economy exploited by many immigrants was obviously mining, and the early mines typified the entire economy. According to Henry George, "mining gave a color to all California thought and feeling. It fostered a reckless, generous, independent spirit, with a strong disposition to 'take chances' and 'trust to luck.' Than the placer mining, no more independent business could be conceived. The miner working for himself owed no master." He "worked when and only when he pleased," and "when his claim gave out, or for any reason he desired to move, he had but to shoulder his pick and move on."[21]

Geologic conditions produced the opportunities for early California miners. The precious metal had originally been deposited deep within the Sierra Nevada when a subterranean intrusion of molten ore formed countless gold-bearing veins. An era of erosion brought the gold nearer the surface. After that, seismic upheavals lifted the entire area and tilted it to the west. This change in the pitch of the land increased the force of streams and, consequently, their eroding power. In other words, two periods of erosion succeeded the one of vein formation. Consequently, the western foothills of the Sierra Nevada were one of the richest placer mining regions in the world, an area in which great wealth lay on or near the earth's surface.[22]

This is not to say that all or even most of the forty-niners struck it rich; only that opportunity beckoned all men equally, at least for a few years. Skill, capital, and knowledge were not essential prerequisites to success; anyone could master the simple technology of placer mining. Working alone or in a small group, the prospector gouged some earth from a glacial or alluvial deposit called a placer and swirled it around in a pan of water. The heavy gold dropped to the bottom, and the light, extraneous matter flowed over the rim. This procedure remained the basic technology of gold mining for years. Improvements such as the cradle or rocker, the long tom, and the sluice appeared, but each refinement merely elaborated the basic technique by allowing the miner to wash larger quantities of dirt.[23]

The influx of miners combined with California's isolation to create opportunities in another sector of the economy, commerce. In the first two decades after statehood, enormous quantities of goods had to be imported from the East, China, Europe, Latin America, and even Australia. Letters sent across the Isthmus of Panama took nearly a month to reach New York, and, after a Manhattan supplier received an order, it might take him several weeks to locate shipping. Thus, between the time a California merchant ordered goods from Gotham and received them, six months might elapse.

Under these conditions, a trader had no way of anticipating the market. It might be overstocked or undersupplied. Nor could a merchant learn what others had ordered. Cargo manifests listed many items only as sundries and frequently described the contents of a package without indicating quantities. Furthermore, merchants could not keep large stocks on hand. High interest rates made it preferable to sell goods immediately rather than wait for higher prices. Warehouses were few, expensive, and insecure. Storeships charged high tabs and lighterage imposed additional burdens.[24]

Because merchants could not maintain a reasonable supply of goods, prices fluctuated violently. Shortages multiplied prices ten, a hundred, or even three hundred times; then, oversupply caused prices to collapse just as quickly. The arrival of one ship could change the market from scarcity to glut, making or breaking a man. In the fall of 1849, lumber brought $400 per thousand feet. By the spring of 1850, it sold for less than the cost of freight. At one time, tobacco brought two dollars a pound; at another, boxes of it served as stepping-stones. Dried apples fluctuated between five and seventy-five cents a pound, whiskey between forty cents and two dollars a gallon, and butter between six and eighty cents a pound.[25]

Given such a market, commerce offered great opportunities, and any man could dream of mercantile success. Eastern contacts and sources of credit in a difficult money market did help. Merchants had to know the mining seasons, master steamboat schedules, and keep books. But chance market conditions, which individual merchants could neither predict nor control, often determined success. Anyone with a daring and adventurous spirit could try his hand at trade. David Hawley, typical of these early San Francisco merchants, once bought a shipload of potatoes and dry goods in Hawaii, returned to San

Francisco, and sold his cargo for $600,000. At the dedication of the new Merchants' Exchange in 1867, one speaker compared the career of traders to the "white-winged carrier across the trackless ocean." The hidden rocks, dangerous shoals, and violent storms all had counterparts in commerce. The merchant had no written law or method to guide him to fortune; he had only his good sense, strong arm, and manly efforts to rely on.[26]

Like mining and commerce, California agriculture offered the chance of success for some years after the gold rush. At a time when 30 percent of the American people lived in towns and cities, California's urban population rose from 21 percent in 1860 to 37 percent in 1870 and 43 percent in 1880. And, because of the state's isolation and the perishability of food, this large urban population had to be fed locally. In short, there was a demand for farmers, a demand that continued throughout the period. In 1860, agriculture employed only about 16 percent of the state's labor force; in 1870, only about 21 percent; and in 1880, about 23 percent. At the same time nationally, farms employed about 50 percent of the labor force.[27]

The increased number of farms and farm acreage between 1850 and 1880 reflected this need and the opportunities it implied. In 1850, there were only 872 farms in California with a total of about 22,000 acres; in 1860, 19,000 with 9 million; in 1870, 24,000 farms with 12 million acres. Finally, in 1880, 36,000 farms totaled nearly 17 million acres. Thousands of men sought opportunity in farming.[28]

The people who established these farms had a shimmering vision of the future. In short, they foresaw California as a veritable Garden of Eden. In 1858, one of their spokesmen, Samuel Bell, a minister and a founder of the University of California, addressed the State Agricultural Society and claimed that farming had already supplanted mining as the major source of wealth in the state. According to Bell, California poured out agricultural riches more bounteous, more ravishing, and more inexhaustible than its mineral resources. In the climax of his speech, Bell became rhapsodic as he asserted that the farms and farmers of California were unequaled throughout the world. He claimed to have seen beets weighing 125 pounds, turnips 30, and pears 4. Farms yielded 300 bushels of potatoes per acre, 90 of barley, and 100 of wheat. A single acre produced at least 50,000 pounds of carrots, beets, turnips, and onions. The same land gave four crops of peas in a year or strawberries for seven months. This cornucopia resulted from California's magnificent climate. In the Golden State, there was no winter, only eternal spring, summer, and fall. A farmer could work all year and gain "elastic vigor" from his toil but no stiff limbs, rheumatic joints, premature wrinkles, old age, or decay. According to men like Bell, California was an agricultural paradise if there ever was one; and the California farmer had virtually unlimited opportunities.[29]

A fourth sector of California's early economy, manufacturing, offered no less opportunity than mining, trading, or farming. San Francisco experienced chronic labor shortages during the 1850s; thus, California's artisans and mechanics earned the highest wages in the nation. The perception of alternative sources of employment furnished the key to these conditions. As long as men thought they could improve their lives in the mines, they avoided the urban labor market, and they refused to work for less than they received in the hills. In fact, urban laborers frequently demanded a premium to make up for opportunities lost by not being in the mines. San Francisco carpenters demanded twelve dollars a day in 1850 while miners were making ten. In 1849, the federal government had to pay common laborers sixteen dollars a day in San Francisco, the same wage received by paymasters. And longshoremen successfully struck for six dollars a day in 1853, a time when miners were getting only five.[30]

The constant drift of men between San Francisco and the Sierra illustrates the lure of the mines and its effect on wages and the supply of labor in the city during the 1850s. For example, Howard Gardiner first reached San Francisco in July 1849. In August, he left for the mines but returned in December. He stayed at the bay through March and then went back to the gold fields. August found him in the city once again, where he stayed until May 1851. Then it was off to the mines for six years. Finally, in the fall of 1857, he returned home.[31]

Men like Gardiner abounded in California. They tried their luck at mining, got discouraged, and drifted to San Francisco. If they could not equal their income from mining, they returned to the hills. As a result, California laborers demanded and received the highest wages in the country. In 1860, the mean ratio of annual wages in twelve manufacturing categories was two-and-a-half times greater in the Pacific

TABLE 2.2   RATIO OF SAN FRANCISCO WAGES TO
WAGES IN THE MIDDLE ATLANTIC STATES, 1860

Industry	Percentage Ratio to Earnings in the Middle Atlantic States, 1860
Foundries and Machine Shops	458
Cigars and Cigarettes	297
Flour and Grist Milling	281
Agricultural Implements	263
Sawed Lumber	261
Carriages and Wagons	260
Malt Liquors	258
Woolen Goods	237
Leather	216
Distilled Liquors	191
Brick and Tile	182
Paper	149
Mean Average	255

states than in the Middle Atlantic. Table 2.2 compares the annual earnings of workers in Pacific Coast industries to those in Middle Atlantic states. High differentials prevailed in every case.[32]

Of course, prices were also higher in San Francisco, but not nearly two-and-a-half times as high. Some important items, such as food, were actually cheaper. Moreover, confident San Franciscans probably concerned themselves more with the level of income than with the cost of living. Certainly, California's propagandists and publicists emphasized the availability of jobs much more than they did the cost of living.

All in all, during the years after the gold rush, four major sectors of the economy offered widespread opportunity. Mining, commerce, agriculture, and manufacturing all seemed to promise success. Given the undeveloped nature of the economy, the lack of preexisting institutions, and the absence of barriers to entry into the economy, anyone could take a chance. In short, success or failure was as likely to be determined by luck or hard work as by background, the size of one's fortune, or technical skills or knowledge. For parts of two decades, depending on the sector, California's economy remained open. All these conditions contributed to the widespread conviction that any San Franciscan could improve his position.

Nothing seemed to substantiate that notion more than the lives of

San Francisco's wealthiest men. They almost universally exemplified the rags-to-riches myth and provided living evidence of the American dream. Among the city's more notable millionaires were such men as Henry Miller and Charles Lux, who made their money raising livestock; Ben Holladay, whose fortune derived from Wells, Fargo, and Company; and Lloyd Tevis and James Ben Ali Haggin, two brothers-in-law who became rich investing in land, mines, and railroads. Then there was the "bank crowd"—William C. Ralston, William Sharon, D. O. Mills, Alvinza Hayward, John P. Jones, and Elias J. "Lucky" Baldwin—whose wealth came from the Bank of California and the silver mines of Nevada. But when one thinks of San Francisco millionaires of the late nineteenth century, one immediately thinks of two groups, the big four (Charles Crocker, Mark Hopkins, Collis P. Huntington, and Leland Stanford), who built the Central Pacific Railroad, and the bonanza firm (James G. Fair, James C. Flood, John W. Mackay, and William S. O'Brien), who uncovered the heart of the Comstock. By 1880, the wealth of these men was legendary, and they were no longer mere commoners. They had become railroad kings and silver princes.

The immense wealth of the big four and the bonanza firm fascinated the rest of the city because it seemed to prove that anyone could do well there—to verify the dream. Therefore, San Franciscans loved to speculate about the size of their fortunes. In 1871 the *Call* guessed that each of the big four had $10 million. Six years later, another estimate suggested a combined wealth of $50 million, a sum surpassed by the fortunes of the silver barons, supposedly worth a total of $100 million. According to John S. Hittell, these estimates were trifling compared to reality; he figured that the silver kings were worth $150 million. But all these guesses pale beside a claim that John Mackay's $275 million made him the world's richest man.[33]

Not only their wealth but their very lives made these millionaires an important symbol. Like most other San Franciscans, the truly rich had remarkably undistinguished youths. They came from poor families, left home young, made their way to California, and then achieved fame and fortune. To others, these self-made men provided inspiration.

Crocker, Hopkins, and Huntington all descended from families who had suffered hard times. Charlie Crocker's father, once a successful liquor salesman in Troy, New York, failed about 1834, and Crocker remembered his youth as a constant struggle with poverty. Collis Huntington's father couldn't support a wife and nine children on his small farm, a problem compounded by his iconoclasm and freethinking, excommunication and ostracism from the community. Mark Hopkins's family experienced straitened circumstances when his father died leaving a widow and eight children. His death ended Hopkins's formal education, and Mark went to work in the family store.[34]

Poverty precluded much schooling for Crocker and Huntington as well. Like Hopkins, both of them had to help support themselves at an early age. After neighbors ceased trading with Huntington's father, his fortunes declined steadily. The children were so hungry that the town overseers took custody of Huntington and one brother. Bound over to a local farmer, Huntington spent one year on a farm, where he received seven dollars a month plus room and board. The following year he worked for a shopkeeper, then went to New York City. After Crocker's father's business failed, he became the sole support of his mother and sister. At one point, Crocker labored sixteen hours a day for eleven dollars a month. Another time, he sold newspapers to feed the family. Finally, after two years, the Crockers moved to a farm in Indiana.[35]

Stanford's childhood differed in several respects from Hopkins's, Huntington's, and Crocker's. The child of a united family, he received an education and never experienced poverty. His father kept an inn and farmed 300 acres, built roads and bridges, and held contracts for grading part of the Albany-Schenectady railroad. Old Man Stanford had enough money to educate his children, and Leland attended school until the age of twelve. After that, his father hired private tutors to teach him at home. At seventeen, Stanford enrolled in the Clinton Liberal Institute, where he remained for three years. One year at Cazenovia Seminary ended his formal education, and he quit school to read law in an Albany office.[36]

After Stanford's legal apprenticeship, his life began to parallel those of his associates. Each of the four left home and struck out on his own, and each was moderately successful. Stanford spent three years in Albany, was admitted to the bar, and then headed for Wisconsin. He opened an office in Port Washington and became prominent in society and politics. But when fire destroyed his home and library in 1852, he decided to leave Wisconsin. He may have been planning to move even before this calamity; immigration to Wisconsin had slowed noticeably, and his business had declined. In any event, the fire settled his mind, and Stanford joined his five brothers in California.[37]

Crocker, Stanford, and Hopkins left home under somewhat different circumstances. Crocker disagreed with his father one morning, packed up his belongings (one shirt, a clean pair of socks, and a dickey), and made his way to Mishawaka, Indiana. There he worked as a farm laborer for seven months, in a sawmill for four months, and in an iron forge for several years. In 1845, aged twenty-two, he discovered an ore bed and built his own forge. He supported himself for five years, sold the forge, packed up his assets, and headed west. Huntington, too, set out on his own at an early age. At sixteen, he took his life's savings ($84), went to New York City, bought a load of merchandise, and began peddling. On buying trips to New York, he purchased discounted notes and collected them as he traveled. By 1842, he had enough capital to open a store in Oneonta, New York, which soon became the largest in the country. Seven years later, he settled his affairs, pocketed $2,000, and made for California.[38]

Nothing about their early lives foretold the enormous success awaiting these men in California. Their immediate families were undistinguished and rather poor, except for Stanford's. Three of them had no particular education, and all four left home at an early age. Each probably went to California with a small amount of capital, but no more than thousands of other men. In essence, they were as anonymous as anyone who trekked across the country during those first years.

The early lives of the silver kings, although more veiled than those of the railroad kings, began just as inconsequentially. Poverty stricken, uneducated, and from broken families, their backgrounds made them poor candidates for success, but they too became millionaires, "proving" that the dream was real and that anyone had a chance in California.

Like many other San Franciscans, they were Irish. James G. Fair was born near Belfast, John W. Mackay in Dublin, and William S.

O'Brien in Queen's County. Only James C. Flood claimed birth in the United States, possibly an affectation he adopted after becoming rich and famous.[39]

All four men, moreover, came from poor families whose poverty precluded formal education. Flood had no schooling; Mackay had little. The death of Mackay's father forced him to support his mother and sister by selling newspapers. For the rest of his life, his lack of formal schooling embarrassed him. His handwriting was labored and cramped, and he always asked a friend to write his letters. O'Brien also came from mean circumstances. He arrived in San Francisco barefoot, whereupon a stranger gave him a pair of boots. According to local legend, O'Brien spent the rest of his life trying to find the stranger. What we know of Fair's story essentially duplicates his partners'. His father fled Ireland in 1843 with four children, left them with a friend in Illinois, and went to Alabama. He hoped to establish a farm but died unexpectedly, leaving the children to fend for themselves.[40]

Other than these few scattered details, almost nothing is known about the silver kings before they came to California. But because their backgrounds were so typical, other San Franciscans could identify with them and hope to emulate them. Journalists, commentators, and social critics regularly pointed out that not one of the city's millionaires had inherited his money and that they had come from the barefooted strata of society. The conclusion seemed inescapable. No place else on earth offered a society with so little stratification. Nowhere else did men have such an opportunity to realize their dreams. Nowhere else could any man become a gentleman, or maybe even a king.

3. Success: Reality and Perception

By objective standards, many San Franciscans accomplished their primary goal in the late nineteenth century: they experienced social mobility. The Irish became better off, more Chinese got jobs, immigrants generally moved into the white-collar ranks. And yet, for contemporaries, the gleam on California's shine began to tarnish.

Denis Kearney became the WPC rabble-rouser, its champion of gloom and doom, but he too had begun to succeed. Kearney's life and career support the theory that San Franciscans were improving their lives, at least economically. His example, therefore, generates curiosity about the sources of discontent in the city. What made Kearney, a man doing well and well on the way to greater success, lead a popular protest? The answer to that question, and to the larger problem of discontent in a city of mobility, begins to emerge only if we change our frame of reference. We need to cease considering what was actually happening and begin to contemplate what Kearney and his followers thought was happening in San Francisco.

As for Kearney himself, like many of his fellow San Franciscans, he was an ambitious immigrant who had come to the city seeking a better life, and by the middle of the 1870s he had achieved some success. Born in Oakmount, County Cork, Ireland, in 1847, Kearney remained there until his father's death forced him to become self-supporting. He signed on as a cabin boy and eventually became a master mariner. In 1863 he migrated to America and, five years later, settled in San Francisco. For several years, he worked on California coastal steamers, but in 1872 he bought a drayage firm. By 1877, he was doing well. Business prospered, and three drays brought him a comfortable in-come. As he proudly wrote Lord Bryce, he was "the owner of a fine house."[1]

Throughout these years, Kearney tried to educate and improve him-self. He frequented newspaper offices, where he made friends with re-porters, and he was well-known at the Lyceum for Self-Culture, a local educational and debating society.[2]

By 1890, Kearney would achieve many of the goals that had im-pelled him to San Francisco. As early as the 1880s, he was on friendly terms with Leland Stanford. Jane Stanford later recalled how the erst-while drayman "became an ardent, most devoted and loyal friend" of her husband, and Kearney sent a letter of condolence when their son died in 1884. Now running an employment agency, Kearney also asked Stanford to tell his wife that he "would select the proper and necessary help for her . . . , that is, if [he] was deemed worthy of the honor." Kearney himself knew William H. Crocker, the banker son of Charles, and he occasionally dropped in at the Crocker Bank "to see 'his good friend Will.'" When the former agitator became fatally ill in 1907, one of his daughters was visiting Paris, another was in Japan on part of a world tour, and the third was singing in Europe.[3]

Denis Kearney was a man who wanted to do well; he sought money, culture, and the company of successful men. He was proud of his suc-cess and gloried in his accomplishments. Late in life, he resented statements that he had been "merely an agitator" and asked an inti-mate friend, "Haven't I been a success in life?" He recounted how he had gone to sea as a cabin boy but became a first officer. Then he took up a new business and "in a short time . . . was making good money as a drayman." Afterward, when he found himself broke, he went into the grain market, bought stocks, and held his own. He had money in the bank and in 1899 was described as a "prosperous speculator in wheat, sugar, and oil. His powerful hands were no longer knotted and clenched, but white and soft. The chin no longer protruded, and the jaw had less of the appearance of aggressive prominence."[4]

Kearney's history replicates that of many other San Franciscans—as well as that of Americans in general. In recent decades, an impressive number of historians have studied urban social mobility in the United

States—in the East and the West, in large cities and in small towns. The results of their work have been striking—widespread social mobility characterized American cities. Like other cities, San Francisco has attracted analysts of mobility. Three studies, each focusing on a slightly different time and a somewhat different group of people, have shown that social mobility was occurring in San Francisco before 1880. At least statistically, San Franciscans were improving their stations in life, and the career of Denis Kearney was typical.

One of these analyses measures mobility between 1870 and 1900 by studying changing proportions of white-collar workers in the city's nine major ethnic groups. It reveals moderate to substantial gains in status for all ethnic groups but a somewhat more varied pattern for the working class. Irish, Chinese, and Canadian working men scored major gains but remained underrepresented in white-collar ranks. Germans, English, and Yankees slightly increased their proportion of white-collar jobs while the percentage held by Scandinavians and Italians in 1900 had actually declined. In general, the Bay Area Irish moved more rapidly from working class to middle class status than did their Irish brethren in the East. The Chinese matched their rate of economic progress, and both the Irish and the Chinese did better than working class Italians, Scandinavians, or blacks.[5]

A second study seeks to determine the degree of mobility among San Francisco's Irish between 1852 and 1880 (see table 3.1). This analysis shows that the pattern of Irish women's occupations did not change because San Francisco did not offer women any greater opportunities in 1880 than in 1852. However, between 1852 and 1870, "the occupational status of Irish-born males . . . improved slowly but surely." Then, after 1870, the depression halted further advances.[6]

One last study focuses on white-collar mobility in nineteenth-

TABLE 3.1   OCCUPATIONAL STRUCTURE, IRISH-BORN
MALES IN SAN FRANCISCO, 1852–80

	% 1852	% 1860	% 1880
White-Collar	15.4	15.8	19.9
Skilled Blue-Collar	19.6	20.5	18.6
Semiskilled Blue-Collar	17.3	26.7	30.0
Unskilled	47.7	37.0	31.5

century San Francisco, particularly among merchants. It too reveals that occupational mobility occurred during these thirty years. For the sample used, 60 percent of the men with low manual jobs in 1850 had improved their occupational status by 1880; 23 percent of the skilled workers, and 57 percent of the low white-collar employees.[7]

But the experiences of upwardly mobile San Franciscans—of men like Denis Kearney—present a paradox. If San Franciscans were upwardly mobile and had improved their economic status, why was there widespread dissatisfaction in the late 1870s, dissatisfaction manifested in both the July riots and the formation of the WPC? Why were people unhappy if they were fulfilling one of their basic desires—getting ahead?

This question has several possible answers. Maybe the protesters were complaining about some condition other than economics in general and the improvements in their own lives in particular. However, this explanation seems unlikely because the July riots occurred in an economic context. Demonstrations were called to support eastern strikers; and the speeches, pamphlets, and broadsides of the WPC broadcast economic concerns. It is impossible to consider the Workingmen's Party of California without thinking about economic conditions in California in the 1870s.

A second explanation for the seeming contradiction between concurrent mobility and widespread dissatisfaction is that the protesters had not gotten ahead. After all, not everyone was improving himself. For example, the study of mobility among San Francisco's Irish shows that in 1880, 31.5 percent of the Irish-born men remained unskilled laborers. Another 30 percent still performed semiskilled blue-collar work. Altogether, the proportion of Irish-born males in the two lowest occupational groups had decreased only from 63.7 percent in 1860 to 61.5 percent in 1880.

This is an intriguing explanation for the existence of discontent during a time of mobility. Nevertheless, it too remains problematic. For one thing, it is not susceptible to proof. We can characterize the WPC only in aggregate (rather than individual) terms, so we cannot determine if the movement was made up only of San Franciscans who had not improved their lots. But it does seem unlikely. This hypothesis directly counters the description of party members given by the

WPC itself (see chapter 1). Also, it explicitly contradicts the clearest statement of party membership we have from a participant: Frank Roney's claim that "the staunchest members" of the WPC were small property owners.

Finally, the theory that the WPC included only people with frustrated desires contradicts the case of Denis Kearney. His life certainly does not support the theory that Workingmen were San Francisco's failures. Some other explanation is needed.

That explanation comes to light if we change our basic viewpoint. We need to consider what people believed was happening as well as what was happening in fact. Some years ago, Stephan Thernstrom, one of the first American historians to study mobility quantitatively, wondered if determining how much mobility actually occurred provided an adequate analysis of the historical record. According to Thernstrom,

> the meaning of mobility—whether a given level of it is perceived as high or low, whether it satisfies the people who experience it or only whets greater appetite—is influenced by societal values. Even if 40 percent of American working-class children found their way into middle-class callings and only 10 percent, say, of French working-class youths, Americans may have *expected* to experience four times as much mobility; indeed, they may have expected something like 100-percent upward mobility and have been more frustrated and embittered than their objectively less-mobile French counterparts. This extreme example is perhaps implausible, but the general point—the need to examine subjective perceptions and expectations as well as objective measurements—must be kept firmly in mind.[8]

This statement provides an essential clue to understanding what was happening in San Francisco in 1877, to Denis Kearney and to his followers. Kearney had advanced, but he felt insecure, and he began to realize how easily his gains could disappear. He had already lost a sizable amount of money in the stock market, and a monopoly of the customs' house drayage limited his business. Because only one firm in San Francisco was a "United States bonded drayman," other teamsters lost about $70,000 worth of business a year. Kearney, along with other draymen, protested and tried to destroy the monopoly. They failed, and he believed that powerful interests had blackballed him. He began to doubt that he would ever acquire "the palace and thousands of acres" that crystallized his goals.[9] The thought of failure scared and angered Kearney, and he began to wonder what had gone wrong.

Others felt similar emotions. Some feared losing the small gains they had made; others worried that they could not continue to better themselves. Still others doubted that they would ever find the success that brought them to San Francisco in the first place. It was not the past and its success that concerned them. It was the present and the future—a present and a future that they had begun to doubt. And this doubt created dissatisfaction in a city of social and economic improvement.

According to the Workingmen, the state had changed. California no longer offered every man the chance to improve his life. "Zero" spoke for his fellows when he explained that men "driven from the East" knew what the West was really like: "alluring and fascinating . . . a dreamland as long as unreached." But once men arrived, the dream became a "nightmare." William Wellock, an English immigrant and the vice president of the WPC, told a Thanksgiving Day crowd in 1878 that "hundreds of thousands" had been "induced to move to the Golden State by the glittering vision." But they had "found themselves cruelly mistaken" and had gradually been "oppressed and degraded" until they were now "most bitterly ground down to poverty."[10]

Frank Roney experienced more than disappointment in the city. He confided to his diary that a friend from Denver wanted to come west, but Roney refused to encourage him. Two months later, he felt "a stronger desire to return" to Omaha than he had "thought . . . possible." His discontent finally culminated when he imagined a "fearful" end for the city with "no soul remain[ing] to tell the terrible calamity that befell" it. San Franciscans reminded him of "a crowd of roisterers" during an epidemic, people who "drank to the success of King Death and sang in chorus the glories of the plague while the victims writhed before them in all the agony which the horrors of the plague inflicted." As Mrs. Fremont Older wrote some years later, "the peach-blossom hue [had] left the air." San Francisco was "a hard world of reality after all. One could be sad in California as well as in the East, South or across the seas."[11]

In pamphlets and brochures, the WPC asserted that California had turned. What had once been "the fairest" and "most promising" of states now presented a "pitiable spectacle."[12] The transformation was total. This state had been truly blessed by nature and stood "unsurpassed" in the fertility of its resources. Its fields produced "plenteously, and without excessive labor to the efforts of the husbandman." Its pastures and meadows were "sufficient for the flocks of the nation," and its minerals "justified [its] proud name as the El Dorado of the world." To citizens of other, less favored lands, California appeared "pre-eminent in resources and capability." But, instead of being rich and prosperous, California was prostrate. It no longer attracted "poor and oppressed laborers of other lands in search of homes for themselves, their wives, and their children." In fact, California's decline was so total and so fearful that its "very name" struck "terror" in "the hearts of all honest workingmen" who were looking for "new fields of labor and new lands for homes." As conditions now stood, "no capitalist, comfortably-fixed mechanic, or farmer, would think of leaving his home in the States east of the Rocky Mountains, and coming to the Pacific coast." And, with a plaintive cry, the Workingmen asked, "Why is it that with those who are already among us there is neither content nor happiness?"[13]

What had happened in San Francisco? Why had thousands of San Franciscans begun to worry about the future, become anxious during a time of prosperity and seemingly widespread success? The explanation for unhappiness, and the source of disgruntlement, can best be found by examining the social and economic context of San Francisco between 1849 and 1877, especially depression, economic development, and social contrasts.

To begin with, although San Franciscans remained generally optimistic and seemingly believed in William Wellock's "glittering vision," they also had darker forebodings. At some level of consciousness, they had always understood that fortunes could be lost as well as won and that failure was inextricably linked to success. To remind them of this, the figure of Joshua Norton stood before them. Perhaps the profound understanding that downward mobility was just as possible as upward explains the strange fascination and affection of San Franciscans for this odd character.

Norton, an Englishman, had arrived in San Francisco and entered business around 1847 or 1848. At one time, he bought goods for several mercantile houses in the interior of the state and achieved some success. He speculated in real estate and owned valuable property. After acquiring a sizable fortune, Norton tried cornering the rice market. He purchased all the rice in the city and as much in transit as he could. He bought at high prices and figured that his corner would justify the risk. Just as the plan reached culmination, several ships laden with grain entered the harbor, ruining Norton. When he was unable to fulfill his contracts, a protracted lawsuit followed. During the trial, Norton's mind snapped, and he became convinced that he was Emperor of California and Protector of Mexico. As his first official act, he wanted to settle the dispute, marry a creditor's daughter, and make her his empress. San Franciscans immediately took Norton to heart. Restaurants served him free meals, and shopkeepers accepted the bills and bonds he had printed (free of charge) at local printshops. San Franciscans saluted and bowed to him on the streets. He reviewed cadets at the University of California and marched at the head of the annual police parade. The city directory even listed him as "Norton, Joshua (Emperor), dwl. Metropolitan Hotel."[14]

At least one San Franciscan consciously understood the significance of lives like Joshua Norton's. While Mark Twain lived in San Francisco between 1864 and 1866, he wrote two stories that illustrated the vagaries of fate, the injustice of life, and the inability to predict who would succeed or fail. Significantly, the *Call* reprinted both stories in the early 1870s.

The first to appear was "The Story of the Bad Little Boy." In it, Jim stole, lied, bullied, and cheated, yet nothing ever happened to him the way Sunday school books predicted; he never received his just punishments. Instead, he led "a charmed life." When he grew up, he got married, "raised a large family, and brained them all with an axe one night." He "got wealthy by all manner of cheating and rascality" and became "the infernalest wickedest scoundrel to sit in the legislature."[15]

Twain's other story, that of "The Good Little Boy," told about Jacob, who always obeyed his parents, studied his books, and arrived at Sunday school on time. He never played hooky or lied, and his life's ambition was to become the hero of a Sunday school book. "But somehow nothing ever went right with this good little boy; nothing ever turned out with him the way it turned out with the good little boys in the books." His good deeds always got him in trouble, and he always received the blame for other boys' mischief. He came to an untimely end when he tried to stop a gang of boys from tying dynamite to a string of dogs. When Alderman McWelter appeared, all the other children fled. Jacob, full of innocence, tried to explain. The alderman never waited to hear Jacob's story and proceeded to spank him. "In an instant, that good little boy shot out through the roof and soared away toward the sun, with the fragments of those fifteen dogs stringing after him." Finally, a part of him "came down all right in a tree-top in an adjoining county," but the rest "was apportioned around among four townships, and so they had to hold five inquests . . . to find out whether he was dead or not, and how it occurred." [16]

Although San Franciscans could dismiss Emperor Norton as an eccentric, and Jacob and Jim as fictional characters, no one could miss the lesson of William C. Ralston and his untimely death. He provided the most spectacular and obvious example of failure to a city built on the cult of success. In 1875 Ralston was one of the city's richest men. He had arrived in San Francisco in 1854 and quickly made a fortune in banking, commerce, mining, and industrial development. As president of the Bank of California and as a leading mining man, he had poured millions into the growth of the city's economy. But in midsummer 1875, rumors began flying that he was in financial trouble and that the bank itself was in danger. On August 29, these stories reached a fever pitch, and a run began. By early afternoon, the bank was out of cash, and the greatest financial institution in the West closed its doors. The next day, the bank's board demanded Ralston's resignation, and he surrendered his entire personal fortune to cover a debt of nearly $5 million to the bank. That afternoon, Ralston went for a swim in the bay, as he frequently did. While in the water, he apparently suffered a stroke and died. [17]

To San Francisco, Ralston's sudden, unexpected collapse and death carried a symbolic meaning. His demise suggested that financial security was nonexistent—not even for one who had fulfilled every dream. On the Sunday after Ralston's death, many San Francisco ministers preached this lesson. Reverend W. H. Platt, rector of Grace Church, wondered, "If this great moneyed power could go down, might not less conspicuous ones?" Reverend T. K. Noble of Plymouth Church based his sermon on the biblical text, "How are the mighty fallen," and the Reverend Dr. Stone of the First Congregational Church spoke on "The Insecurity of Earthly Riches." He told his congregation that "fortunes melt and collapse." Individuals could "not be made secure." One journal summed up the consternation in San Francisco: "The community stands aghast and confounded at the fearful spectacle of this man deprived of life, and ask 'who is to be the next victim?'"[18]

Ralston's was only the most notable collapse in San Francisco. A year earlier, the *Call* had written about "Broken Down Men" and commented that "numbers" of once successful men had become "poor." Those who "held their own" were "not very numerous." A few months later, the newspaper reprinted a list of the wealthiest men in the city in 1851, noting that many of those mentioned had "died by the wayside . . . committed suicide" or "lost their whole possessions." By the mid-1870s, only one person on the list still counted among the city's economic elite. Even more startling, in 1878 one historian of San Francisco claimed that half the millionaires in California at the start of 1875 had dropped from the group, and a sizable number were "reduced to bankruptcy or its verge."[19]

By the middle of the 1870s, signs everywhere suggested that failure might be just as likely as success. In other times, San Franciscans might have shrugged off these signs. In a different decade, they might have dismissed Norton, Ralston, and all the other sometime millionaires as aberrations. But in the middle of the 1870s, these stories could not be dismissed so easily. Economic transformation and depression marked this decade, and the very foundations of the city's economy seemed to totter.

Throughout the 1870s, San Francisco experienced depression. The crisis began in 1869 with the completion of the transcontinental railroad. Expected to stimulate the economy and create jobs, the railroad produced a full-scale commercial panic. Eastern merchants suddenly had easy access to California markets. They responded by rushing trainloads of goods into the West, and San Francisco markets became glutted. Prices fell, and stagnation of trade resulted. The commercial depression lasted several years until local merchants learned to function as part of the national market.[20]

At the same time, other sectors of the economy also experienced uncertainty, and mining was particularly hard hit. Gold production had been declining steadily since 1864, when $57 million in bullion passed through the Golden Gate. Six years later, exports were down 40 percent to only $33 million. The next year, they decreased another 50 percent to $17 million. Agriculture also suffered as a calamitous drought plagued the state. Rainfall at San Francisco declined from an all-time high of 40.5 inches in 1867–68 to 21.6 inches in 1868–69, 20.2 inches in 1869–70, and 13.1 inches in 1870–71. That last season was truly disastrous. Crops withered, and thousands of animals died.[21]

With three primary sectors of the economy depressed, the San Francisco real estate market collapsed. San Franciscans had been speculating in land for several years because they expected the railroad to generate unprecedented growth. Prices continued rising during the first three quarters of 1869 but plummeted in the fourth. Monthly sales dropped from $5 million to less than $2 million, and the total value of transactions in 1870 was barely half that of 1869. The collapse destroyed millions in paper values and caused the money supply to contract. Banks called their loans, and many people could not meet their obligations.[22]

Conditions stabilized for a few years in the early part of the decade, but in the middle of the 1870s things became worse than ever. The first omen of impending disaster appeared in 1875, when mining stocks tumbled. The value of Comstock shares declined more than $100 million and sank nearly $43 million in a single week. That fall, the Bank of California failed, and its closing precipitated a near panic. Two other banks suspended, and the stock exchange took a holiday. On top of these crises, a fire destroyed Virginia City, Nevada, and San Francisco took a loss of about $5 million. Only the reopening of the Bank of California and the resumption of trading on the stock exchanges prevented the city's financial ruin.[23]

New disasters were yet to come. Drought hit the state once again, and rainfall in San Francisco declined from 28.2 inches in 1875–76 to 9.7 inches in 1876–77, the lowest in many years. Losses in crops and livestock exceeded $20 million. This agricultural crisis severely affected San Francisco's commerce and manufacturing. Grain exports declined precipitously. In 1876, dealers shipped nearly 10 million centals of wheat worth $17 million. The following year, cargoes decreased by one-half and receipts by one-third. At the same time, the total value of merchandise exported by sea collapsed. Outbound ships carried $31 million worth of goods in 1876 but only $23 million in 1877. Moreover, industries dependent upon agricultural commodities found prices rising and shortages everywhere. Costs rose, and manufacturers were unable to compete with eastern imports. They discharged employees and cut back production.[24]

Then the Consolidated Virginia mine suspended its monthly dividend of $1 million, and San Franciscans watched its shares decline from a total value of $80 million in January 1875 to $10 million in December 1877. Stock in the California mine collapsed as well. In three years, the paper worth of the mines shrank by about $140 million. The total value of Comstock shares declined 90 percent, from $300 million in early 1875 to $30 million in late 1878.[25]

In one sense, California's depression was unique and resulted from purely local factors. In another, the crisis was a microcosm of national events. The Panic of 1873 officially began during the week of September 13 as several major New York banks suspended payment. Within days, a full-scale financial panic occurred as the New York Stock Exchange closed down, and President Grant raced to the scene. Six years of severe depression followed, but trouble had actually preceded the panic itself. In 1872, about 4,000 businesses failed nationally and suffered a collective loss of $121 million. However, these figures seem small compared to 1878, when 10,000 firms with aggregate assets of $234 million went under. The nation's industrial giants suffered along with its small businesses. During the depths of the crisis, the majority of the country's railroads entered bankruptcy proceedings, and about 70 percent of the iron mills and furnaces shut down. Not until 1879 did prices rise and recovery begin; not until the early 1880s was the economy actually healthy.[26]

The explanations given for the national depression closely parallel those for California. Commercial dislocations resulting from completion of the Suez Canal are reminiscent of the effects of the transcontinental railroad; and huge losses from the Boston and Chicago fires bring to mind the catastrophe in Virginia City. The collapse of Jay Cooke and Company evokes images of William Ralston and the Bank of California. More important, both the country and the state had experienced significant economic problems since the 1860s: excessive railroad construction, currency inflation, and overbuilding of plants and factories. Even though California's economy remained largely independent of the nation's, it suffered from many of the same ills, and so it tumbled. By 1870, San Francisco was in the throes of a major depression. Businesses failed, banks closed, agriculture suffered, and factories shut down. The city faced the most serious economic crisis in its history, one that lasted throughout the decade.

Unemployment was the most serious manifestation of this depression, both nationally and in San Francisco. The extent of national joblessness remains unknown, but contemporary estimates placed unemployment at 3 million, or about two-thirds of the nation's nonfarm workers. One modern historian has found this guess "a bit wild" and lowered his own estimate to 1 million, which still provided "misery enough to go around."[27]

In San Francisco, thousands found themselves out of work. As early as 1870, perhaps 20 percent of the labor force was unemployed, and an incident in March 1870 indicates the magnitude of the crisis. To alleviate unemployment, the state legislature passed several bills providing relief and temporary work. One act authorized San Francisco's Board of Supervisors to spend $50,000 grading and improving Yerba Buena Park. On March 22, the first day of the project, a thousand men nearly rioted for the 115 available jobs. The crowd swelled daily until, at week's end, 2,000 laborers clamored for work. Their frustration and dissatisfaction culminated in the formation of the San Francisco Workingmen's Society, which survived about a month and then faded away after doing little more than publishing resolutions and calling for mass meetings.[28]

Unemployment remained chronic throughout the 1870s but worsened after 1876. The Panic of 1873, the grasshopper plague in the Great Plains, and the Comstock bonanza induced thousands more to go west, a massive immigration that contributed to the crisis. From 1873 to 1875, about 150,000 immigrants settled in California, more than the total in the previous ten years combined. Tens of thousands gravitated to San Francisco, and the compiler of the city directory estimated that the city's population increased 50 percent between 1872 and 1876.[29]

Once again, reports of massive unemployment circulated, and the winter of 1875–76 proved particularly hard. Widespread destitution prevailed in some parts of the city, and the San Francisco Benevolent Association proclaimed conditions the worst in years. In July 1877, the *Alta* suggested that 5,000 men lacked work. Less than a week later, the *Argonaut* raised the figure to "twenty or thirty thousand," and the *Bulletin* concurred. Swollen as these estimates may seem (in 1880, the total labor force of the city stood at only 105,000), they were probably accurate. Even Hubert Howe Bancroft, who usually provided lower estimates of unemployment than other observers, guessed that 15,000 were unemployed in 1878.[30]

The activities of charitable organizations confirm the high rate of unemployment. Between April and June 1877, the San Francisco Benevolent Association made 4,000 calls. By July 1878, its members had visited more than 20,000 families. The *Call* reported that charities fed 14,000 people a day, and the *Chronicle* explained that privation went far beyond hunger. Thousands also "lacked sufficient bedding, and in many cases were unable to attend the [free] lunches by reason of not possessing enough clothing to hide their nakedness."[31]

The temporary nature of many jobs compounded the problem of unemployment. Because of the oversupply of labor, employers retained workers only if they had work to be done, unconcerned about letting men go during slack periods. There was no difficulty in replacing them later. Once again, San Francisco's situation paralleled that of the nation, where about 570,000 were out of work and unemployment was a source of constant anxiety. In his diary, Frank Roney vividly described the uncertainties an iron molder faced in the city. After he arrived in San Francisco in April 1875, Roney worked at the Pacific Iron Works. Although desperate for money, he felt unable to request an advance because he feared losing his new job. He therefore worked six weeks before he was paid or even knew his wages. While at the Pacific, Roney worried constantly about being let go; in July, he was. Then he found a job at City Iron Works, but it lasted only until August 5. Until the tenth of September, he had no work. At one point, things seemed so hopeless that he applied for a job in Hawaii. Finally, in September, Roney found work and thought things were looking up. Three weeks later, "contrary to all expectations," he was laid off again. He had no work at all during October and November. In December, five days of odd jobs brought in ten dollars. In January, he loaded coal on a steamer for two days and received five dollars; another day he earned two dollars in a freight house. He passed day after day without finding steady work. In the middle of the month, he started laying sidewalks and drives, again for two dollars a day. That job, too, lasted only a short time. Finally, in late January, Roney went to work at the Union Iron Works, and this new job lasted for at least several months.[32]

Roney's experience was far from atypical. After 1870, significant numbers of men worked only irregularly—if at all. In September 1884, the San Francisco Labor Council reported an oversupply of labor and irregular employment in nearly every trade. On the average, painters had been idle half of the time since April. One man reported not working a full week since July, no more than three and a half days in any one week, and remaining entirely idle for three weeks. Similar conditions prevailed among the coopers. One man worked less than a month between May 1 and the middle of September. He personally knew others who had been completely unemployed for six months. Of the eighty wood carvers in the city, only four or five had regular jobs. Bricklayers averaged five months of work a year, and city laborers felt lucky if they could count on three days a week.[33]

Unemployment and the rapid growth of the labor force drove wages down and made life harder even for those with jobs. In 1898, the United States Department of Labor studied wages in twelve cities between 1870 and 1880 (see table 3.2). The survey included twenty-five occupations, and the department drew its data directly from the payrolls of two firms in each city. The study indicated that, in nineteen of twenty-two occupations, wages in San Francisco decreased between 1870 and 1880. The rate of decline ranged from less than 1 percent for plumbers to 25 percent for bricklayers.[34]

These figures become even more meaningful when compared with the decennial change for the entire country. For, while daily wages fell in San Francisco, they rose nationally. Whereas wages declined in nineteen occupations in San Francisco, they increased in the same nineteen occupations across the country. Furthermore, because the national figures included San Francisco (where daily wages were dropping), they understated the percentage increase in wages elsewhere.

San Francisco's workingmen did benefit from a small decrease in the

TABLE 3.2   PERCENT CHANGE IN AVERAGE DAILY
WAGES, SAN FRANCISCO AND USA, 1870–80

Occupation	SF	USA
Blacksmiths	−6.3	+7.0
Blacksmiths' Helpers	−10.7	+4.9
Boilermakers	−5.0	+10.6
Bricklayers	−25.0	+1.2
Carpenters	−13.0	0.0
Compositors	−3.5	+5.0
Conductors (RR)	−10.2	+6.8
Engineers (RR)	−4.4	+21.4
Firemen (RR)	−16.0	+11.4
Hod Carriers	−16.7	+4.6
Iron Molders	−5.7	−1.5
Iron Molders' Helpers	−9.8	+5.2
Laborers, Street	−20.0	+2.7
Laborers, Other	0.0	+6.4
Machinists	−10.1	+6.1
Machinists' Helpers	−16.9	+6.6
Masons, Stone	−2.0	+11.1
Painters, House	−16.4	+8.1
Pattern Makers	+3.0	+4.4
Plumbers	−0.8	+6.5
Stone Cutters	−11.4	−7.8
Teamsters	+1.5	+18.8

cost of living. Food prices fell during the decade, but increasing rents canceled much of the boon. Furthermore, the overall gain fell far short of the reduction in income. In order to make ends meet, many people did without nonessentials. New clothes, furniture, books, amusements, newspapers, alcohol, and tobacco became luxuries rather than a normal part of life.[35]

Life was hard in San Francisco at the end of the 1870s. Depression had created a context in which people could easily believe that the experiences of William Ralston and Joshua Norton would become the future norm, in which the gains of the past two or three decades seemed threatened. The economic collapse of the 1870s had a directness, an immediacy, and a power that overshadowed the growth of the past. For many San Franciscans, the "glittering vision" had indeed become a nightmare.

4. Economic Transformation

Other factors contributed to the grotesque quality of massive unemployment in a seemingly Edenic California. The transformation of the state's economy must not be overlooked. For, even as the state was growing, it was changing, and economic changes seemed to have made it harder, and less likely, for San Franciscans to succeed. Henry George, soon to begin writing *Progress and Poverty*, was one of the first to understand this condition. Envisioning the looming impact of the transcontinental railroad, he proclaimed that San Francisco had entered an era of greater business and greater population. But he also predicted that only those already prosperous stood to benefit. Those who had would become richer, but for those who had not, it would become "more difficult to get." Those already prosperous would find increased opportunities, but those who could count only on their own labor would become poorer "and find it harder to get ahead—first because it will take more capital to buy land and to get into business; and second, because as competition reduces the wages of labor, this capital will be harder for them to obtain."[1]

In the long run, George erred. Economic growth raised the general standard of living even as it created greater maldistribution of wealth. The paradox evaporates when we realize that economic development increased total wealth so that even a smaller percent of the total was a greater amount. But, despite the incorrectness of his long-term prognostications, George certainly *appeared* to be correct in the short run. Economic transformation seemed to be narrowing opportunities by increasing the scale of business enterprise, demanding new skills, and requiring greater sums of capital. The nature of the most successful businesses during the 1870s suggested that achieving success would be harder in the future than in the past.

Men no longer succeeded in traditional ways—by filling buckets with gold nuggets, working fertile land as yeoman farmers, producing and selling goods as independent artisans and craftsmen. Instead they became entrepreneurs, businessmen who took risks and carried them out successfully. They saw people, money, land, machinery, and resources as factors of production, and they integrated those factors into continuous processes. They created enormously profitable organizations, and they built companies of an unprecedented scale. They understood the division of labor, the differentiation of function, and the intensive use of capital. In short, they apprehended the workings of a modern economy. First in mining, then in commerce and agriculture, and finally in manufacturing, they transformed California's economy. Hydraulic and quartz mining replaced solitary prospectors, and huge mechanized ranches superseded yeoman farmers. Integrated factories supplanted independent artisans. As a result, other San Franciscans doubted that they could compete and wondered what the future held for them.

Mining became the first sector of the economy to develop. By 1852, placer mining had peaked; thereafter new processes dependent upon the application of capital, the utilization of machinery, and the hiring of wage labor displaced the older method. Hard-rock, or quartz, mining actually began in 1849, when discoveries revealed tremendous gold deposits embedded in quartz veins, or lodes. However, hard-rock mining posed technological problems. First, the ore had to be excavated, then crushed in order to break out the gold. Finally, ore and metal had to be separated. But the companies involved in quartz mining between 1849 and 1851 knew little about the elaborate technical apparatus needed. They scarcely understood the nature of ore-bearing veins in California and frequently built plants in poor locations. As a result, the earliest attempts failed, and the nascent boom collapsed. Only after 1851 did technological advances permit the slow but steady growth of hard-rock mining. By 1858, various companies had erected 279 quartz mills at a total cost of $3,270.00 Moreover, the total capital invested was probably twice that in the mills alone.[2]

The complicated processes required to extract the gold had raised capital requirements. After excavation, gold-bearing ore was crushed in stamps at a quartz mill. But since these machines left pieces too large to free the maximum amount of gold, the crushed rock required pulverization. Different processes then retrieved the gold. One method involved adding water to the powder, thus creating a pulpy mass. Mercury, which amalgamated with gold under certain conditions, was then introduced, and the gold was recovered. Another process involved pouring the pulpy mass over coarse blankets, thus catching the finer particles. Neither of these methods worked if the gold was found in metallic sulfides. In that case, heated ore was exposed to chlorine gas. This procedure converted the sulfides into a solution from which gold could be precipitated.[3]

Because the technology of quartz mining differed so radically from that of placer mining, it demanded a different business structure. The great risks and the high cost of development led to incorporation and issuance of stock. By the end of 1860, mining shares were bought and sold daily at the principal business houses of San Francisco. Two years later, California's first stock exchange was established there, with Stockton and Sacramento quickly acquiring similar institutions. Quartz mining had become a highly sophisticated business requiring an understanding of corporate finance as well as managerial skills and technical knowledge.[4]

Hydraulic mining developed about the same time. Prospectors soon realized that they were uncovering only the outcroppings of buried channels, and they dreamed of recovering the rich but hidden treasure. Ground sluicing ultimately revolutionized California gold mining. A miner simply dug a gully down the side of a hill, built a flume to the top of the gully, and sent water cascading over the edge. Finally, he used traditional methods to extract ore from the accumulated debris.

Several elaborations turned ground sluicing into hydraulic mining. In 1852, Antoine Chabot replaced flumes with hoses; the flexibility of the hose gave him more freedom in sluicing (the flexibility was also more convenient). The following year, Edward E. Matteson attached a nozzle to his hose and directed it at the base of a hill. The effect was simple and obvious: the hill collapsed. Then, in 1858, miners discovered that they could blast a hill before they hosed it. Three years later, the invention of the crinoline hose tripled the available water pressure. These latter two technological developments ultimately led to mining on a scale vastly larger than anything previously attempted.[5]

Julious Poquillon typified the new entrepreneurs. In 1866, he decided to excavate an entire region, formed a partnership with two other men, took options on hundreds of acres in the North Bloomfield region, and headed for San Francisco. There he formed a syndicate that included William Ralston of the Bank of California; S. F. Butterworth, superintendent of New Almaden, one of the largest quicksilver mines in the world; F. L. A. Pioche, head of a prominent investment firm; and L. L. Robinson, president of the Giant Powder Company and proprietor of the Riverside Land and Irrigation Company. Their firm, the North Bloomfield Gravel Mining Company, controlled more than 150,000 acres of valuable mining property. The partners spent eight years and several million dollars developing it. They ultimately built two reservoirs, one hundred miles of canals and ditches, and a drainage tunnel two miles long. By 1874, they employed over five hundred men.[6]

Similar technological and organizational changes took place in agriculture. Just as mining developed from a simple enterprise into a complex industry, so the family farm gave way to the large, organized, mechanized ranch. To be a successful rancher, sowing and reaping no longer sufficed. One had to compete in a market where large-scale rationalized producers were gaining increasing dominance. Instead of yeomanry, California developed an agricultural structure geared to the international wheat trade.

California contains only a small amount of arable land. According to the 1940 census, the state encompasses about 100 million acres. Of this vast domain, only 13 million acres is actually suited for farming, and less than 7 million acres was cultivated in 1940. In other words, only about 7 percent of the state's total area is worth farming. However, these statistics tell only part of the story. In 1940, 3.5 million irrigated acres constituted the core of California's agricultural heartland and produced nearly 83 percent of her agricultural income.[7] No boundless tracts of fertile land awaited nineteenth-century immigrants.

Concentrated landholdings compounded the scarcity of arable farmland. Some have argued that landownership was more restricted in California than anywhere else in the country, and by 1871 the state's 122 largest farms comprised a total area exceeding the other 23,315 combined. In 1860, the four principal farm counties of the Sacramento Valley (Yolo, Colusa, Butte, and Tehama) contained 55 farms larger than 1,000 acres. By 1880, there were 417 such farms, with 71 exceeding 5,000 acres. The number of great ranches increased relatively as well as absolutely. In 1860, fewer than 4 percent of the state's farms were larger than 1,000 acres. In 1880, more than 11 percent were at least that large. There were eight times as many great holdings while the total number of farms had not even tripled. Similar patterns held in the state's other agricultural counties.[8]

Land concentration occurred because a handful of men set out to construct agricultural empires in the San Joaquin and Sacramento valleys. Most settlers considered the area worthless because it looked like a barren plain during the dry season. The first farmers planned to raise fruit, dairy, and vegetables for the burgeoning markets of San Francisco and Sacramento, and they saw little value in the arid acres. The valley seemed worthless for the purposes they contemplated.[9]

William Chapman viewed the land differently, recognized its potential, and made plans for its development. He realized that wheat could grow where grass grew and understood that wheat needed the same growing time as grass and that it should be sowed at the beginning of the rainy season. Used for wheat, the land would be more profitable than any manufacturing or mercantile business. But Chapman also knew that wheat was most profitable when grown in large tracts, and he began to buy as much land as he could. He invested his own money, borrowed more, and induced others to join him. Before long, he controlled 200,000 acres.[10]

By the middle of the 1860s, men like Chapman had acquired a large chunk of California's prime agricultural land, and two factors—the grain trade with England and mechanization—guaranteed their predominance, ensured the growth of large ranches, and inhibited the development of family farms. By 1865, fleets of grain ships sailed yearly between California and the British Isles. As a result, the acreage devoted to wheat tripled between 1866 and 1872. From July 1, 1865, to

June 30, 1866, the state exported about 1.8 million centals of wheat. The amount nearly tripled during the following year, and by 1872, the annual cargo was about 10 million centals.[11]

This enormous trade did not necessarily bring success to individual farmers. Furthermore, the wheat trade drastically altered farming because marketing became as important as production. Farmers became subject to the vagaries of the worldwide grain market, but they knew little about functioning in a market of that size. At every moment, they were threatened by those who understood the wheat trade and used their knowledge to control it.

The annual shortage of sacks illustrates the necessary knowledge and acumen. California grain was customarily shipped in bags rather than bulk because captains feared that bulk cargo would shift and overturn their vessels. Therefore, farmers needed thousands of sacks every year, but most did not realize the importance of bags and ordered them at the last moment. In the meantime, brokers who did understand the situation stepped in, bought up the supply, and drove up prices. These events happened year after year, and farmers lost part of their profit to speculators. Had they realized that bags were indispensable, they could have placed orders at stipulated prices months in advance. San Francisco bag dealers profiteered annually because wheat growers did not understand a crucial part of their business.[12]

Shipping was equally important. Wheat had little value unless it could be transported to England, and whoever controlled shipping controlled the grain trade. Isaac Friedlander, the "Grain King," understood this fact first, and every year, before farmers thought about shipping, he hired every available boat and chartered a commanding part of the necessary tonnage. At his funeral, one eulogist proclaimed that he gathered the grain crop of California in the hollow of his hand.[13] And yet, Friedlander was only tangentially involved in growing wheat. His success resulted from the fundamentally changed nature of agriculture.

The spread of Hugh Glenn, a major rancher in the San Joaquin Valley, illustrates how mechanization, the wheat trade, and land concentration altered California agriculture. By 1874, this "farm" exceeded 50,000 acres; it had 15,000 miles of fence, 16,000 sheep,

1,000 cattle, and 800 horses and mules. Subdivided into nine individual farms, each had its own foreman who collectively supervised a work force of 700 men and distributed a monthly payroll of $30,000. The work itself took place on an equivalent scale. For plowing, 100 eight-mule teams pulled gang plows in formation. The teams began at dawn, plowed nine miles north, turned west, and stopped for lunch. In the afternoon, they plowed south for nine miles, and then returned to the starting point. At the end of the day, they had circled 20,000 acres. To harvest this kingdom, Glenn had three monstrous steam threshers. The largest, known as the Monitor, required fifty-six men, seven headers, twenty-one header wagons, and ninety-six animals for its operation. However, it took only fifteen minutes to bag the cut grain, and the Monitor could thresh 3,000 sacks a day. Glenn's annual harvest amounted to about 20,000 tons, or 320,000 sacks, worth more than $500,000. It required twenty large ships to carry the 1880 crop to Europe, and Glenn's shipping bill ran $230,000.[14]

At the same time that mining and agriculture were changing, commerce too was being transformed. Before 1869, merchants profited from the imbalance of supply and demand caused by San Francisco's isolation. But the completion of the transcontinental railroad equalized supply and demand, thus destroying the chance for windfall profits. Any item now ordered from the East became available in roughly two weeks. Most important, improved transport limited the total cost of an item to its New York price plus the cost of transportation and a reasonable profit. From then on, a merchant's success, like that of a farmer or miner, depended largely on skill, ability, and knowledge. After 1869, a merchant needed exact knowledge of business conditions and sources of supply as well as of how to strike the best deal and anticipate the market.

Changes began as early as 1855, when greater warehouse space and lower lighterage fees enabled merchants to start manipulating supplies and controlling prices. The changed nature of imports also stabilized markets. About 1854, California started producing more of its food. As a result, grain and flour imports all but disappeared by the end of the decade. Meat, too, ceased to be a major import. Food had provided merchants with an ideal speculative commodity because of its inelastic demand; and the substitution of imports with a more elastic demand diminished speculative chances. If merchants forced prices too high, consumers simply refused to buy.[15]

The telegraph line between California and Missouri also furthered stabilization. On October 23, 1861, San Francisco and New York came into virtually instantaneous communication. Merchants could telegraph orders directly to New York to discover prices, shipping conditions, and other market news.[16] The telegraph enabled them to make rational decisions because they were no longer isolated. However, goods still took three weeks to reach San Francisco. The merchant knew enough to make rational decisions but could not always act on them.

Ultimately, the completion of the transcontinental railroad produced the most radical alterations in the pace, precision, and scale of business. Before 1869, San Francisco merchants adjusted their business to the rhythm of the steamship, and "steamer day" had a special meaning for the commercial population. Merchants remitted payments on the steamer twice a month. Several days before each sailing, they started to raise the necessary cash. They dunned obstinate debtors, beseeching, wheedling, and bullying them for money. Funds failed twice a month, and specie became scarce in San Francisco. But the merchants' honor and business depended upon payment. Therefore, they did everything possible. They borrowed money at 4, 5, or even 10 percent interest per month. They made cash sales at any price, and they hid from their creditors. Then the steamer departed, and calm prevailed once again. For ten days, the merchants relaxed. Then, the cycle began all over.[17]

The completion of the railroad destroyed this pace of business. Day after day, week after week, the train inexorably pulled into the station bringing goods, bills, messages, and a multitude of affairs. Merchandise had to be taken to the warehouse. Bills had to be paid. Instructions had to be sent. Nothing could wait, and commerce demanded a new discipline. A merchant always had to be ready.[18]

After 1869, San Francisco merchants also had to confront eastern competitors. Before completion of the railroad, all freight and passenger traffic to western America arrived by water and passed through

San Francisco. Now the merchants of the East, and particularly those of Chicago, coveted enormous new western markets. As the Union Pacific pushed west, eastern traders secured business that had once belonged exclusively to San Francisco. The railroad freed the city's hinterland and forced a readjustment of the mercantile mind. Merchants could no longer profiteer. From now on, they competed with traders accustomed to more stable business climates and smaller profit margins. They had to accommodate to the market since it would no longer adjust to them.[19]

Like mining and agriculture, commerce had become rationalized, and its scale increased. By 1871, a few large firms dominated the dry goods business. There were twenty-three principal houses, but a few controlled an inordinate share of the business. One of them, "the monster, the Stewart's of this city," accounted for perhaps 20 percent of the volume. It imported three times as many goods as its nearest competitor, and a few large houses together did 40 percent of the volume. Men who understood the changes in commerce controlled the most successful firms. They had seen how transportation, communication, and finance destroyed the speculative world, and they had seized opportunities to launch enterprises on a new scale. As a result, commerce came to resemble mining and agriculture. Large-scale rationalized enterprises based on capital investment replaced individual proprietors whose business was based on their own effort.[20]

At the same time, artisans and mechanics discovered diminished opportunities. Between 1860 and 1870, the level of wages in California declined substantially, both in absolute terms and in relation to wages in the East. Table 4.1 compares average annual earnings in five regions of the country in 1860, 1870, and 1880. During these twenty

TABLE 4.1 COMPARATIVE WAGES
BY REGION, 1860–80

Region	1860	1870	1880
Middle Atlantic	100	100	100
Northeast	106	108	104
South	91	73	70
Central	101	99	99
Pacific	255	138	136

TABLE 4.2   WAGES IN NEW YORK AND SAN FRANCISCO, 1870–80

| | 1870 | | 1880 | | Ratio SF / NY | |
Occupation	SF	NY	SF	NY	1870	1880
Blacksmith	$3.81	2.25	3.57	2.68	169	133
Blacksmiths' Helpers	2.34	1.49	2.09	1.53	157	137
Boilermakers	3.38	1.84	3.22	2.17	184	148
Boilermakers' Helpers	2.24	1.40	1.97	1.50	160	131
Bricklayers	5.00	3.16	4.00	3.12	158	125
Carpenters	3.85	2.88	3.35	3.41	133	98
Compositors	3.41	2.53	3.29	2.98	134	110
Hod Carriers	3.00	1.96	2.50	2.03	153	123
Iron Molders[1]	3.72	1.95	3.51	2.21	192	158
Laborers, Street[1]	2.50	1.49	2.00	1.57	167	127
Laborers, Other	2.00	1.76	2.00	1.39	114	144
Machinists	3.37	2.27	3.03	2.53	148	120
Machinists' Helpers	2.25	1.55	1.91	1.70	145	112
Masons, Stone	5.00	2.89	4.89	2.50	173	196
Painters, House	3.72	2.44	3.10	3.00	152	103
Pattern Makers	3.00	2.45	3.08	3.15	122	98
Plumbers	3.66	2.76	3.63	3.39	133	107
Stonecutters[1]	4.14	2.85	3.66	2.49	145	147
Teamsters	2.64	1.70	2.68	2.14	155	125

[1] Philadelphia figures; none available for New York.

years, the percentage ratio of average annual earnings in the Pacific region relative to those in the Middle Atlantic was halved, with almost the entire reduction occurring in the 1860s.[21]

A series of figures compiled by the United States Department of Labor indicates a substantial decline in the ratio of average daily wages between New York and San Francisco between 1870 and 1880 (See table 4.2).[22]

Declining wages resulted partly from a substantial increase in the labor supply during the 1860s and 1870s. Large numbers of Chinese immigrants arrived in San Francisco as did newcomers from eastern states. As table 4.3 indicates, the Chinese segment of the population grew from less than 5 percent in 1860 to almost 10 percent in 1880. However, at least 15 percent of the labor force was Chinese, and this estimate is probably understated since the figure of 104,650 includes entrepreneurs, managers, and businessmen—all more numerous among the non-Chinese. A reasonable estimate would be that in

1880, 20 or 25 percent of the wageworkers (hired labor) in San Francisco were Chinese.[23]

Other new laborers joined the Chinese in San Francisco. As the transcontinental railroad neared completion, a wave of immigrants flowed westward. As early as 1868, a steady stream of immigrants started pouring into California, annually surpassing the volume of any year since the early 1850s. In 1868 and 1869, the actual gain in the state's population may have exceeded 50,000.[24] Many newcomers ended up in San Francisco because they lacked real alternatives. The placers were long since exhausted, so the mines provided no viable option. Few immigrants understood the nature of California ranching, and even fewer had money to buy land, so agriculture held few attractions. Therefore, newcomers flocked to the city.

There they found a new industrial economy. The Censuses of Manufactures for 1870 and 1880 disclose a marked increase in the number of plants based on the intensive use of capital and subdivision of labor. In 1870, only nineteen firms had an investment between $50,000 and $100,000. Thirty-one others were capitalized at more than $100,000. But, during the 1870s, the number of firms in the first group increased by 184 percent and in the second by 222 percent.[25]

These factories operated on a larger scale, employed more men, consumed more raw materials, and produced more goods than was customary. By 1880, more than one hundred companies employed twenty-five to fifty men (an increase of 189 percent since 1870). These la-

TABLE 4.3   CHINESE LABOR IN SAN FRANCISCO, 1860–80

	1860	1870	1880
Total Population	56,802	149,473	233,959
Labor Force	—	68,352	104,650
Chinese Population	2,719	12,022	21,745
Chinese Labor Force	—	9,054	(16,200)[1]
Chinese as Percentage of Population	4.8	8.0	9.3
Chinese as Percentage of Labor Force	—	13.2	(15.5)[1]

[1] The 1880 census does not list the number of Chinese who were employed in San Francisco. These figures assume that the same percentage of Chinese worked in 1880 as in 1870.

borers no longer relied on their own muscle to transform raw materials into finished products. Many of them operated machines, and the number of firms using steam power increased from fewer than two hundred to more than five hundred during the decade.[26]

Larger labor forces (and more machines) processed more materials and turned out more goods. The number of plants utilizing $25,000 to $100,000 worth of material tripled, and there were four times as many firms consuming more than $100,000 of supplies. Larger quantities of material yielded a larger output. Nearly three times as many firms produced goods worth more than $100,000 in 1880 than in 1870.[27]

As factory production became more common, traditional crafts and skills began to disappear. Because of the changing mode of production, labor became relatively undifferentiated and unskilled. Whereas it had once taken years to learn a trade, it now took days, or even hours, to learn a job. Many men became laborers instead of craftsmen or artisans. Conditions in the building trades clearly illustrate the decline of traditional crafts and skills. When William Laird MacGregor, a Scotsman, visited the city in 1876 he found the building technology fascinating, and the speed of construction astounded him. One morning, he walked past the site of a new house and saw the foundations being laid. Two weeks later, the building was framed and roofed. MacGregor had apparently never seen a balloon frame before because he noted that a good hammer and nails were everything needed to put up a house. Window sills, architraves, doors, cornices, and interior fittings were all fabricated in a joiner's shop and added when the frame was complete. The technique, clearly new to MacGregor, accounted for most construction in San Francisco and diminished the role of the skilled carpenter.[28]

Other trades were also changing. In 1874, the contractor for the Palace Hotel decided to use novice lathers and plasterers. His decision suggests that he could get a satisfactory job from new men and indicates that new techniques had jeopardized the position of the master.[29] Of course, skilled artisans still practiced their crafts in San Francisco, especially in the building trades—the elaborate mansions atop Nob Hill provide ample evidence of that—but the look of the future was clear: unskilled labor was going to perform an increasing share of the work.

A letter from Patrick J. Healy, a shoemaker, to Henry George, the editor of the *Post*, reveals the extent of the change in his industry. He argued that labor-saving machinery had utterly destroyed the position of master craftsman and made apprenticeship unnecessary. "The proprietors of large factories, with the control of money and machinery and a few skillful experts, can go on grinding out shoes and calicoes regardless of those who had given early years of their life to the acquirement of the technical knowledge necessary to follow such occupations." Healy suggested that anyone who doubted him should visit a local factory that used machines. Boys with only a few months' experience were swiftly and easily turning out products that their fathers had only recently produced slowly and laboriously.[30]

This change in the nature of labor also allowed unskilled Chinese immigrants to find work in San Francisco and to compete successfully for jobs. Unfortunately, the 1880 census does not indicate the occupational structure of the Chinese in San Francisco. Nonetheless, the evidence it does provide allows reasonable approximations. The vast majority of San Francisco's Chinese performed unskilled labor. In 1880, San Francisco's labor force contained 27,885 persons born in "Other Countries," including China. We have already seen (table 4.3) that about 16,200 Chinese worked in the city. Therefore, the Chinese comprised about 60 percent of the non-enumerated nativities. The jobs most commonly held by members of this group, in order of numerical importance, were domestic servants (3,836), cigar makers and tobacco workers (2,602), launderers and laundresses (2,465), laborers (2,226), and boot- and shoemakers (1,985). All of these occupational groups fall into the category of unskilled workers, and all five were known to provide work for substantial numbers of Chinese immigrants. The transformation of San Francisco's economy was essential in providing job opportunities for the Chinese.[31]

Thus, by 1880, San Francisco had become an industrial city. Thirty years before, it had almost no manufacturing, a condition that prevailed for the better part of two decades. Then, after 1870, the city rapidly transformed itself into a center of production, and fully integrated factories became common. But manufacturing was not the only part of the economy to have changed. Within scarcely a quarter of a century, at least four sectors of California's economy had undergone a transformation that seemed to have changed the conditions of opportunity.

The transformation of California's economy reflected the national trends toward industrialization and the development of a rationalized economy. During the nineteenth century, every sector of the American economic system metamorphosed. In 1813, the Boston Associates founded the Boston Manufacturing Company and invested $500,000 in the first integrated textile factory in the country. Ten years later, they turned Lowell, Massachusetts, into the Manchester of America, and within twenty years the manufacturing corporation had begun to spread across the land. Between 1849 and 1879, the number of manufacturing establishments increased from 123,000 to 509,000; between 1879 and 1899, the capital invested in manufacturing grew from $2.718 billion to $8.168 billion. The value added by manufacturing increased from $240 million in 1839 to $5.044 billion in 1899.[32]

Although the growth of industry most dramatized the changing nature of nineteenth-century America, agriculture and commerce underwent similar transformations. In the world of trade, eastern merchants, particularly those in New York City, used new transportation technologies and methods of organization to expand their markets and increase the scale of their operations. A few New York import firms turned auction privileges into great fortunes, and during the 1820s a handful of Gotham auction houses sold $160 million worth of goods— about 20 percent of the entire country's imports! At the same time, New York traders increased the size of their city's hinterland by building the Erie Canal, taking advantage of the steamboat, and inaugurating regular packet line service between Manhattan and Liverpool. No Yankee peddlers these, and no wonder that A. T. Stewart's store at the corner of Ninth and Broadway became the world's largest retail establishment in 1862. The general store had become the department store, and Montgomery Ward had become a multimillionaire.[33]

Meanwhile, American farmers broke new ground on the plains and prairies. In addition to the legendary yeoman, thousands of "capitalist estate-builders" set up midwestern plantations worked by hired farm laborers. The censuses of 1850, 1860, and 1870 disclosed noticeable increases in the number of large farms and an expanding volume of hired hands. Paul W. Gates, one of the great historians of American agriculture, has concluded that "these estate-builders were to be found in every portion . . . of the Corn Belt," that some of them had investments of hundreds of thousands of dollars and, "for a score or more," of up to several million. Their bonanza farms experienced enormous gains in productivity as the proprietors used new and improved plows, harvesters, rakes, drills, and reapers to increase output—perhaps by 20 percent in the 1850s alone. Cattle ranches, hog ranches, and wheat ranches fed the nation's cities while Americans eulogized the family farm.[34]

Economic modernization extended throughout the nineteenth century and peaked in the years after the Civil War. In San Francisco and California, it was well under way by 1870 even if only a few astute observers recognized it. Before long, however, an altered climate of opportunity seemed apparent to thousands of residents as it combined with depression to make success harder to achieve, at least for the time being.

5. Social Contrasts: Nob Hill

Along with economic depression and transformation, social contrasts contributed to discontent among San Franciscans. During the 1870s, class differences seemed to become more obvious and created diverging styles of life that were increasingly difficult to understand or accept. A new social attitude seemed to foretell the development of a new—and very unpleasant—kind of society. Although the entire class system became more complex with the development of a managerial and professional middle class—as well as a petite bourgeoisie of clerical workers, shopkeepers, and artisans, and the differentiation among skilled, semiskilled, and unskilled laborers—the aspect of the class system most perceived by contemporaries was a tremendous social and economic chasm yawning between the new industrial elite and the new industrial masses, between Nob Hill and South of Market.

A few San Franciscans (especially the silver princes and railroad kings) acquired more wealth than anyone had ever imagined, and they created an extremely visible style of life that reflected their extraordinary wealth. The acquisition of these fortunes created a psychological problem for the new multimillionaires, one that they could not ignore. They found the transition from poor New England farmboy (or penniless Irish immigrant) to king of the hill an unsettling experience. Nothing in their backgrounds or early lives had prepared them for vast riches. As a result of their great success, these new millionaires no longer knew who they were. As Eliza Dolittle plaintively wondered after her own transformation, "What am I fit for? . . . Where am I to go? What am I to do? What's to become of me?"[1]

To answer these same questions, San Francisco's millionaires created the world of Nob Hill, where they mimicked the English aristocracy, just as New Yorkers created Fifth Avenue and Chicagoans their Gold Coast. To these people, Nob Hill became more than just a promontory in the heart of San Francisco. It became a unique social environment that gave form and substance to their lives. It told them what to do, how to behave, and (most important of all) who they were.

Obviously, the world of Nob Hill derived from the enormous fortunes that the railroad kings and silver barons had acquired. Today, it is impossible to determine exactly how rich they were, but all evidence suggests that their wealth was stupendous. Even estate valuations, which are notoriously low, reveal the extent of their wealth. According to these figures, James G. Fair had $12,228,998.07 when he died in 1894, and William S. O'Brien $9,377,819.65 in 1878. Crocker's assets were valued at $24,142,475.84 at his death in 1889.[2]

Another way to grasp the wealth of these millionaires is to look at income and dividend figures for their companies. The two bonanza mines, California and Consolidated Virginia, paid out $74,250,000 between 1873 and 1880. As major stockholders, the silver kings gathered in the lion's share of this money. The Central Pacific Railroad (CPRR) was also profitable: between November 6, 1869, and June 30, 1878, it reported net earnings of $37,428,608.93. Between 1874 and 1884, the CPRR distributed $34 million in dividends. Much of this money went directly into the hands of the company's principal owners, the big four.[3]

Of course, these figures consider only income and earnings, not the actual worth of the companies. Huntington's private correspondence with Hopkins reveals the ever increasing value of their stock. Huntington apparently owned about 93,000 shares of the CPRR with a par value of $9,300,000. In late 1871, he offered to sell out for 50 percent of par, $4,650,000. However, the worth of the shares rose quickly. Huntington's letters indicate that he would accept $70 apiece in April 1873, $90 in May, and $95 in September. In other words, Huntington's stock in the CPRR had a value of nearly $9 million only four years after the road was finished.[4]

One of the most accurate indications of net worth appears in the capital accounts of the CPRR. On October 29, 1877, Crocker sent Huntington a list of these accounts: Stanford, $6,084,048.81;

TABLE 5.1 CAPITAL ACCOUNTS OF THE BIG FOUR, 1878–86

	LS	CPH	CC	Estate MH	Mrs. MH
June 30, 1878		7,863,388	7,972,040		
July 20, 1879	7,084,823	8,330,479	8,609,323	8,367,634	7,788,686
December 31, 1882	14,374,256	17,589,245	18,362,110	10,270,959	11,687,467
September 30, 1883	18,334,284	18,823,295	21,518,976	10,270,959	6,915,527
December 31, 1884	12,972,632	15,704,669	17,131,899	11,147,333	7,797,009
December 31, 1885	15,644,496	18,620,110	19,697,120	11,816,173	6,875,564
December 31, 1886	16,545,198	19,688,956	19,769,995	12,442,448	

Huntington, $6,903,809.86; Crocker, $7,091,385.88; and Hopkins, $7,515,620.74. In his personal books, Huntington kept a list of "Comparative Statements of Account," which indicates the size of the railroad kings' capital accounts in their various mutual enterprises (table 5.1).[5]

Huntington's inventory of Mark Hopkins' estate, made on December 31, 1878, provides an even more exact sense of the men's wealth (table 5.2).[6]

Finally, one of Huntington's few remaining personal ledgers provides the balance in his personal account. On January 2, 1892, he valued his assets at $37,157,381.17 and on December 30, 1893, at $38,253,293.01.[7] These sums were truly remarkable—especially when a quart of milk cost a dime, a dozen eggs twenty cents, and a pound of steak a quarter.

The size of these fortunes demolished their holders' original sense of identity. They no longer felt like the same people, and they stopped enjoying what had been their favorite activities. Mackay once complained that he no longer liked playing poker. He won a large pot one night and rose to leave almost immediately. Asked to stay, the silver king responded, "Leave me out, Boys, I'm through. When I can't enjoy winning at poker, there's no fun in anything." As a poor man, Mackay had figured every penny; as a rich man, he didn't know what he spent. Poor, he'd liked winning and hated losing; rich, he just didn't care. He had no taste for cards, and he missed it."[8]

Wealth also disrupted personal relationships. Millionaires lost old

TABLE 5.2	ESTATE OF MARK HOPKINS
Cash	271,784.90
Stocks	7,534,981.04
Bonds	6,984,341.00
Shares of Jointure	1,450,957.04
Livestock, Wagons	9,781.00
Household Items	247,945.34
Debts Due	
Open Accounts	2,719,728.90
Bills Receivable	558,699.90
Jointure	7,433.36
Joint Real Estate	909,109.88
Total	20,694,762.36

friends and had trouble replacing them. James G. Fair complained of loneliness and feared that other people cared only about his money. Moses Hopkins recalled that his brother Mark disliked social gatherings and seldom ventured into public; he let his wife socialize for both of them. A business associate noted that Leland Stanford was a man without intimate friends. No one in California had more admirers, but "no man" had "fewer confidential friends."[9]

The wives of the new millionaires suffered similar dislocations. Across the country, William Dean Howells understood the inner turmoil experienced by women like Theresa Fair, Jane Stanford, and Mary Hopkins. He could easily have been quoting one of them when he had Mrs. Lapham tell Silas, "We don't, either of us, know what to do. You've had to work so hard, and your luck was so long in coming, and then it came with such a rush, that we haven't had any chance to learn what to do with it."[10]

A letter from Mary Crocker, wife of the railroad king, suggests how money had altered her feelings toward old friends. In 1881 Mrs. Crocker received a note from Hannah, once a dear friend with whom she had shared every confidence. The two women had not corresponded for twenty-five years, and Mrs. Crocker was surprised to hear from her. The railroad queen replied that she had "not heard of" Hannah "for a long, long time, do not often see your brother or any of the old friends." Furthermore, she had "lost all interest" in her girlhood home and would never return there. However, Mrs. Crocker politely told Hannah that if she ever came to California "and I am here, we will have a visit." In closing, Mrs. Crocker commented that writing the letter had made her nervous and that she could not think.[11]

San Francisco's richest men starkly exposed their loss of identity when they talked about their early lives. In essence, they obliterated the past and recreated it in ways more meaningful to their new economic positions. They talked not about the lives of struggling farmboys and immigrants but rather about the lives of future millionaires. In doing so, they literally became self-made.

They had the opportunity to indulge in this kind of mythmaking in 1891–92, when historian Hubert Howe Bancroft decided to publish a new biographical series, *Chronicles of the Builders of the Commonwealth: Historical Character Study*. The volumes were to include sketches of leading westerners, and for inclusion a subject had to subscribe. The amount an individual paid determined the length of his biography, and Bancroft tailored the accounts to suit the subscribers' wishes.[12]

George H. Morison interviewed James G. Fair for the project, and Morison's correspondence with Bancroft shows how the silver king wrote his own life story. According to Morison, Fair was "a sort of Munchhausen" who magnified his own importance by saying things that were not quite true but not quite false either. Fair emphasized the leadership qualities evident in his early life. "He has never, as a man, followed anybody's lead, but has always been a leader," and Fair stressed that "he has never taken hold of anything that he did not succeed in." These self-perceptions allowed Fair to claim total credit for the bonanza firm's success. He downgraded the contributions of Mackay, Flood, and O'Brien and assumed responsibility for creating the partnership, discovering the ore, and organizing the enterprise.[13]

During the interview, Fair ignored his ancestry almost entirely. Although he admitted to having Scots-Irish parents, "he declined quietly, without saying that he declined, to speak about his father and his mother and his grandfather and grandmother and so on down the line."[14]

Fair's refusal to discuss his origins is understandable within the context of his self-conception. His ancestors had little importance because, in Fair's mind, they had little to do with producing him. Fair considered himself the master of his own destiny. As he discussed his early life, Fair virtually created a new person, one who corresponded with the man he now understood himself to be. Jim Fair, Irish immigrant and poverty-stricken miner, hardly resembled James G. Fair, silver king. Therefore, the first Fair yielded to the second, a man destined to be a leader of men, a holder of money and power.

Like Fair, Louise (Mrs. John) Mackay rewrote the story of her life. Mamie Hungerford, as she was once known, came from a family of little distinction. Her father had cut hair in Virginia City, Nevada, and her mother had sewed to help make ends meet. At sixteen, Mamie married a successful doctor, Edmund G. Bryant, who soon took to drink and abused his family. A separation followed, and Mrs. Bryant supported herself by sewing and embroidering. Her plight was common knowledge in Virginia City, and neighbors, including the

James G. Fair family, often helped out. Widowed in 1866, Mrs. Bryant married John Mackay the following year.[15]

But in 1875, she recounted her life story as that of Marie Louise Antoinette Mackay, wife of one of the richest men in America. The father of this chatelaine descended from an old English family, and the mother emerged as "one of the most accomplished and fascinating ladies of the present age." Mrs. Mackay herself, "a lady of rare culture" and "a celebrated linguist," was "noted for her great talent in singing and the languages, speaking French and Spanish as fluently as her mother tongue." Because of her beauty and culture, the most gallant men of the coast had courted her, but she "turned a deaf ear" to them all—except for John Mackay. So much for Mamie Hungerford.[16]

James G. Fair and Louise Mackay probably believed what they told the interviewers. The stories they narrated must have been more real to them than reality. Looking back, they needed to know how they had achieved prominence and success. By indulging themselves with the luxury of creating new pasts and developing new identities, they could begin to answer that question. Only remapping their early years so that they retrospectively appeared as continuous, unbroken paths without major disruptions could accommodate the overwhelming changes in their lives.

Remolding their pasts, the new millionaires created identities based on a common denominator—money. After all, their great wealth had changed them and necessitated the new selves. Money had made Louise Mackay feel like a spoiled, extravagant child,[17] and it exhilarated others as well. One of them told a group of wealthy guests that they could never guess how he felt that night, "one of the richest men in the world, giving the biggest ball ever given in Frisco." Five years before, none had ever heard his name, and butlers would have barred doors against him. Now, here he was, "the proudest man that ever lived."[18]

The new millionaires spent money lavishly, but selectively. They bought things that reflected their new self-images and freshly minted social status—things like jewelry. After all, gems were not just decorative but also quickly convertible into cash. Unlike specie, however, they could be worn. When millionaires covered themselves with precious stones, they were literally wrapping themselves in riches. They appeared inseparable from their money, and they felt that way. One night, Mrs. Mark Hopkins swathed herself in diamonds enough to hide the color of her dress. One grande dame compared her to a crystal chandelier. "Six rows on her neck, and one necklace down to her knees," a "stomacher" as big as "a mustard plaster, a tiara and bracelets enough to fill Shreve's [Jewelry Store] window." The dowager was amused, but Mary Hopkins yearned for status, and she dressed to win it, or so she thought.[19]

Jane Stanford (the "queen of diamonds") owned one of the largest jewelry collections in San Francisco. Some claimed that her collection of rubies surpassed any in the world, and her baubles had a value estimated at well over a million dollars. Among her stones were four matched sets of diamonds, each including a necklace, corsage, earrings, tiara, bracelets, and brooches. She also owned a large pear-shaped black diamond, a necklace of varicolored stones, and sixty pairs of diamond earrings.[20]

An incident that occurred many years later, in 1897, indicates the importance of jewels to the millionaires. To raise money for the Stanford University Library, Widow Stanford decided to sell her jewels in London. She had all the various boxes brought to her in Palo Alto "for a last look at them as a collection." While they were spread out, Mrs. Stanford had them photographed so that she could always remember them. Taking the pictures became a major enterprise since Mrs. Stanford wanted "each piece, in turn, to occupy the central position because of the precious memories attached to it." After the photographs were taken and enlargements made, Mrs. Stanford wanted the gems painted in their exact size and color, almost like close relatives whose painful departure had to be delayed as long as possible. Only after dozens of pictures had been taken and the portrait painted did they all leave for London. In the end, not too surprisingly, she received no satisfactory offers and brought her collection home again.[21]

The millionaires' great wealth made them feel special, and they believed that their money entitled them to rank and privilege. After all, they had achieved what others had only attempted. They felt that their fortunes made them somehow better than other people. As one interviewer wrote of Fair, he seemed to think that "God Almighty" had used "a little superior clay" to form him and used "the odds and ends for the rest of mankind."[22] Or, as Louise Mackay supposedly said to Theresa Fair, "With wealth like this, we can queen it anywhere we've a mind to."[23]

But San Francisco's established social elite snubbed the silver barons and railroad princes, just as Mrs. Astor cold-shouldered Mrs. Vanderbilt and the Coreys cut the Laphams. They claimed to value lineage, taste, and culture as well as wealth, to have created a world of gentility and refinement reminiscent of the great cities. The reigning community aped their counterparts in New York and Philadelphia, Boston and Charleston by concerning themselves with architectural styles, interior decoration, landscape gardening, manners, the arts, charity, society, and a mode of life.[24] Therefore, they excluded the new millionaires. "Toward the close of the Seventies, and even in the beginning of the Eighties, the disposition to brand as upstarts and parvenus all the aspirants to social recognition began to assert itself," and the old guard decided to "retreat behind its lace curtains and watch, rather than accept, for a long time, these . . . upstarts."[25]

The old elite had country estates south of San Francisco at places like Atherton and Menlo Park, where they maintained an urbane sort of existence and thought it shameful for interlopers to live nearby. The novelist Gertrude Atherton referred to "the impertinent invasion of Menlo Park" by James C. Flood and his family. She said that their arrival "annoyed and agitated" the entire country. Only when their husbands demanded it for business reasons did the Atherton women leave calling cards. The return visit confirmed their fear that the Floods did not belong. Instead of dressing in simple summer frocks, Mary Flood and her daughter "got themselves up for the occasion. Mrs. Flood wore a flowing dark blue silk wrapper, discreetly ruffled, and 'Miss Jennie' a confection of turquoise-green flannel trimmed with deep flounces of Valenciennes lace!" Confronted with these apparitions, Gertrude Atherton "was stricken too dumb to take any part in the conversation."[26]

The new millionaires could not accept rejection by the old guard. As they saw it, great wealth entitled them to social preeminence. Assuming that their fortunes would provide entree to society, they found their ambitions thwarted. Prior claimants challenged their assertions and ridiculed their pretensions. Unaccustomed to unfulfilled aspirations, the kings created a separate world in San Francisco, the world of Nob Hill.

This world rested upon money and its expenditure, what Thorstein Veblen called "conspicuous consumption." On this San Francisco hilltop, just as on Chicago's Gold Coast, New York's Fifth Avenue, and Philadelphia's Main Line, the rich consumed "as an evidence of pecuniary strength." Nabobs not only ingested goods far beyond the minimum needed for subsistence but also far in excess of the quality needed for utility. They consumed "freely and of the best, in food, drink . . . shelter, services, ornaments, apparel, weapons and accoutrements, amusements, amulets, and idols or divinities." Partaking of these superior goods became a sign of wealth, and failure to have done so would have been "a mark of inferiority and demerit."[27]

But millionaires needed to do more than display money; they needed to create new selves. And so they consumed selectively as well as conspicuously. On Nob Hill, they recreated aristocratic England in the heart of San Francisco. The new millionaires replicated noble settings and a rhythm of life divided among town house, country estate, and exclusive spa. They mimicked noble rites of life and copied ceremonies of marriage, birth, and death. San Francisco's upstarts donned the habits of the English nobility—landscape gardening, country sports, and entertaining. They supervised stewards and agents and oversaw local affairs including church, charity, and education. In short, the new millionaires modeled themselves after, and presented themselves as, aristocrats.

For the new millionaires, this particular form of conspicuous consumption fulfilled several needs. It let them display their fortunes and reinforce the idea that they were special; no one else could spend as lavishly and ostentatiously. Also, in their minds, successful imitation would establish their own transcendence. If they created an analogy between themselves and the nobility, they would unquestionably garner status, respect, and prestige. But, most of all, this kind of imitation provided norms that told them how to behave in any situation, and the interrelationships among the various forms made them more meaningful. In other words, the model gave the nabobs an elite identity and self-conception.

The millionaires began building the world of Nob Hill in the mid-1870s by reconstructing their physical environment. They erected enormous new residences, and, like the aristocracy, they built two types of homes, city mansions and country estates. In San Francisco itself, they located high atop Nob Hill, creating an unquestionably "aristocratic" neighborhood. Their "truly palatial" mansions would "presently transform that quarter into the Belgravia of San Francisco."[28]

These houses became the West Coast equivalents of French chateaus on Fifth Avenue and Gothic castles on Prairie Avenue. Every Philadelphia palazzo had its San Francisco counterpart, each more fantastic than the last, each carefully calculated to heighten the contrast between its occupants and hoi polloi. Here lived no ordinary mortals; here lived a railroad king, a silver baron, a merchant prince, an illusion intensified in many ways, not least of them Nob Hill itself, one of the highest points in the city. Perched atop it, these mansions "dominated the heights of San Francisco like medieval fortresses." Visible for miles around, no one could miss them.[29]

As one drew nearer and saw the walls and fences surrounding the mansions, one's astonishment grew. Solid granite encircled Crocker's house. Flood's brownstone wall sported heavy bronze railings that gleamed in the sun. San Franciscans believed that Flood kept a servant to do nothing but shine it. "Passing [by at] any hour of the day, one discovered him polishing away at some section." The Stanford and Hopkins homes boasted the most monumental walls of all; Stanford enclosed his palace with a granite blockade fourteen feet thick at the base and thirty feet high. Next door, an even mightier fortress surrounded the Hopkins castle as though some great lord lived there. One observer reported that "the massive oak doors swung on iron hinges to permit the entrance, not of armored knights on horseback, but of basket phaetons, the family barouche, rockaways, and broughams."[30]

Inside the gates, the mansions themselves heightened the illusion of nobility and aristocracy. The immense buildings and their architectural styles made them seem more like palaces than homes. The Stanford mansion had more than fifty major apartments. Two blocks down California Street, the Crocker residence was only slightly smaller. Flood's house rivaled those of Stanford and Crocker in size. A massive building of brown sandstone, it was surmounted by a thirty-foot-square tower that projected out from the main building.[31]

Perhaps the greatest of these great houses belonged to Mark and Mary Hopkins, but its significance resulted less from its size than from its appearance: it truly looked like a castle. When Hopkins decided to join the growing colony on Nob Hill, he hired the architectural firm of Wright and Saunders to design his chateau. They created a building described variously as a "hundred-turreted, glorified gingerbread, three million dollar castle," a "weird aggregation of towers and cupolas," a "highly-ornate box stove," and a "bit of Carcassone [brought] to the shores of the Pacific." Its "gray towers could be seen from the bay and far south of the city," and it was, perhaps, the strangest of many "strange homes, these Nob Hill palaces, the amazement of visitors from the Old World which had nothing like them." [32]

The great lords of San Francisco lived in urban palaces, but to emulate the English nobility they also needed country estates. They located these manors south of the city in San Mateo County, near enough to be easily accessible, far enough to seem rural. Set in large parks, these villas allowed San Francisco's wealthy men to play the role of country lords. James C. Flood called his seat Linden Towers, where he lived near the likes of D. O. Mills (Millbrae), Milton Latham (Sherwood Hall), and William C. Ralston (Belmont), whose riches ranked them just below the silver princes and railroad kings in the pantheon of San Francisco wealth.

Of all the San Francisco squires, the noblest was Leland Stanford, who bought an estate in 1876 and built a fine country residence. Although not nearly so elaborate as his San Francisco palace or in any way comparable to the Vanderbilt mansion at Hyde Park, no one would have called the house unpretentious, and the Stanfords furnished it with costly rugs, furniture, and objets d'art. The clearest indication of Stanford's motives in acquiring this second fine home appears in a painting, *Palo Alto Spring*, which he commissioned from Thomas Hill in 1878. Stanford had Hill paint an open-air conversation piece reminiscent of mid-eighteenth-century works by Hogarth, Gainsborough, and especially Arthur Davis. In it the Stanford family and a large group of friends and relatives take their ease in the lush green serenity of Palo Alto. The house itself provides a somewhat hazy background for children playing croquet on the lawn, infants resting on a tiger skin, and servants bringing trays of liquid refreshment. One young girl swings in the branches of a stately old tree, while her elders sit and talk in elaborate wrought-iron chairs. Stanford himself admires a newly painted canvas, and the inevitable dog stands nearby.[33]

After successfully demonstrating possession of that key characteristic that "all" English aristocrats "had in common"—"the ability to support both a country mansion . . . and a metropolitan life"[34]—San Francisco's new millionaires added a final dimension to their aristocratic world. They built the Hotel del Monte.

The English nobility had been traveling to the great European spas and watering places for several centuries. Although many San Franciscans including Crocker, Stanford, Flood, Fair, and Mackay made the grand tour, a trip to Baden-Baden or Bad Kissingen was too lengthy for them to make regularly. They required someplace closer to home. After 1880 the Hotel del Monte near Monterey Bay, south of San Francisco, satisfied this need. The Central Pacific financed this West Coast version of Saratoga or Newport, the Greenbriar or the Homestead, and it was the special project of Charles Crocker. He personally supervised its construction, and upon completion the place became his favorite residence. The grounds were arranged in the manner of an English landscape with flower beds, rose gardens, and choice shrubbery. The lawns were kept "fresh as an emerald," and guests could stroll through acres of lush greenery. Those who preferred more strenuous activities could use the croquet plats, archery range, or swings. In the morning, guests swam in seawater tanks; in the afternoon, they drove carriages brought from San Francisco; and, in the evening, they danced. But regardless of what they were doing, the nabobs always dressed elegantly. No lounging robes or casual costumes at del Monte. Worth gowns of velvet, silk, or satin sparkled at the dances, and elaborate costumes *en promenade*. Del Monte was the Marienbad of California. Before long, it became a major element of the Nob Hill world.[35]

Once newly wealthy San Franciscans had placed themselves in the proper physical milieus—the conjunction of urban palace, country estate, and exclusive spa—they had to create a life-style appropriate to the new settings. Hugger-mugger activities wouldn't do in such surroundings. Therefore, San Francisco's elite modified their behavior to comport with their elegant surroundings. And so they mimicked the ways of the English nobility. Birth and death became ritual occasions on which to celebrate the maintenance, continuity, and passage of the family line.

When Leland Stanford, Jr., was born, he did not receive a twenty-one gun salute, but he *was* introduced to the world on a silver platter. The Stanfords gave a dinner party when the infant was only a few weeks old, and after everyone had been seated, a waiter brought in a large, covered, silver tray. He placed it in the middle of the table, and Stanford rose to address the guests. "My friends, I wish now to introduce my son to you." He removed the cover from the tray, and there lay the Prince of Palo Alto on a bed of flowers. Carried around the table and presented to each guest in turn, the baby smiled and went through his introductions very nicely, behaving in a manner befitting the heir apparent to the house of Stanford.[36]

When one of the millionaires died, newspapers frequently called the funeral arrangements simple and unpretentious, but they found enough material to jam column after column. They commented on the paucity of the floral pieces but overstuffed lines describing them. They emphasized the restraint but devoted paragraphs to the splendor. Convention mandated understating the magnificence of rich men's funerals, but no one who saw their mausoleums could mistake the self-conception of these men—they were beings who deserved tombs, not graves. For her husband, Mrs. Mark Hopkins erected a $150,000 vault with walls of highly polished, rose-colored marble and massive bronze doors. William S. O'Brien, generally considered the most retiring and least pretentious of the bonanza quartet, was entombed in a granite mausoleum decorated with stained glass windows and bronze doors that proclaimed for all the world to hear, "This is the last resting place of a graveyard aristocrat."[37]

Between the major turning points of birth and death, the new millionaires behaved as aristocratically as possible, but few trappings of nobility rivaled the importance of their horses. Fine animals symbolized aristocracy, so San Francisco's new millionaires spent vast sums on magnificent animals, housed the beasts in palatial stables, and showed them off in public places. The upstarts' horses seemed almost part of their families and garnered a corresponding amount of concern and affection.

In their majestic homes, the equine humanoids basked in far greater luxury than the majority of San Franciscans. At William C. Ralston's Belmont, the horses "stood in stables of polished inlaid wood, and their harness was silver-mounted." Just north, at Flood's Linden Towers, stalls of polished mahogany contained sterling silver knobs and fittings. To light his horses' domain, Milton Latham provided a crystal chandelier. The *Argonaut* wryly observed that when a San Franciscan became extremely wealthy, he built a "palace of a stable, with marble halls, Brussels carpets, and hot and cold water in every stall."[38]

Like their other possessions, the new millionaires displayed their horses. Unless seen and admired, the animals did not demonstrate a family's aristocratic qualities. The new millionaires therefore went driving. They loved trotting out their nobility and their horseflesh, spending Sunday afternoon behind the reins of a beautifully matched pair. After church, anyone could see "gold-mounted carriages of every approved pattern, drawn by richly-caparisoned steeds, driven by uniformed liverymen." The vehicles contained "beautiful belles and gallant beaux" who went "whirling swiftly over the open road . . . rivaling each other in display, as well as emulating each other in merrymaking and jollity." Mrs. Ben Holladay, the queen of Wells-Fargo, preened in her "well-appointed dark green brougham, drawn by two large bay horses in showy harness. . . . Upon the box were seated the coachman and footman in green cloth liveries, bright gilt buttons, and tall hats." Her footman, the first seen in the city, "attracted as much attention as if he had been a Fiji Islander in native costume." Other striking turnouts belonged to Milton Latham (a dark brown carriage with yellow wheels, pale blue interior, and a pair of milk white horses), Lucky Baldwin (who had the first regular English coach in the city), and J. B. Haggin (who had one of the first four-in-hand teams). Indeed, all the new millionaires indulged their tastes for fine horses and elegant carriages.[39]

Once equipped with these aristocratic trappings, the new millionaires needed a place to display them. Driving out Point Lobos Road to the Cliff House to view the ocean and watch sea lions frolic on the rocks below provided a favorite diversion; but Golden Gate Park offered the preferred venue. Opened in 1871, the park was meant to be a resort for the entire city, but its location on the western edge of

town and the lack of public transportation limited the number of visitors. Those who could not afford to hire a horse or carriage had to
forgo the pleasure. Soon, the park became a play place for the rich.
The *Argonaut* revealed the significance of the site when it urged the
city to build a "'Golden' Avenue to the Golden Gate Park." Unless
San Francisco had "parks and drives, avenues and boulevards, where
fashion" could "display itself and where folly" could "air itself," millionaires would "go away to the East—to Europe—and spend their
money in Central Park, at Long Branch, on the Champs Elysees, and
the Bois de Boulogne."[40]

Horses also allowed rich men to participate in the "sport of kings," a
sure-fire sign of nobility. What, after all, could be more aristocratic
than the Derby or Ascot opening day? Therefore, a number of San
Francisco millionaires, like their counterparts in eastern cities, raced
horses. During the 1880s, men like James Ben Ali Haggin and Lucky
Baldwin raced thoroughbreds, but the first of the new millionaire
horsemen, Leland Stanford, chose to breed and race trotters. He
bought his first horse, Occident, in 1870 and spent the next twenty
years turning his Palo Alto stock farm into one of the finest in the
world. At one point he employed eight trainers to handle 71 colts and
775 horses altogether. His prized Electioneer became the world's
champion sire of trotting champions, and its offspring earned universal
fame. Besides the animals themselves, Stanford's establishment included blacksmiths, wheelwrights, and millers. According to one visi-
tor, Palo Alto was "probably the most complete horsebreeding establishment in the world."[41]

Racing horses linked the personal and public sides of aristocratic
life. Through houses, estates, resorts, and ceremonies, new millionaires
copied aristocrats. But true nobles also had public responsibilities,
doing things for "the people." Raising and racing horses provided enter-
tainment that everyone could enjoy; the animals generated tremendous
enthusiasm, and the entire state rooted for their success. In addition,
the rich demonstrated nobility (and fulfilled their obligations to society) through philanthropy, patronage of the arts, and government
service. In each of these endeavors, aspiring aristocrats exercised
leadership while showing the proper relationship between themselves
and the common folk.

Some of San Francisco's new millionaires acquired special reputations for generosity (and others for parsimony), but almost all of them contributed to charitable and philanthropic causes. As aristocrats, their sense of noblesse oblige dictated helping the less fortunate. However, their manner of giving suggests a less than selfless motive. They used money in ways that *they* thought would benefit others and rarely allowed recipients to spend the funds at will. Thus, their seeming generosity allowed the new millionaires to make decisions and control the behavior of others, and, at the same time, demonstrate that they knew what was best. In short, charitable activities helped enthrone them in positions of leadership and superiority.

The history of San Francisco's Jackson Street Kindergarten Association demonstrates how a group of parvenus could use their money to ennoble themselves and dictate the behavior of others. Founded in 1871 under the auspices of Mrs. Sarah Cooper's Bible class, the association located its first kindergarten on Jackson Street in "the very heart of the Barbary Coast." Private donations funded the organization, and Sarah Cooper proved an adroit fund-raiser who knew how to appeal to the new rich. In 1881, Charles Crocker sent a check for $200, and Mrs. Stanford donated $500. In coming years, Mrs. Stanford contributed $100,000 to the project. These aristocrats, who could have given their money to any number of worthy causes, found the aims and objectives of this group particularly appealing. According to Mrs. Cooper, the kindergarten did a "child-saving work" designed to correct "the hereditary defectiveness of the masses." She hoped to build "character—genuine character" by getting "hold of the little waifs that grow up to form the criminal element just as early in life as possible." Mrs. Cooper believed that "the pliable period of early childhood" offered "the time most favorable to the eradication of vicious tendencies." She therefore argued that the kindergarten, which has "rightly been termed the 'Paradise of childhood,' . . . the gate through which many a little outcast has re-entered Eden," could lay "the foundations for national prosperity and perpetuity."[42] The doctrine that kindergartens could better humanity appealed to the new millionaires. By supporting the organization, they implied that they had already risen and knew the path that others should follow. Identifying themselves with the best, as opposed to the worst, elements of society, they used their money to reform other people and thereby the city.

Practicing philanthropy was only one way the new millionaires made decisions for others, enforced their own values, and established their superiority. Because they assumed that wealth gave them leadership, they passed judgment on what belonged and what did not. In the process, "culture lost all connection with function other than that of establishing an identification with that narrow society which had made itself the custodian of values attached to the arts." Consequently, architecture, literature, art, and music became primarily status symbols. That very fact provided the new millionaires with a "justification of . . . [their] aristocratic pretensions."[43]

A tour of Europe launched many new millionaires on the road to cultural leadership. On these journeys, they experienced European traditions firsthand. When they returned, they presented themselves as cultural authorities. While away, they became patrons of the arts, buying sculpture and paintings by the shipload and sending them back to San Francisco. During these travels, the millionaires often experienced a rebirth. They returned to San Francisco with new identities and felt ready to assert themselves as arbiters of taste and beauty. Such claims might have flopped if James Flood or Collis P. Huntington had simply moved to the top of Nob Hill and tried to affirm his superiority; San Franciscans knew their backgrounds and recent histories too well. But, by withdrawing for a year, traveling, and allowing the rest of the city to read of their doings abroad, the new millionaires prepared San Francisco for the return of new men, connoisseurs of the arts. As such, they attempted to dictate the style and content of art.

About 1875, Leland Stanford decided to commission a great historical painting depicting the completion of the transcontinental railroad. He approached the noted California artist Thomas Hill and agreed to pay $25,000 for a canvas eight feet by twelve feet. Hill began the project and soon discovered that he was expected to portray what Stanford wanted to see, not what had actually happened. On one occasion, the railroad king demanded that Thomas Durant, president of Union Pacific, be given a less prominent place; on another, he threatened to "annihilate" the painter if he did not leave out Fred Mc-

Crellish, the editor of a San Francisco newspaper and political oppo-
nent of Stanford. Time after time, Stanford ordered Hill to relocate
some individuals, delete others, and add still others who had not even
been present.[44]

In a similar incident several years later, Louise Mackay hired the
popular French artist Jean-Louis Ernest Meissonier to paint her portrait. But she found his treatment of her hands "unpardonable. Great
gnarled things . . . with big bony wrists," and she compared them to
Napoleonic horses. Dissatisfied, she hired another French artist to
paint her. The difference between the two works betrays the new millionaires' perception of the function of art. In the words of John
Mackay, the original portrait had her "eyes down pat" and captured
her "expression . . . cleverness . . . determination." It was a good psychological portrait. But Louise Mackay wondered, "What woman
wants a portrait like that?" so she had herself painted by an artist who
"always made a lady look so pretty." The second artist understood her
and portrayed her as she wanted to see herself, as a young and beautiful woman. In her mind, art should depict the world as she, not the
artist, saw it.[45]

Using their money to encourage (and discourage) artists was only
one form of cultural imperialism practiced by the would-be aristocrats.
In 1882, D. O. Mills actively assisted New York's Metropolitan Museum of Art, and in 1878 John Mackay underwrote the cost of the
American exhibit at the Paris International Exposition. Each Nob
Hill palace had its private library, and Leland Stanford, Jr., began a
museum of antiquities. One of the shrewdest assertions of cultural
leadership was patronage of the opera. San Francisco's wealthiest citizens attended performances conspicuously and made sure that the city
had a splendid opera house. In 1873, Dr. Thomas Wade, a successful
dentist, conceived the idea of building an opera house to rival any in
the country. Its three thousand seats provided the third largest seating
capacity, its mezzanine was the first diamond horseshoe, and its crystal
chandelier was the most splendid in the land. Though Wade ran out of
money before finishing the building, James C. Flood and John Mackay
came to his rescue. Just as New York nabobs underwrote the Met,
these silver princes advanced funds, took a mortgage, and, when
Wade defaulted, took over the opera house themselves.[46]

The new millionaires consolidated their positions as nobles by patronizing the arts and donating to charity. They understood the traditional relationship between aristocrats and the rest of society (the former was to guide the latter), and they tried to establish themselves as unchallenged leaders. Therefore, it also made sense for them to seek political position. High public office symbolized the rank to which they aspired.

The most desired office was membership in the United States Senate, what Ernest Crosby called "the House of Dollars." Five San Francisco millionaires attained this lofty position. In order of election they were John P. Jones, William Sharon, and James G. Fair, who all represented Nevada, and Leland Stanford and George Hearst, who represented California. Here they joined economic peers like Nelson Aldrich and Chauncey Depew in the most exclusive club in the nation, the American version of the House of Lords. As such, they considered it worthy of their presence and fought bitterly to gain admission, a battle that inevitably cost money. John P. Jones supposedly spent half a million dollars in 1872, and William Sharon spent at least as much two years later. James G. Fair's election may have cost him $350,000, and Fair estimated that Stanford's seat cost him a flat million.[47]

Unhappily, the new senators seemed not to enjoy their duties. Stanford found them "irksome." Only a month after taking office, he started to complain. He found Senate procedures tiresome and inefficient. Rumors soon circulated that he wanted to resign. Although he remained in office for eight years, he addressed the Senate fewer than two dozen times and frequently absented himself for long periods.[48]

Except for John P. Jones, who actively participated in the Senate for thirty years, other rich men seemed to have the same feelings. Sharon has been categorized as having "one of the worst" records in the history of the United States Senate. "His record of inaction is unbelievable. He was seated at only five sessions and was recorded on less than one percent of all roll calls. He never introduced a bill, and if he spoke on one, it is not recorded." He did not even arrive in Washington until a year after his election, preferring to remain at home with his mistress.[49]

Fair's record was slightly superior, even if his feelings hardly differed.

He remained in Washington, answered his mail, and tried to help his constituents. But he, too, "took no initiative whatever" in Senate proceedings and seemed to take little pleasure from his work. He told Senator Johnson Camden of West Virginia that he "really had no desire to return to the Senate for another six years," and when Camden retired, Fair wrote that they both had "too many other cares to be bothered with the Senate." He was glad that his friend would be "troubled no more with that hateful Senate" and he knew that Camden would be "much more happy."[50]

Given this behavior and these attitudes, one wonders why the new millionaires paid the costs of running for office. Why did they spend the money needed to run successful campaigns? Apparently these men liked being senators even if they disliked the Senate. Being a senator was the closest to being a lord that an American citizen could get. Men who aspired to the aristocracy logically aspired to the Senate. As senators they saw themselves above the mass of men and thought it their duty to serve as impartial leaders of all the people. After Fair's election, he looked out for everyone's interests. He tried to treat all political parties alike because he "hardly knew" which one he belonged to, and he was a Democrat only because he had to sit on one side of the aisle. However, he had received many Republican votes, so he refused "all documents and everything . . . that were unpleasant for the Republicans to hear." His only responsibility, as he saw it, was "keeping everything going" to Nevada "that it was entitled to." As a leader of all the people, Fair considered himself above partisan politics.[51]

By the late 1870s, San Francisco's new millionaires, like those throughout America, had differentiated themselves from everyone else in the city. Their aristocratic pretensions, as well as their money, set them apart. Harriet Lane Levy's "forehead . . . brushed the sidewalk" in front of the Mackay's house, and one Stanford University faculty member's wife thought of Jane Stanford as "royalty." One was always conscious of the "queenly" widow's "great wealth and power, her wonderful knowledge of the world, for she had been everywhere and seen and heard everything and all sorts of people," and the "poor faculty people must have seemed rather insignificant to her." Even Jessie Knight Jordan, wife of the university president, was awestruck by Mrs.

Stanford's "somewhat impressive figure with her rather massive frame" and by her manner, which, "though extremely cordial, was distinctly that of a woman with an assured position in the social and financial world." Only after Mr. Stanford's sudden death did she come to seem "very human."[52]

6. Social Contrasts: South of Market

The world of Nob Hill was not the only new world in San Francisco. Comfortable middle-class bungalows were rising on the sand dunes of the Western Addition, and adventurous San Franciscans would soon ride trolleys into the Mission District. There they bought the famous San Francisco Victorians, constructed in the Queen Anne, Italianate, or Stick-Eastlake styles, all characterized by flamboyant carpentry and the ubiquitous bay window. In Chinatown, San Francisco's most oppressed minority was trying to improve its condition, despite extraordinary social, physical, and economic handicaps. And, barely a mile from Nob Hill, clearly visible from the heights, separated from the pinnacle by the city's broadest boulevard, was South of Market, the home of San Francisco's "other half."

Unfortunately, San Francisco's other half had no Jacob Riis to record their existence or memorialize their lives, and their story must be pieced together from fragmentary evidence scattered through newspapers, government reports, and an occasional letter or diary. All of that evidence reveals a misery comparable to that depicted by Riis for New York's Mulberry Bend, Hell's Kitchen, or Five Points.

By the late 1870s, South of Market had a reputation as San Francisco's crowded quarter. It included most of three wards, the seventh, ninth, and tenth, a habitable area of just about nine-tenths of a square mile. Streets made the region a bit larger, perhaps one and a quarter square miles. In 1880, these three wards housed 55,323 people, a density of about 46,000 per square mile. Put somewhat differently, the section encompassed 3 percent of San Francisco's total area but almost 25 percent of its population.[1]

Fifty-five thousand San Franciscans could cram into fifty-eight square blocks because "nearly one-third of the city's boarding houses, a quarter of its hotels, and half of its . . . lodging houses were located there." In addition, one-third of San Francisco's restaurants served meals South of Market. But terms like *boarding house*, *hotel*, and *lodging house* fail to convey an adequate impression of the squalor that characterized this neighborhood. One reporter investigated living conditions in the area and actually rented a room in one of the "shabby, unclean-looking houses" that advertised "Lodgings—single beds, 50, 37½, and 25 cents per night." There, he found himself consigned to the upper story of an old warehouse subdivided into cubicles furnished with a cot, chair, and no window. A burlap sack filled with straw and fleas served as the mattress. The stench was insufferable. Two years later, another reporter found conditions no different and concluded that "on the whole, the accommodations obtainable by the poorer classes . . . are not at all what they ought to be."[2]

Housing was not simply small, dirty, and unpleasant. Landlords frequently allowed property to deteriorate and "get into a state highly prejudicial to the public health." In 1876, the city health officer began his description of living conditions South of Market by noting the obvious—that the area was densely populated, mostly by members of the working class. He also asserted that overcrowding, poor drainage, lack of ventilation, and filth made many residences unfit for human habitation. Imperfect drains, open cesspools, and inadequate sewers caused diphtheria, typhoid, and other diseases to germinate and spread, frequently with fatal results. During the fiscal year ending June 30, 1877, San Francisco experienced a smallpox epidemic and many deaths from diphtheria. The health inspector perceptively concluded that these conditions attracted those who could afford nothing better.[3]

Despite this situation, rents rose throughout the 1870s. A survey of classified advertisements in the *Chronicle* suggests that housing costs increased from 6 to 80 percent between 1870 and 1880, depending on the size of the flat or house. The shortage of inexpensive housing was so severe that one San Franciscan believed "no city in the world" experienced "the want of cheap dwellings suitable for the mechanic and

TABLE 6.1   BUILDINGS AND
POPULATION IN SAN FRANCISCO,
1860–80

Year	Number of Buildings	Population
1860		56,802
1861	11,265	
1865	15,518	
1870	19,459	149,473
1875	23,700	
1879	28,700	
1880		233,959

families of moderate means" that San Francisco did. Real estate was "so high" and interest "so exorbitant" that property-owners felt compelled to ask high rents.[4]

Other factors also drove housing costs up and made it difficult to acquire decent lodgings. Most important, the population had grown more rapidly than the supply of housing. Between 1860 and 1880, the population had more than quadrupled, but the city's building stock had not even tripled (table 6.1).[5]

At the same time, San Francisco's geography and topography limited the land available for homes. Surrounded on three sides by water and covered with steep hills, the city boasted relatively little flat land. San Franciscans attempted to increase the land supply by filling parts of the bay, scaling hills with cable cars, and cutting through rocky mounds, but there was never enough land.

The working class found the problem particularly acute. As in other cities, workingmen walked to their jobs, spending the minimum of time and money on travel. As late as 1880, 80 percent of San Francisco's laborers lived within half a mile of their jobs. Horsecars, cable cars, and streetcars began to revolutionize land use during the 1870s and were generally thought to be the poor man's friend, supposedly enabling him to avoid the congestion and filth of the industrial city. But to a struggling laborer, even ten cents a day was too much for carfare. Therefore, workingmen continued to live South of Market, along the Embarcadero, on the Potrero, in Butchertown— always within walking distance of wherever they found employment.

Only those with steady jobs and a guaranteed income could move to the Western Addition or the Mission and commute downtown. The majority of laborers lived in the heart of the city in tenements, lodging houses, or rooms where the scarcity of land and competing uses determined rents.[6]

As early as 1870, some San Franciscans recognized the seriousness of the housing problem. One complained that exorbitant rents made it almost impossible for a laboring man "to procure a house sufficiently large for his family . . . in a good location, at a price that the wages he receives will justify him in paying." This grievance persisted throughout the decade. Many married men could barely keep their heads above water, and "only the most prosperous artisan . . . could afford to have a house all to himself; usually, he had to rent two or three small rooms." In some cases, several families took up "rooming," which could be "very miserable" indeed. Three families and several young men might jointly rent a house. Each family would have a room or two for itself, but they shared the stove. Under these conditions, asked one reporter, how could "a wife, accustomed to obtaining her meals at the restaurant, and to looking at her room merely as a temporary sleeping place, have any idea of what home is?" Or how could children "have any affection for home? They do not know what the name means."[7]

These questions certainly imply nineteenth-century attitudes toward women and families, but they also indicate the difficulty inherent in establishing and maintaining traditional family life. For one thing, hundreds of men never married. Since the gold rush, San Francisco had suffered a serious sex ratio imbalance and, in 1880, had four adult white men for every three adult white women. One-fourth of the city's white men thus had no choice but bachelorhood. This burden fell especially hard on common laborers, who had difficulty finding the money and lodgings needed for housekeeping. Women could wait for the best offers, and common laborers had difficulty competing with more successful men.[8]

San Franciscans who did marry and establish families might well encounter a disappointing family life. Their wives expected them to provide and establish a household; love and affection depended upon their ability to do so. But many laborers could offer little more than squalid rented rooms, so they lost the respect of their wives, and divorce rates began to climb. In 1864–65, one divorce was requested for every 9 marriage licenses issued. Ten years later, one divorce was requested for every 4.5 licenses. In 1864–65, one divorce was actually granted for every 16.5 marriage licenses. Ten years later, one divorce was granted for every 7.6 licenses. Furthermore, the sex ratio meant that a divorced woman could probably remarry, and many wives sought release from unsatisfactory husbands. Women sought more than 75 percent of the divorces issued in San Francisco during the 1870s.[9]

Poverty generated severe conflict between husbands and wives. Frank Roney wrote in his diary both about arguing with his wife and about the guilt he felt afterward. Fortunately, they "made the matter all right at night."[10] Other couples fared worse. On May 6, 1870, Annie Blake, a resident of the Seventh Ward, appeared in police court and charged her husband James with assault. As evidence, Mrs. Blake pointed to her black eye. When asked to defend himself, Mr. Blake stated that he had found only a few days' work in the last seven weeks and when he did earn a little money, his wife squandered it on beer. If he complained, she called him "hard names" and threw dishes. "At the time he was arrested, she had just broken a cup on his head, and he had to strike her to keep her quiet."[11]

James Bowlan became even more violent. On June 17, 1879, he murdered his wife, Nellie. They had been married four years, and at first, Bowlan proved himself an "affectionate, loving husband." Then he suffered an accident, broke his leg, and lost his job. "As he had not been very economical, he soon found himself without funds to support his wife in the manner he had been wont to keep her." A coldness developed between them, and they separated. When Bowlan began working again, he begged his wife to return and promised her "all those luxuries which his means would permit." She refused him and announced that she wanted a divorce. Bowlan continued to press his affections, but when he discovered that she intended to remarry, he arranged a meeting and shot her.[12]

With marriage ties strained, parental authority too lost force, and children achieved a new independence. They began looking outside the home for leadership and guidance. San Francisco youth formed new social organizations more significant to them than their families. Gangs of hoodlums roamed the city, especially South of Market.

These youths had no jobs and could not afford high school, so they hung around corners, ogled women, rang doorbells, and unhinged gates. They sang obscene songs and uttered horrid oaths. They also picked pockets, clubbed businessmen, and outraged working girls. In no way did these youths behave as society expected.[13]

The annual reports of the San Francisco Industrial School provide an indication of the change in parent-child relationships. Founded in 1858 "for the reformation and care of idle and dissolute children," for about ten years this institution housed urchins convicted of "leading an idle and dissolute life." Every year, 65–90 percent of the boys received their sentences for this reason. However, in 1868, one boy was committed for a new reason: he was "ungovernable." Two years later, eleven boys were incarcerated for being "unmanageable." Moreover, no law enforcement agency committed them; they were simply "surrendered." The number of these cases increased to forty-eight the following year, and in 1872, fifty-five boys were "surrendered as unmanageable by parents and guardians."[14] In other words, a growing number of San Franciscans did not understand their children, could not control them, and therefore handed their progeny over to the city.

In February 1871, for example, the father of a girl charged in police court with leading an idle and dissolute life "testified that his child was beyond his control, that she ran away from home, and would not mind him." The man swore that he did all he could for the girl but could not afford to dress her in the fine clothes she craved. Eighteen months later, a mother testified against her son, who had been arrested for stealing five dollars. She said that the boy was "very wicked," had run away from home three weeks ago, and "was beyond his father's or her control." She then informed the judge that he could "do what he pleased with the boy." In both instances, the court committed the children to the industrial school.[15]

Perhaps a courtroom scene of February 19, 1877, sums up how relationships between husbands and wives, and parents and children, had deteriorated in some families.[16] Five boys ranging in age from ten to fourteen had been arrested for running away from home and sleeping in a stable. The officer asked one of them,

"What is your father's name?"
"I don't know," he replied.

"Don't know . . . a boy of your age ought to know. Now what does your mother call your father?!"

"She calls him old man, that's all."

"Well, what's your mother's first name?"

"Don't know."

"What does your father call her?"

"Old woman, that's all he calls her."

Sad to say, some San Franciscans would have found the dilapidated flats, hoodlum children, disagreeable spouses, and semiemployment an improvement over their own lives. Some citizens camped out in haybunks along the wharf, eked a living out of the garbage dumps south of the city, or huddled in the lumberyards along the waterfront. A series of newspaper articles published in 1878 vividly described their miserable existence.[17] An investigative reporter for the *Post* began his assignment by donning rags and smearing himself with a mixture of grease, beeswax, lard, and yellow ochre—then finished his ensemble with an old clay pipe and plug of tobacco. Thus arrayed, he meandered down Pacific Street. Near Dupont, he struck up a conversation with an old drunk, who ultimately invited him to spend the night. Thus, he began studying the lives of homeless, jobless, and starving people in San Francisco.

His new acquaintance led the reporter to the Vallejo Street wharf. There lay a pile of hay bales a block long and two hundred feet wide. The men clambered over this mountain of fodder, passing hundreds of sleeping bodies. At every step, voices called to protect territorial rights. Finally, the guide reached his own place, a crevice between two rows of bales. A barrel at one end blocked the wind, loose hay served as a mattress, and old canvas provided bedding.

The tramp soon fell asleep, but the reporter lay awake and pondered the contrast between this pile of hay and the pleasant homes he knew. As he stared into the night, he glanced at two schooners gently floating beside the dock. Suddenly, he spied a dark object creeping from the wharf to the rigging of one, and from the rigging to the deck. Then the form disappeared. Curious, the reporter made his way to the ship, where he found, wrapped in every sail of the schooner, dozens of tramps huddled and sleeping. From one of them, the journalist learned that sleeping on the decks was common, an accepted practice among sympathetic captains. In exchange for a nesting place, the homeless pulled up the sails and swabbed the decks.

Utterly amazed, the journalist headed for Tar Flat and the lumberyards south of Market and east of Beale. Here, too, he discovered a nightly rendezvous of homeless tramps and penniless men. The towering stacks of building material formed nooks and crannies where these men took shelter from the fog and wind. Leaving the lumberyard, the scribe headed for the Pacific Mail Steamship docks at the foot of Brannan Street. There he found a dilapidated house with paneless windows and boarded-over doors. Seeing a single entrance, he entered. Peering into the dim room, he beheld a spectacle of utter wretchedness. People of all ages covered the interior. They had no bedding except old pieces of carpet, sacks, or oilcloth; no stoves, no chairs, nothing but four walls and sleeping shadows. Heartsick at the misery, faint from the stench, the reporter groped his way outside and found a flophouse for the rest of the night.

Next morning, he headed for the city dump, where he witnessed another aspect of life among San Francisco's poor. People of all nationalities, wan and pinched, unwashed and unkempt, dogged and dejected, sifted through every cartload of garbage. Nothing was too small or insignificant. People collected rags of every description as well as bottles, cans, scraps of iron, glass, cork, wood, brick, even oyster shells. Half-rotten fruits and vegetables were genuine prizes. For this miserable, degrading work, people earned perhaps two dollars a week.

The *Post* reporter undoubtedly witnessed life as the most pitiable people in the city lived it—people without homes, jobs, or families. Although relatively few actually lived in the garbage dumps, haybunks, or lumberyards, others worried that they too might sink to this miserable level of existence. Frank Roney, for example, constantly suffered from anxiety, fear, and insecurity. He worried about losing his job and fretted about his health. Suspicious of friends and relatives, he wondered why people failed to answer his letters, thought that his brother-in-law was using him, and suspected his wife of deceiving him. Roney's apprehension peaked when he fantasized the cataclysmic destruction of San Francisco and all the city's residents. His fragile world seemed likely to implode at any moment.[18]

Thousands of San Franciscans constantly struggled to survive with some measure of dignity and self-respect intact. Roney described the battle vividly when he recorded how a used furniture man repossessed the few things that he and his wife had bought. The poor woman, pregnant and alone in the house, was pushed, shoved, and insulted when she tried to retain a few sticks of furniture. Roney felt powerless to respond and rationalized his lack of action by noting that the man was old and had been somewhat kind at first. But if he came to the house again, Roney vowed to "do something not very agreeable." Ultimately, Roney borrowed from friends, found odd jobs, bought on credit, and did without—just to survive. He kept a diary and confided his innermost fears and fantasies to it in order to maintain his dignity.[19]

Other San Franciscans lacked Roney's economic resourcefulness, literary skills, or self-perceptions. Petty thievery allowed some to survive. Throughout the 1870s, minor thefts dramatically increased as individuals tried to provide for themselves and their families however they could. One man found himself arrested for stealing a piece of street planking worth about five cents. When the case was called in court, his wife pleaded for him. She told the judge that he had not worked in several months and that they had no money. Their youngest child was sick, and she had no firewood. The man had gone looking for scraps and taken some wood, which then led to his arrest. Another woman was apprehended taking a can of milk from a doorstep. She told the court that she had come to San Francisco five weeks before but had yet to find a job. She was "friendless, a stranger in the city, and had absolutely no means of support." She stole the milk to ease her hunger.[20]

Some San Franciscans lacked even the ability to steal to keep themselves alive. One woman gave birth shortly after her husband went to the country looking for fieldwork. Severely weakened, she could not search for a job and had to remain in bed. When her money ran out, she pawned her possessions. When those meager proceeds failed, she went without food for almost a week. Her feeble cries finally attracted a passerby who summoned a doctor. He refused to help because she could not pay. She died a few days later and left her baby in critical condition. Equally horrible was the case of Mrs. Rice, an old woman who died of starvation. Neighbors did not see her for several days, and when a wretched stench began to emanate from her room, they called a policeman. He forced his way in and found her decomposing body. Rats had gnawed the flesh from one hand and part of her neck. Such scenes of hunger and starvation became so frequent in 1870 that one San Franciscan (using the pseudonym Humanitarian) wrote the *Call* suggesting that restaurants give "poor starving families the refuse of their kitchens."[21]

Many citizens balked at the choice between starvation and eating garbage, and they chose to end their lives instead. In 1878 and 1879, for the first time, the county coroner published detailed statistics about suicide in the city. In both years, "want of means" provided the most common "immediate cause" of self-destruction. During the fiscal year ended June 30, 1878, 26 of 103 suicides were explained in this way. The next year, 23 of 86. Patrick Richards, an Irish cooper, was perhaps typical of San Francisco's actual and would-be suicides. He had come to the city a short time before and had found no job. He had no money, no friends, and no home; he slept at the station house to keep warm. Finally, he concluded that "rather than live as he had done for the past two weeks he preferred to die."[22]

Many suicide notes suggest a clear relationship between immigration, disappointment, and self-destruction. Many immigrant victims became despondent because their expectations about life in California had not been fulfilled. Frederick Ruppin, an Austrian who slashed his throat, had been jobless for several months and felt forlorn. His suicide note bewailed his ever leaving home. Margaret Connell, born in Ireland, had lived in San Francisco two years before she took arsenic. Unable to get a teaching job, a failure at running a fruitstand, and without meat for two weeks, she ended her life. Edmund Snively, a Virginian, arrived in San Francisco in 1870. After nine years of not finding "the success he anticipated," he shot himself.[23]

An anonymous letter to the editor of the *Call* summed up the reality of life for many San Franciscans during the 1870s. The author said that citizens would "soon hear of another poor cuss who, tired of life, shot himself, drowned himself, or took poison." He planned to kill himself because he could not "get a dime's worth of work." He was hungry all day long and had no decent clothes. While he still looked decent, he had tried to get respectable employment. But now that he

looked like the devil, he was "shunned like the devil." He had often
been so hungry that he had "eaten garbage." He made a "business of
skulking into coffee-rooms and fruit stores after business hours, beg-
ging for stale rolls and rotten fruit." It just wasn't worth it any longer.[24]

Problems were not just economic. Conditions in San Francisco ultimately forced thousands of citizens to ask what had happened to their
dreams of success and whether they would ever be realized. Throughout the 1870s, San Franciscans gradually began to fear that things had
gone wrong, and their discontent grew.

Henry George and the *Post* blamed discontent as much on the tremendous difference between rich and poor as on the existence of poverty itself: "American pauperism demoralized by contrast." Society in
the United States made people desirous of equality and convinced
them that they deserved it. Sleeping in cellars and eating gruel
produced "a degree of degradation" that "naturally inflamed men and
women to anger." The difference between America's "free political
system" and the "social atmosphere" made "pacific submission . . . almost an impossibility."[25]

The *Argonaut* agreed. Hard times forced the laborer to realize for
the first time that he was poor. Unemployment had given him time to
compare his situation to "the profuse elegance of his rich neighbors."
Although the poor did not complain about those who lived modestly
and charitably, they had come "to loathe and despise" those who displayed "their wealth in brazen monograms . . . on their horses' bridles
and upon carriage doors," who had "imported liveried lackies from
abroad to assist my dainty lady from her carriage."[26]

San Franciscans were becoming hostile toward those who had been
the most successful. Before then, most citizens generally looked up to
and respected the wealthy. There was an easy, friendly relationship
between those who had made it and those who were still striving.[27]
The rich, especially the self-made kind, had a symbolic importance
and signified that the dream could come true. But during the 1870s, as
part of the disillusion that spread throughout the city, the rich often
became objects of ridicule rather than respect. Admiration and honor
slowly turned to envy and scorn.

The aristocratic pretensions of Nob Hill millionaires made an easy
target for satire. In 1877, the *Argonaut* mocked San Francisco's rich by

recounting the rise of MacDooligan, a resident of Grub Street. Ignoring his ancestry, the article deftly emphasized his humble origins and then described his varied career in California, first as a potato farmer, then as a putty manufacturer. Just recently, a friend had repaid a debt to Mac-Dooligan with 5,000 shares of seemingly worthless stock. When they soared to $200 apiece, MacDooligan became an instant millionaire.[28]

After smirking at the millionaires' ethnicity, their early occupations, and the sources of their fortunes, the article poked fun at their backgrounds. MacDooligan's ancestors were "too numerous to mention." Undoubtedly, they had been "kings in the old country" and accompanied Richard the Lion-hearted at the siege of Acre. Their coat of arms displayed a spalpeen rampant on a field of gold and their motto was "De profundis saltare."

Next, satirizing each of the MacDooligan clan in turn, the article derided the family's lack of education, taste, and refinement. Miss Margaret, previously called Peggy, had a countenance "not strictly classical" and an "irregular" beauty. Like Mrs. Malaprop, she possessed great conversational powers and loved to talk. Her tastes strayed from the literary, however, and she feared that reading would destroy her originality. Since the family had acquired its money, each member had displayed "delicate traits of refinement" that they had kept "previously hidden." Their manner now ranked them as "distingué," their society "recherché," their appearance "debonnaire," and all their actions breathed a certain savior faire.

The MacDooligan satire offered good-natured ribbing, but other tales about the life-styles of San Francisco's rich and famous cut more deeply. One anecdote alleged that William Sharon asked Jean-Louis Meissonier, a contemporary French portrait painter, if he was one of the old masters. Another yarn professed that William C. Ralston once walked into an artist's studio, looked around, and asked the price of the whole lot. San Franciscans snickered at the millionaire who bought a painting called *The Agony of Samson* and displayed it proudly in his gallery. It seems that the picture had originally been part of a pair of signs used by a patent medicine salesman in mining camps. *The Agony* represented "after" in a "before-and-after" sequence.[29]

Such gibes seem almost affectionate compared to some contemporary characterizations of Charles Crocker and the other railroad kings.

Crocker reputedly furnished his house so that visitors could not tell if it was "designed for a haberdasher's shop or a stage scene of a modern drama." He purchased "goblin tapestries" and hired someone to tell him if "they should be hung upon the walls as paintings or spread upon the floor as mats." He hoped to "buy pictures from the galleries of the Medici and employ Mr. Medici himself to help him make the selections." His fondest desire was to show the world how wealth could turn "a peddler of pins and needles" into "an intelligent patron of art and literature." In fact, he became a "living, breathing, waddling, monument to the triumph of vulgarity, viciousness and dishonesty."[30]

These attacks on rich men somehow seem out of place in a city that valued success, but they make sense in the context of the time and place. The pretensions of the city's nouveaux riches had exposed them to ridicule. It was hard not to laugh at the affectations of Charlie Crocker or Jim Flood. Throughout the country, newly rich millionaires spent money in ways that violated generally accepted standards of taste and propriety, but rarely did the absence of refinement obtrude as evidently as in San Francisco. Tastelessness alone, however, hardly accounted for the depth of hostility and viciousness of the attacks. That the millionaires made themselves appear ludicrous might explain why many fellow citizens laughed but not why (in the words of the *Argonaut*) they came to "loathe and despise."[31]

Jealousy and envy also contributed to hostility. When times were good and the economy growing, men felt hopeful and optimistic. The rich served as admired role models. But in hard times with thousands unemployed and unsheltered, nabobs riding in carriages and living in pseudo-castles inspired envy, jealousy, and disgust rather than admiration.

An anonymous letter to the editor of the *Argonaut* expressed this clearly. The author commented that much had been written about growing old gracefully but nothing about growing rich gracefully. The problem was acutely felt in San Francisco, and it was obviously "very trying" to appear "as if 'To the Manor Born.'" To sit in a carriage with ease and to bestow charity without bombast were extraordinarily difficult. And for a woman "not accustomed to elegance, and power, and finery, transition sometimes excited more ridicule than envy." Problems resulted from her "diffuse style as hostess, her awkwardness of managing the yard-and-a-half of elegant fantail . . . the promiscuous display of the new diamonds, donning them equally in a superb drawing room . . . [or] a quiet neighborhood lunch." There was always "the suggestion of not knowing what to do with it, like the man who drew the elephant."[32]

Changed feelings and attitudes derived from deeper sources than either the charades of the rich or popular jealousies of them. Hostility and disaffection also emerged from a growing sense that San Francisco's rich had gathered their fortunes in ways immoral, if not strictly illegal—ways that seemed likely to monopolize opportunity and deny others the chance to succeed. By the middle of the 1870s, thousands of San Franciscans had become convinced that the wealthiest people in the city would pursue their own interests regardless of the cost to anyone else.

Charges about the ethics of the railroad kings surfaced almost as soon as they began constructing the Central Pacific, but, from the point of view of many San Franciscans, the crucial episode concerned Goat Island and the western terminus of the line. Because of its location on the west side of San Francisco Bay, the city was effectively cut off from the transcontinental railroad. In fact, Congress had chartered the railroad to extend east from Sacramento, and its connection to the bay posed a critical problem. San Francisco itself had a distinct disadvantage relative to other cities. The only all-land route from Sacramento went south to San Jose, then north along the peninsula and into the south end of town. Because this route was long and circuitous, San Franciscans feared that the western end of the line would be located at one of the other port cities on the bay, perhaps Oakland or Vallejo, where land and sea traffic could meet. This outcome would have destroyed the commercial development of San Francisco.

Anxiety peaked in early 1872, when the big four attempted to locate the terminal on Goat Island, smack in the middle of the bay between San Francisco and Oakland. The railroad directors proposed connecting the island to the east shore and locating their shops, warehouses, and railroad facilities there. Stanford, Huntington and company received permission from the California legislature to use the mud flats north of the island and then sought permission from the federal government to develop the island itself.[33]

To many San Franciscans, the purpose of the plan was all too clear. The railroad kings intended to connect the railroad and the Pacific traffic—building a new city that would dominate the entire region. The fact that the owners of the railroad had recently acquired control of the Pacific Mail Steamship Company did nothing to alleviate this concern. In March and April 1872, a number of civic and governmental bodies passed resolutions condemning the proposal. The usually mild-mannered Chamber of Commerce asserted that ceding the island would be "a $20,000,000 gift to a corporation already gorged and plethoric with national bounty, furnishing them with the means and the opportunity to . . . compete with the legitimate trade of our waterfront, as to reduce the value of property in our city scores of millions of dollars." At a mass meeting, citizens assailed giving "to a single corporation the power to build up an independent rival city in our very teeth, and at the expense of the interest of 150,000 people and $300,000,000." The petitioners beseeched Congress not to "take from the masses and give to a soulless corporation, that has thus far lived by and through an habitual system of magnificent mendicancy." In a series of scathing editorials, the *Call* urged San Franciscans to build a new, publicly owned transcontinental line. If they did, the city could avoid being "squeezed to death by half a dozen men . . . so grasping" that nothing would satisfy them "short of our very life's blood." By May 1872, less than three years after the completion of the Central Pacific, one of San Francisco's leading newspapers saw "Stanford & Co." as men "willing to destroy the value of property in this entire city to enrich themselves."[34]

Within five years, San Franciscans were accusing the silver princes of similar crimes. They charged Fair, Flood, Mackay, and O'Brien with manipulating stock prices to bilk the public and enrich themselves. The circumstances seemed indeed suspicious. The bonanza quartet had announced control of the Consolidated Virginia mine on January 11, 1872, and immediately began exploring their new property. About fourteen months later, in March 1873, they knew that they had made a rich strike; by fall, they knew its full magnitude. Throughout this entire period, they kept their discoveries quiet, and stock prices, although rising steadily, made no tremendous advance.

Then, in October 1874, a full year after they had "lifted the top off the Big Bonanza," Mackay and his partners suddenly threw the mine open to the public. The first person they invited into their chamber of silver was William Wright, editor of the *Territorial Enterprise*. Soon afterward came H. R. Linderman, director of the Carson City Mint, and Philip Diedesheimer, a respected mining man and inventor of the square-set method of timbering mines. The stories that each told rivaled the Arabian Nights. Wright estimated the value of gold and silver *in sight* at $116 million; Linderman reckoned the total yield at $300 million; but Diedesheimer topped them all. He claimed that the mine would ultimately disgorge $1.5 billion worth of treasure.[35]

Such proclamations created pandemonium in San Francisco's financial markets, and the price of shares in Consolidated Virginia and California (the adjacent mine also owned by the princes) skyrocketed. Shares in Consolidated Virginia, which sold for $55 in February, 1874, hit $160 on November 17 and then took off—reaching $710 on January 7, 1875. California went from $37 in September to $90 in November and soared to $790 in January. Just as suddenly, prices collapsed. Consolidated Virginia plummeted 115 points in a week, and 180 more during the next three. It had tumbled to $320 by July 1 and hit $254 in early November. The nose dive in California was just as marked. After hitting its high of $790, it plunged 200 points in one week. That was only the beginning of the end. By February 4, shares had plunged (after adjusting for a 5 : 1 stock split) another 305 points. By December 1, 1875, one of those shares bought for $790 on January 7 was worth a mere $105.[36]

To San Franciscans whose paper fortunes had disappeared in a matter of weeks, the explanation was obvious. They had been "jobbed." Between October 1873 and October 1874, Flood and his partners had deliberately avoided publicizing their strike in order to keep prices low and allow themselves to amass as much stock as possible. Only after they had acquired almost complete ownership did the princes reveal the extent of their treasure trove. Demand for the closely held shares caused prices to soar, and the mineowners rapidly disposed of their overinflated holdings at tremendous profits. The *Alta* termed the whole affair "a great crime" and "a cold-blooded scheme to rob poor people." The *Chronicle* called it a "conspiracy" and feared it would "crush the community," making the average citizen "the slave of a moneyed banditti that in its greed and robbery spares neither age, sex, nor condition."[37]

A contemporary novel of stock gambling in San Francisco named its chief villain Mr. Highwater, a loosely disguised Jim Flood. The author depicted him as a man "never loathe to devise a means to excite interest in the stocks he controlled, to induce his rich neighbors to invest in them, which virtually meant the transfer of their funds to his coffers." At the same time, "he by no means lost sight of the working classes, whose earnings he had been so successful in gathering . . . that there was not one in ten of the entire adult population of whose means he had not received from a small portion to the whole." In this way, he had changed San Francisco from "an active, thriving, growing city, to one of stagnation, with widely extended poverty and distress."[38]

Such accusations signified more than a conviction that San Francisco's millionaires were cheating the public. They implied new suspicions that the California pie might not be unlimited and that not every one might succeed. For twenty-five years, San Franciscans had ordinarily remained upbeat and figured that, sooner or later, a man might become a gentleman. But anxieties about stock-jobbing schemes and rival cities in the middle of the bay unveiled the fear that selfish, evil people had the power to destroy the dream for everyone else. The accusations betrayed fears that a predatory clique could monopolize wealth while depriving others of opportunity.

The *Call* expressed this apprehension on several occasions when it reported the distribution of wealth in the city. In August 1871 the newspaper published a list of San Franciscans supposedly worth $500,000 or more. According to the figures, 143 persons (out of a total population of about 150,000) had an aggregate wealth of $153 million. These fortunes included slightly more than one-half the city's total wealth. If another 207 persons worth $43 million were added to this group, fewer than 400 San Franciscans supposedly owned two-thirds of the city's total wealth. Two years later, the *Call* printed another list of affluent citizens. This time, the catalog included everyone with property assessed at more than $50,000, so it was official rather than estimated. The results were a little different but alarming none-theless: about 500 people owned one-third of San Francisco's riches.[39] A populace that had always anticipated universal wealth found itself confronting a radically different possibility—that a few nabobs might become inordinately wealthy, leaving the majority with very little.

III

FROM CROWD TO PARTY

Introduction

By the late 1870s, thousands of San Franciscans had become discontented and dissatisfied with conditions in their city. They had come to the Golden State expecting to improve their lives, and many had done so. But depression and economic development had seemed to stop the process and raise doubts about the ability to succeed in the future. Moreover, the increasingly visible contrasts between life on Nob Hill and life South of Market caused frustration and bitterness as people wondered why some San Franciscans lived in wealth and luxury, others in poverty and penury.

By the late 1870s, according to Ira B. Cross, San Francisco's masses were just waiting for an opportunity to plunder the city.[1] And, in fact, they did take direct action. In July, rioting broke out. However, it is necessary to make an important distinction—between the existence of dissatisfaction and the form of the expression of that dissatisfaction. Dissatisfied people do not inevitably riot, and historians need to differentiate between the sources of dissatisfaction and the ways in which people express that dissatisfaction.

Chapters 2 through 6 have explained the intensity of the discontent in San Francisco. The remainder of the book explains why thousands of citizens expressed their dissatisfaction first in the July riots and then in the Workingmen's Party of California. People rioted because riot was, for them, a traditional form of political expression. They ceased to riot because constituted authority ceased to accept the legitimacy of the crowd as a means of venting political discontent. Then they joined the WPC because its leaders explained what had happened in a way that satisfied them and because the party taught them how to express themselves in new and acceptable ways—through formal institutional politics. This analysis is particularly significant because of the rapid change from one kind of political expression to another. It therefore helps us understand how and why rioting ceased to be a normal form of political action in nineteenth-century cities, and how and why mass participation in political parties replaced it.

7. Riot

During the past few decades, a number of historians have explained riots and violence as a typical form of political expression in preindustrial European societies. Beginning with the pathbreaking studies of George Rudé and Eric Hobsbawm, historians have used the concept of the *crowd* to analyze and explain urban violence through the nineteenth century. They have argued that crowds possessed distinct forms, structures, modes of behavior, goals, and objectives. They have even identified different kinds of crowds on the basis of their participants, objects, and purposes. More recently, a new generation of historians has linked specific types of crowds to specific stages of urban development, and they have shown that the success or failure of crowd action correlates with the level of urbanization.[2]

In the last few years, several historians have used the crowd concept to analyze violence in urban America. Among others, Pauline Maier and Dirk Hoerder have applied the idea to the Revolutionary Era, and Michael Feldberg has used it to analyze popular behavior in the Jacksonian period. Some years ago, Herbert Gutman called the national violence of 1877 "little understood" and suggested that the riots sprang out of "long-standing grievances that accompanied the transformation of Old [preindustrial] into New [industrial] America." He also argued that "characteristic European forms of 'premodern' artisan and lower-class protest" occurred in the United States before, during, and after industrialization, but he analyzed these forms of protest only "briefly."[3]

A closer, more detailed investigation reveals that San Francisco's July rioters resembled the so-called preindustrial European crowd in several key ways. They lived in a city at a point of development comparable to that of London or Paris thirty years before, a city that had just industrialized but whose people had not yet adjusted to the great changes that had overtaken them. Like Hobsbawm's "primitive rebels," San Franciscans had had industrialism thrust upon them and were trying to "adapt themselves to its life and struggles." Like the European crowd of the transition, the Workingmen were "a mixed population" of the lower orders led by men "whose personality, style of dress or speech, and momentary assumption of authority" marked them as leaders. They were "fired as much by memories of customary rights or a nostalgia for past utopias as by present grievances or hopes of material improvement"; and they dispensed "a rough-and-ready kind of 'natural justice.'" In San Francisco, as in Europe, the crowd acted against unemployment and for a low cost of living; they directed their actions at the rich and powerful, as well as at the city's most despised group of foreigners, the Chinese. In short, the July rioters behaved in ways reminiscent of the age quickly passing.[4]

The statistical analysis presented earlier discloses that members of the working class—craftsmen, factory operatives, and common laborers—provided the basic support for the WPC and the July riots. Blue-collar workers were much more likely to have participated in the disturbances than businessmen, professionals, managers, and white-collar workers. The core of San Francisco's working class in the late-nineteenth century, European, and especially Irish, immigrants participated in the protests much more actively than did native-born Americans.[5] However, it is crucial to remember that these people participated not because they were members of the working class and not because they were immigrants. They participated because they were disappointed and fearful—not so much because of the past but about the present and the future. And it was, of course, the working class and immigrants who had the most reason for disappointment and fear.

The leaders of the July riots also resembled their counterparts in the European crowd; they were essentially anonymous men thrust into positions of prominence by virtue of their forceful personalities. The individual most clearly identifiable as a leader of the crowd was described in similar terms by the *Examiner* and the *Chronicle*. According to the former, he was an "excellently-dressed dapper little fellow, with jockey cap, who appears to have made out in advance a complete plan of the night's campaign, as he would walk to and fro through the crowd and give the exact location of the places to be attacked." The *Chronicle* offered a similar physical description but added a few more details about the nature of his power. The young chap was "headstrong and loud in his exhortations to the crowd," and it seemingly followed his orders without question, simply because of the strength of his character.[6]

In guiding the crowd, this young leader and his followers had specific objectives, like their counterparts in Europe. They were out to get the Chinese, San Francisco's most hated minority and the common scapegoat of the city's disaffected. For three nights, the crowd swirled through the streets attacking and destroying Chinese homes and businesses. They particularly sought out laundries and washhouses, and the only other places they attacked were businesses that employed large numbers of Chinese or businesses mistaken for those of Chinese.[7]

In this regard, there was total discipline, as with European crowds. On the night of July 23, as the mass meeting in front of city hall broke up, John Griffin fired three shots into the crowd from a nearby house, hitting three demonstrators. Both the *Bulletin* and the *Examiner* reported that the crowd rushed to the scene, ready to fire his house, but police had already arrested the perpetrator. Since no one could identify his house with certainty, the crowd built a huge bonfire rather than risk burning the property of an innocent person. The following night, as the crowd attacked a laundry on Mission Street, they learned that a man lay gravely ill next door. According to the *Examiner*, "the idea of a white man in danger roused the generosity of the rioters, who proceeded to undo their own work by aiding in putting out the fire." The next night, a similar incident occurred. The crowd began attacking a laundry, presumably Chinese. When the dude in the jockey cap discovered that it actually belonged to an Irish washerwoman, he remonstrated with his men, and they left the scene in high spirits.[8]

That San Franciscans acted in ways so reminiscent of European crowds is not surprising. In 1880, nearly one-third of all San Franciscans were European born, and these immigrants participated actively in the protests of 1877. Moreover, the more recently immigrants had become citizens (and registered to vote), the more likely they were to take part in the riots and demonstrations. Although many historians of the European crowd focus on the eighteenth and early nineteenth centuries, seeming to suggest that crowds had lost their importance by the late nineteenth century, others have studied the continued prominence of the late nineteenth-century crowd. Donald C. Richter has written an entire book on English crowds after 1860.[9] More important for this study, several books have recently treated the Irish crowd during the latter half of the century. Samuel Clark has revealed the *Social Origins of the Irish Land War* between 1879 and 1882, and Charles Townshend has analyzed *Political Violence in Ireland: Government and Resistance since 1848*. Both these volumes, as well as the collection of articles edited by Samuel Clark and James S. Donnelly, Jr. (*Irish Peasants: Violence & Political Unrest, 1780–1914*), demonstrate that the most typical form of political protest by Irish peasants in the late nineteenth century was crowd action and forcefully argue that crowd violence was endemic in Ireland. Townshend begins *Political Violence* with the straightforward statement that "the Irish propensity for violence is well known," and Clark and Donnelly note that "Ireland became almost synonymous with rebellion during the late eighteenth and early nineteenth centuries." George Rudé himself noted that Irish rebellion in the early 1830s "by its intensity and violence, eclipsed all others."[10] Thus, the crowd that developed in San Francisco in July 1877 was the transplantation of a common form of European, and especially Irish, action to a new setting. San Franciscans formed and participated in a crowd that summer because it was, to them, a normal and acceptable kind of political behavior.

In this regard, San Francisco's Irish were also following in the footsteps of New York's Irish. Less than fifteen years before, "an overwhelming percentage" of the city's draft rioters were Irish, and "one extremely strong and persistent motive was deep-rooted hatred of Negroes." A comprehensive study of those riots has pointed out that "the Irish, New York's largest ethnic group, had a tradition of political violence" and has concluded that one explanation for New York's regular riots in the nineteenth century can be found in Europe.

> Some of the disturbances of the 1830s proceeded from an older European tradition of civil disorder, in which the mob was in a symbiotic relation-

ship with the authorities. Rioters acted as a loyal opposition in a society that had not yet developed institutions of political opposition and battled the king's evil councillors or unscrupulous merchants or landowners who were trying to oppress the poor. The Flour Riots of 1837, caused by unemployed and starving workmen attacking the warehouses of flour dealers whom they believed to be charging exorbitant prices, closely resembled the "natural justice" riots so common in Europe in earlier centuries.[11]

Thus, the question of why San Franciscans rioted in July 1877 is answered by understanding who the rioters were and what their typical patterns of behavior had historically been. This knowledge raises two equally important questions. Why did the crowd stop rioting so quickly? And why did this crowd never begin again? We need to ask What happened to the crowd? and Why did it evaporate so quickly?

Two historians have recently analyzed crowd disappearance in different contexts, and their answers are intriguing. Although their interpretations differ, they are not inconsistent, and both clarify the situation in San Francisco. In his study *Riots and Community Politics in England and Wales, 1790–1810*, John Bohstedt argues that riots ceased to be the predominant form of popular politics in England by the early nineteenth century. He interprets riot and crowd behavior as a form of community organization that functioned best under certain precise social conditions: strong horizontal relationships among crowd members (enabling them to interact with one another) and strong vertical relationships between the crowd and the official hierarchy (allowing effective bargaining to take place between the two opposing factions). According to Bohstedt, the crowd lost its effectiveness when urbanization overwhelmed tightly knit communities, destroying the optimum conditions for successful riot and crowd action. As that breakdown became more common and as issues receded beyond the ability of local participants to resolve, riot became less common as a means of resolving political conflict.[12]

Bohstedt's argument applies to San Francisco. By 1877, tightly knit social networks had failed, if they had ever existed. A large proportion of the population, and an especially large proportion of the July rioters, were immigrants, newcomers from dozens of different countries. Many of them had come recently, only been newly naturalized, and had even more recently registered to vote. They had not created the horizontal community ties that Bohstedt shows were necessary to create a powerful and effective crowd. For the same reasons, the lower orders of San Francisco had not yet been able to forge vertical links with the new social, political, and economic elites. The rioters had not been able to traverse the great distance between Nob Hill and South of Market.

Michael Feldberg's analysis of the crowd in Philadelphia provides another explanation for its disappearance. According to him, the crowd dissolved as American cities developed paramilitary police departments in the middle of the nineteenth century. In other words, the crowd lost its effectiveness when the larger society ceased to recognize its legitimacy as a means of political expression (and used force to suppress it). Additionally, cities developed an entirely new set of institutions, one of whose primary functions was to spread an ideology of order—institutions such as public schools, temperance societies, and electoral politics.[13]

This interpretation also applies to San Francisco's July crowd. Even before the first rioting had begun, municipal authorities turned the full power of the city, state, and federal governments against the crowd. On the afternoon of July 23, in response to notices that a meeting was going to be held expressing sympathy with striking railroad workers in the East, San Francisco's chief of police, H. H. Ellis, wrote Brigadier-General John McComb, commander of the Second Brigade of the National Guard of California, that he harbored "serious apprehensions" that a riot would occur. He requested prompt action to suppress it, asking that troops of the National Guard be held in readiness. McComb replied by ordering three infantry regiments, a cavalry battalion, and an artillery company to be ready to march on a moment's notice. Ellis himself mobilized the entire police force, positioned men in every part of the city, and maintained a strong reserve at city hall.[14]

The city had begun to respond in a way that would remain consistent throughout the trouble: no crowd action would be tolerated. The next day, after rioting had broken out despite these early precautions, newspaper editorials attacked the crowd. The *Chronicle* thought that officials could not deal too roughly with "the hoodlum element." It avowed that the mob would have gotten its just deserts if the military had used bayonets and grapeshot. The *Bulletin* tried to speak for the whole city in proclaiming that "public sentiment" was "against all violent demonstrations." There was "no possible excuse for attempting to precipitate" in San Francisco "such a condition of things as exists in Pittsburgh and other large cities."[15]

Despite military preparedness and public exhortation, further rioting occurred that night, and city leaders intensified their response. The navy put its force at Vallejo on alert and made ready to descend on San Francisco. The police force acquired new weapons and issued patrolmen heavy-caliber batons, double the length and weight of ordinary clubs. Their manufacturer guaranteed them "more effective than any other instrument in the business of skull-cracking." Newspapers continued their barrage of anticrowd editorials, and Mayor Andrew Jackson Bryant issued an official proclamation. He advised all citizens to stay off the streets and away from large groups, asking them to leave public places and thoroughfares free for the authorities. He announced that he would not shrink from suppressing the riots and would ensure that all offenders received appropriate punishment.

> All assemblies and crowds of persons will be dispersed, and should resistance be made, arrests and punishment will follow. In doing our duty, should unfortunately the criminal and riotous resist and inaugurate bloodshed, on their hands rests the responsibility. The law is supreme and shall be maintained at all hazards.[16]

Active responses to the crowd came from unofficial as well as official sources. On July 24, William T. Coleman, the lion of the vigilantes, the leader of the San Francisco Vigilance Committees of 1851 and 1856, announced the formation of a third vigilance committee, the Committee of Safety. According to Coleman, it was both a preventive and a remedy. He believed that the "mere organization of this force will probably prevent any occurrence demanding its active efforts." He strongly hoped that the committee's "moral effect would prevent what . . . force and bloodshed might [otherwise] be required to put down." Within twenty-four hours, according to the *Alta*, 2,500 men had signed up, and the very night of its formation, the committee put 1,000 men on the streets.[17]

Rioting continued into a third night. In response, more authorities appealed for order, and the city was more closely patrolled. The Committee of Safety issued a proclamation stating its purpose: to sustain the constituted authorities. It followed the mayor in asserting that "peace and security" would be maintained at all costs, and it tried to unite the entire populace under its flag. The committee claimed to include citizens "of all sects and all parties, holding all shades of opinion, each ready . . . to lay aside all differences, and to refrain for a time from urging individual views." In addition to its public proclamation, the committee placed an advertisement in several mass-circulation daily newspapers. Addressed to the "Workingmen of San Francisco!" the notice requested their aid in suppressing the rioters and asked them to enroll "in the ranks of the friends of order." It justified this request on the basis of a "common heritage in the glorious history of our State, in the hope of its still more glorious future."[18]

Archbishop Joseph Sadoc Alemany, the leader of San Francisco's Roman Catholic community, also got in the act. He wrote a circular letter praising authority. It was never lawful, he wrote, to join a mob to gain redress of grievances, no matter how great the provocation. Remedy could never be found in "the torch of anarchy."[19]

Mayor Bryant issued a second proclamation. He felt compelled "once again, and for the last time, to warn all good citizens" to stay at home. Streets and public places had to be "left free and unobstructed for the operations of the police, the military, and the Committee of Safety," who would "see that order . . . [was] maintained at all hazards." Coleman and the Committee of Safety echoed the mayor's caution "against being on the streets after nightfall." They deemed this advice "necessary because more vigorous means than have hitherto been used will be employed to suppress riotous proceedings."[20]

Those more vigorous means took several forms. The Board of Police Commissioners issued Remington revolvers and fresh ammunition to every policeman in the city. The commissioners authorized their use and empowered officers to shoot into any crowd that attacked them with weapons, including stones. The police were to accept no risks to themselves and were to use their weapons without regard for the consequences. The Committee of Safety also armed itself, some members with carbines and shotguns, others with breech-loading rifles, still others with weapons supplied from the arsenal at Benicia. Even a group of Civil War veterans, armed with Springfield rifles, formed a battalion to help crush the uprising.[21]

State officials, too, prepared for all-out warfare. Governor William Irwin asked the commanding officer of the naval base at Mare Island to put his entire force of sailors and marines at the ready, and the officer agreed. The commander of the state arsenal at Benicia sent 10,000 additional arms and 80,000 cartridges to the city, and that night San Francisco was an armed camp. The *Bulletin* provided a list of the total peacekeeping force on July 26. It included 252 policemen, 1200 militiamen, 5,000 members of the Committee of Safety, four Parrott guns, and one Gatling gun. As the newspaper put it, the "spirit of order" had been thoroughly aroused.[22]

No further rioting broke out in San Francisco. The crowd disappeared as quickly as it had formed, and there can be no doubt about the reason: the decisive response of all levels of officialdom had suppressed the crowd. San Francisco's authorities simply refused to recognize the legitimacy of the crowd, would not negotiate with it, and turned the full power of government against it. The *Alta* pointed this out explicitly when it claimed that "the firm stand taken by the authorities, seconded most nobly by the military and citizens," had brought an end to the disturbances. When it became known that arms and ammunition had been distributed—and would be used—the crowd "were cowed."[23]

This analysis, as convincing an explanation as it is for the demise of the crowd, actually leaves still another fundamental question unanswered. *Why* did constituted authority cease to accept the legitimacy of crowd action as a means of political expression? Beginning with Hobsbawm and Rudé, historians have argued that crowds were an integral part of the body politic throughout the seventeenth and eighteenth centuries. They have analyzed the structure of crowds, the ideology of crowds, and the relationship between crowds and other social structures. What we find in San Francisco in 1877, and what Feldberg discovered in Philadelphia several decades earlier, is that the formal political hierarchy ceased to accept the existence of the crowd. The question is, why?

The usual explication of crowd theory implies that the nature of the crowd became transformed. Early crowd historians identified it with a particular era in social development, and they typically referred to the crowd they were studying as "the preindustrial crowd." Such explanations assumed that another kind of crowd, "the industrial crowd," was out there just waiting to be found and analyzed in its own right. How-ever, not too many years ago, Robert J. Holton criticized the notion of a fundamental dichotomy between preindustrial and industrial crowds as he pointed out basic continuities between crowds of the two eras. In particular, Holton interpreted all crowds as social phenomena that need to be understood in the context of social development and the evolution of society.[24]

In fact, the crowd was not simply—or even primarily—a social phenomenon. It was principally a means of political expression; dissat-isfied people banded together to express their discontent. The object of discontent might well have been social conditions, but the crowd itself was a form of political action. Moreover, crowds formed for a very simple reason: their members were prohibited from participating in formal political institutions, in either Europe or America. They could not take part in political meetings, could not vote, and could not hold office—just to mention a few of the more obvious forms of political expression. Since they could not do any of these things, and since the powers-that-were did not want to grant them a recognized role in formal political institutions, the crowd existed as, and was accepted as, a means of political protest, a way by which the *menu peuple*, to use Rudé's phrase, could express displeasure.

This changed during the nineteenth century. The democratization of politics in Western countries, in England, France, and especially the United States, diminished the role of the crowd. Members of the lower orders were now allowed to participate in normal politics, and, having received that right, they were no longer allowed to express themselves in extralegal ways. The crowd was crushed as part of that process of democratization.

During the nineteenth century, restraints on suffrage gradually eased in the United States. By the 1840s, most American states had enfranchised all adult, white male citizens, and the degree of partici-pation in presidential elections increased. About 50 percent of the eli-gible Americans voted in presidential elections from 1824 to 1836, 70 percent from 1840 to 1872, and nearly 80 percent from 1876 to 1900. According to Michael McGerr, increased voting resulted from a new intensification of party feelings and loyalties. The development of popular parties and popular politics changed the nature of political participation and increased the importance of the vote as a form of political expression. Of course, other forms of political activity still existed, but during the late nineteenth and early twentieth centuries, "the majority of Americans" had nothing to do with other forms of political behavior; "the vote was their only political weapon."[25]

Thus, the so-called preindustrial crowd was actually a manifestation of "predemocratic society." It was a means of political expression for people whose access to formal political institutions was blocked. When those people were given access to political parties, especially the vote, they were also denied access to their traditional, customary, and long-respected form of political protest—the crowd. That explains why it has been so hard to find and to analyze the "industrial" crowd. The crowd, or rather its members, was forced to learn a new kind of political behavior, electoral politics.

This is all very clear in the context of San Francisco during the summer and fall of 1877. No sooner had rioting begun in July than San Francisco's authorities began teaching the crowd and its members what forms of political behavior were acceptable. On July 24, even as the *Bulletin* criticized the previous night's turmoil and denied that conditions justified a protest meeting, it asserted that citizens always had the right to meet peacefully to talk. Even as the *Chronicle* suggested that the riotous mob deserved to have been shot by the military, it proclaimed that the right of the working class "to meet peaceably, discuss and adopt resolutions and to express sympathy for their class, anywhere and everywhere, must not be assailed. They have just as good a right to do these things as the Presidents and Directors of railway and mining corporations have to meet and adopt resolves."[26]

This is not to say that no members of San Francisco's working class had previously participated in electoral politics. We know that many of them had; we know that the Democratic Party had tried to win power by stressing class and race as election issues. But we also know that before the mid- to late-1870s, the appeal was unsuccessful. Between 1860 and 1873, the party elected only one mayor, less than one-fourth of the Board of Supervisors, and an equivalent number of major executive officers. Before the late 1870s, the constituency sought by the Democratic Party was not sufficiently acculturated to electoral politics to provide a base for electoral success.[27]

Other factors also discouraged the lower classes from participating in electoral politics before the late 1870s. Although the Democratic Party tried to appeal to the working class, it never nominated candidates who truly excited the masses, spoke their language, or raised their spirits. In addition, practice never precisely squared with ideology. Despite "universal suffrage," institutions such as voting registration limited political participation. In California, between the time of statehood and 1880, in addition to being twenty-one years old, male, and a United States citizen, a voter had to have been a resident of the state for six months, and a resident of his election precinct for thirty days before the election in which he wished to vote. That these requirements were specifically intended to inhibit voting by some groups is revealed by events in 1880. After San Francisco's Workingmen had moved so actively into the political arena, the state legislature tightened the requirements for suffrage. To vote, one now had to have been a resident of the state for one year, of the county for ninety days, and of the precinct for thirty days.[28]

This kind of inconsistency between expressed belief and legal usage should not surprise. It is, after all, far less jarring than the existence of slavery in a nation that espoused the principles of the Declaration of Independence. The inconsistency also reveals that other members of the community as well needed to adjust to the newly democratized political culture. When political participation was limited, or when Hubert Howe Bancroft commented that Workingmen's delegates to the California Constitutional Convention of 1878 "were scarcely identified with the community and more fit to clean legislative halls than to sit in them," it becomes clear that the passage of laws meant to democratize politics did not mean that everyone understood or accepted the new institutions. Workingmen needed to learn to use new political techniques, and other San Franciscans needed to learn to let them be used.

Statistics of voting registration and participation also substantiate the generalization that the working class increased its participation in electoral politics after 1877. Table 7.1 indicates the number of registered and actual voters in San Francisco between 1875 and 1880. It reveals two significant trends. First, the absolute number of registered voters increased consistently throughout the period. The decline be-

TABLE 7.1   REGISTRATION AND VOTING IN
SAN FRANCISCO, 1875–80

Year	Number Registered	Number Voting	NV / NR
1875	33,848	25,653	.758
1876	46,671	41,646	.892
1877	50,004	33,663	.673
1878	37,915	27,098	.715
1879 (special)	47,740	38,034	.797
1879 (general)	44,765	41,612	.930

tween 1877 and 1878 is readily explained by the statement of the registrar of voters that "a great number of names were stricken from the Register [of Voters] by the Election Commissioners . . . very materially reducing the number from the Register of 1877." The decline between the special and general elections of 1879 is explained by his statement that "judicious and careful examination of the registration was made during the interval . . . and many names were eliminated."[29]

The election commissioners were acting under provisions of a law enacted by the state legislature on March 18, 1878, almost exactly three months before the election of delegates to the state Constitutional Convention. The law decreed that new ward registers should be prepared for that election, and that only the names of persons who had voted in either the election of September 5, 1877, or October 15, 1877, could be included. In other words, in the two years of greatest electoral participation by the Workingmen, thousands of names were purged from the voting register, presumably to limit their participation and influence on the outcome of crucial elections.[30]

The other major trend shown by the table is the increasing percentage of registered voters who actually voted. As the stakes increased, the Workingmen voted more regularly. From a low of 67.3 percent in the municipal election of 1877, held just several weeks before the formation of the WPC, the percentage of eligible voters who cast ballots climbed to 71.5 in 1878 (the election of delegates to the Constitutional Convention), 79.7 in the special election of 1879 (to ratify the new Constitution), and 93.0 in the general election of 1879 (in which the WPC ran a full slate of candidates). As one historian recently put it, "In San Francisco . . . the vaunted voice of the people was actually the voice of some of the people some of the time." Moreover, since voting is both age- and class-specific, "it is likely that the core of the city's active electorate was older, more prosperous, and of higher occupational status than the male population as a whole."[31]

This analysis clearly implies that increases in registration and voting resulted from greater political participation by members of the WPC, not the established citizens of the city. The statement also coincides perfectly with the analysis that the July rioters and members of the Workingmen's Party of California were younger, less prosperous, and of lower occupational status than their opponents. They were men just learning to use electoral politics as a way of expressing political positions and oppositions.

The summer and fall of 1877 was the time when San Francisco's working class made the decisive shift from using traditional to more modern forms of political expression. That year they discovered what forms of political protest were now acceptable and how to use new political institutions. Having gained that knowledge, they began to act differently. The crushing of the crowd by the forces of law and order left the lower classes with two choices: not to participate in politics at all or to learn a new form of politics. Obviously, they chose the latter, and the months after the July riots were a time of intense ferment as the working classes began to participate in organized political parties and to use alternative modes of political behavior.

8. Alternatives and Explanations

Historians who have studied the summer of 1877 in San Francisco have actually examined only the two most obvious examples of working-class political activity and organization, the July riots and the Workingmen's Party of California. In fact, the working class districts of the city were ablaze with passion as people determined how to commit themselves politically and how to achieve their goals. The riots and the WPC were only two alternatives available to workingmen: the old form of behavior that was no longer accepted and the new political party that most ultimately joined.

But other parties also sprang up. Most have left few traces, and it is challenging to determine what they championed and how they behaved. The remaining evidence does establish that each of them differed from the others, and those differences help us understand the decision that most workingmen finally made, to side with the WPC.

The first important choice pitted riot against party. Having made that choice or, more accurately, having had it forced upon them, the workingmen had to pick between an existing party, especially the Democratic, and a new one.

Less than a week after rioting had ended, the *Examiner*, a mouthpiece of the Democratic Party, reported that "certain ill-advised persons" were trying to start a workingmen's party. However, this attempt could have no good result. The newspaper urged workingmen to rely on existing parties and asserted that labor could gain nothing by forming its own organization. Such an effort would leave workingmen prey to sham leaders who knew nothing about political management and neither knew nor cared about the interests of the working class. The proper alternative was the Democratic Party.[1]

A few days later, just before San Franciscans voted for municipal officials, the *Chronicle* joined the *Examiner* in urging workingmen to support already existing parties. The *Chronicle* suggested that it was too late for new parties to be effective and tried to persuade workingmen to support the Taxpayers' Ticket. The *Examiner* followed the line it had laid down in late July. It attacked all workingmen's parties and asserted that they were "composed of venal and vicious small-fry politicians" who did nothing more than dupe the workingmen. The only party really looking out for their interests was the Democratic. It was "itself the workingmen's party," with a thorough organization, power at all levels of government, and the ability to benefit workingmen. New parties had "no power whatever to aid or promote the cause of any—least of all that of the workingmen." They were "ephemeral, fruitless, worthless, baneful, and too often noxious." To the Democratic Party, the workingmen, if they were "wise and true to themselves," should "contribute their support in the election . . . to strengthen it, and to enable it all the better to champion their cause."[2]

Workingmen spurned this advice and flocked to the WPC. But even as they did, a host of other parties vied for their support. Having rejected the Democratic Party as advocate and savior, San Francisco's workingmen could choose among a crowd of entrants to the political arena. Between July 1 and December 31, 1877, San Francisco newspapers reported (sometimes briefly) the activities of eight additional parties. The Workingmen's Party of the United States (WPUS) and the Workingmen's Party of San Francisco; the Workingmen's Legislative Committee of the Eleventh Senatorial District, the Workingmen's Municipal Convention, and the Workingmen's Union; the Workingmen's Independent and Labor Reform Club of the Twelfth Ward and the Workingmen's Trade and Labor Union of San Francisco (WTLUSF)—all entered the fray. Perhaps just for variety, one party abjured use of the denomination *workingmen's* and called itself simply the National Labor Party. Altogether, at least ten organizations, including the WPC and the Democrats, contended for working class favor.

Each of these parties urged workingmen to form their own political organization while it denounced the Republicans and Democrats alike. At the mass meeting of the Workingmen's Party of the United States on July 23, the organizer of the party attacked the older parties as slaves of the money ring and tools of monopolists. He blamed national economic woes on both parties equally, criticizing them for devoting time and energy to securing the spoils of office, not the welfare of the people. A month later, Patrick J. Healy, a party member, wrote a letter expressing the same sentiments. He personally felt the need to "cut aloof" from all existing political parties. They controlled the government, had brought the country to the verge of bankruptcy, impoverished the people, and sent beggars throughout the land.[3]

The Executive Committee of the Workingmen's Union had somewhat different reasons for supporting a separate party. Those men simply believed that workingmen had never been fairly represented. By way of contrast, the Workingmen's Party of San Francisco (a different organization from either the WPUS or the WPC) claimed that the Republican and Democratic parties were disintegrating and that the candidates of both were corrupt. The leaders of the National Labor Party had more positive reasons for advocating a new party. Rather than criticizing the older parties explicitly, they simply felt that workingmen needed their own party to ameliorate the conditions of life and meet the wants of the masses. They would recognize neither Republicans nor Democrats but only workingmen, irrespective of political opinion and party feelings.[4]

The leaders of the WPC accepted many of these justifications for a new party. In late August, Denis Kearney attended a meeting of the short-lived Workingmen's Trade and Labor Union of San Francisco. There he advocated a new party to promote integrity and honesty in politics. He wanted to bring about a "new deal in politics," crushing the old parties that had ruined California. Later, after he had organized the WPC, Kearney told a journalist essentially the same story. He had seen that "thieves and corrupt men got into the legislature and obtained possession of the reins of government," and so he "advocated the building up of a great party to overthrow them." His sole object was to "organize the oppressed laboring classes into a political party" to obtain "through the ballot box a redress of the wrongs which had afflicted the downtrodden laborer." He intended to organize a workingmen's party to drive the "thieves and corrupt rascals" from power.[5]

The vast majority of workingmen threw their support behind the WPC, its candidates, and its program. But understanding this outcome requires an understanding not only of the WPC but also of the other parties, what they said and what they did, in order to see what workingmen rejected as well as what they accepted. Unfortunately, the documentary record does not permit an investigation of every party. The newspapers mentioned several very briefly, and these probably existed just long enough to field candidates in the municipal election of September 1877. When they failed, they disappeared. Included among this group are the Workingmen's Independent and Labor Reform Club of the Twelfth Ward, the Workingmen's Municipal Convention, the Workingmen's Union, and the Workingmen's Legislative Committee of the Eleventh Senatorial District. These parties are most useful as an indication of the extent of political ferment in San Francisco that summer and fall.

One additional party, the Workingmen's Trade and Labor Union of San Francisco, is best considered as a precursor to the Workingmen's Party of California. Its early members included both Denis Kearney and John G. Day, and it too collapsed in the aftermath of the September elections. Historians of the WPC sometimes discuss the WTLUSF when they describe the early history of the WPC and the beginning of Kearney's political activity. Since this organization disappeared with the founding of the WPC, and since there is no reason to believe that it differed substantially from the WPC, this approach seems reasonable.[6]

In considering the alternatives to the WPC, we can examine three in depth: the Workingmen's Party of the United States, the Workingmen's Party of San Francisco, and the National Labor Party. Although the available information is limited, these parties offer useful contrasts to the WPC. Their explanations for the problems that had overtaken San Francisco, their solutions to those problems, and their characteristic modes of political behavior reveal what San Francisco's workingmen were not seeking, as well as what they were, at this critical time in the evolution of their political consciousness.

One major difference among the parties lay in the varying explanations they offered for the plight of San Francisco and its workingmen. Only one party, the Workingmen's Party of the United States, offered a Marxist interpretation, emphasizing class differences as the reason for San Francisco's crisis. The WPUS is especially intriguing because of its close contemporaneity with the July riots. On July 22, the party held a well-attended meeting at Charter Oak Hall, and its chairman suggested that some action be taken to support striking railroad workers in the East.[7] As a result, notices appeared the next day announcing a mass meeting to be held on the sandlots in front of city hall. Its purpose was "to express their sympathy and take other action in regard to their fellow workmen at Pittsburgh and Baltimore." During the day, men paraded through the streets with banners reminding the city of the meeting and trying to drum up an audience. Police arrested one demonstrator in the afternoon, but they soon released him although they did confiscate his streamer.[8]

That evening a crowd estimated at six or seven thousand gathered across from city hall. At 8:00 sharp, a Mr. French called the meeting to order, and a series of speakers addressed the throng. As this meeting disbanded, the crowd began to bolt through the streets of the city and rioting began.[9]

This temporal conjunction between the WPUS and the July riots should not be interpreted causally. No historian has ever claimed that the WPUS plotted the violence, and no evidence supports such a conclusion. Just the opposite. The July riots and the WPUS seem to have been totally dissociated from each other, and the differences between them suggest a great deal about what San Francisco's workingmen were seeking, in both policy and style of political action. Had the speeches at the meeting of July 23 captured the hearts of San Francisco's working class, the riots would not have occurred.

The Workingmen's Party of the United States was organized in late July 1876 at a convention of socialist organizations meeting in Philadelphia. Various socialist groups from around the country sent delegates, hoping to reconcile the conflict between Lassalleans, who favored political action by workingmen, and Marxists, who believed that the organization of the working class into effective trade unions had to precede political struggle.[10]

The Declaration of Principles adopted in Philadelphia tried to reconcile Lassallean and Marxist principles, but it began with a clear expression of Marxist ideology. It proclaimed that "the emancipation of the working classes" had to be effected by "the working classes themselves, independent of all political parties of the propertied classes." All "social misery, mental degradation, and political dependence" resulted from the subjugation of workingmen to the "monopolizers of the means of labor," and the "economical emancipation of the working classes" was therefore "the great end" to which all political movements had to be subordinated. This struggle for freedom meant "not a struggle for class privileges and monopolies" but, ultimately, a struggle for "the abolition of class rule."[11]

San Francisco's section of the WPUS accepted these goals and reiterated them at the mass meeting on July 23. Leaders of the party introduced a series of resolutions condemning the American class system and demanding its destruction. The current depression resulted from "the active and ever-grasping policy of the capitalistic and governing classes." The working classes had been "despoiled of their homes and property and virtually disfranchised" by means of "the systematic grabbing of public lands, and the granting of subsidies to railroad and steamship lines, and the giving away of every possible franchise, together with a false and labor robbing monetary system." The resolutions concluded by asserting that there was "a gradual encroachment of capital upon the rights and liberties of the people," that all legislation was being "made and executed in the interest of the moneyed and propertied class," and that the producing classes were "being rapidly reduced to a condition of serfdom."[12]

The Workingmen's Party of San Francisco explicitly rejected the theory of social relations propounded by the Workingmen's Party of the United States. The surviving evidence indicates that the WPSF had a very short existence indeed. First mentioned in newspapers on August 24, it disappeared from view a week later. During that time, it nominated a slate of candidates for the municipal elections of September 5, and it issued a platform. Moreover, its founders held a relatively inflated opinion of themselves and their ability to satisfy the city's working class; at a meeting of delegates on August 27, the party voted to expel any member who helped organize another political party.[13]

During its short life, either the party did not have time to elaborate and express a coherent explanation for the woes of San Francisco, or the newspapers did not think its analysis worth reporting. We know only that the WPSF denied the existence of class conflict in the city. At a mass meeting on August 30, it issued a platform that directly challenged the Workingmen's Party of the United States, asserting that "a real unity of interests underlies the present apparent diversity." It did "not hold . . . any class responsible for evils incident to [the] vicious social and political conditions."[14]

We know almost as little about the history of the National Labor Party (NLP) in San Francisco. This organization first received newspaper attention in early November, and its activities attracted infrequent notice through the end of the year. On November 3, the *Chronicle* reported that the party had been formed about a week after the election of September 5 and that a platform had been drafted then. The party had not publicized this document because its founders thought that they should try to win public support only slowly. By late fall, they felt that the time had come, and the NLP issued its platform. Taken alone, this document contained a hint of class consciousness. The preamble declared that "the industrial classes" were "confronted . . . by capital centralized in the hands of an arrogant and unscrupulous minority." It called for the destruction of a "power which oppresses the people, makes the poor poorer, lowers the dignity of labor, threatens the safety of life, the security of property, and the very stability of the Government itself, and for building in its stead a Government of the people, for the good of the people."[15]

Nevertheless, later statements contradict the idea that the NLP was class oriented. In mid-December, one leader said that the party had not declared war against capitalists but only against capital wrongfully gained. Even more significantly, the NLP lashed out at its chief rivals for the allegiance of San Francisco's workingmen, Denis Kearney and the Workingmen's Party of California. According to the NLP, the WPC and its leaders were "misguided and radical in their method of procedure, though their object is praiseworthy."[16] Hardly the words of a Marxist organization, especially considering the almost total lack of class consciousness displayed by the WPC.

Some contemporary observers did consider the Workingmen's Party of California to be communist. Contemporary newspapers frequently referred to the communist agitation in San Francisco, and as far away as New York, Thomas Nast castigated Kearney and his followers for their communist tendencies. Hubert Howe Bancroft, the contemporary historian of California and the West, also considered the party communistic.[17]

Nonetheless, this interpretation provoked challenges almost as it appeared. In describing the California constitution of 1879, for which the WPC claimed exclusive credit, Henry George called it "anything but . . . communistic, for it entrenched vested rights—especially in land—more thoroughly than before." All in all, George thought that the new constitution actually "sacrificed the interests of the laboring classes . . . to what the land-owners regarded as their interests, while in other respects its changes . . . were out of the line of true reform." In short, the new constitution was "anything but a workingman's Constitution."[18]

The Workingmen themselves denied the communist label. In May 1878 the party drafted a platform, and its second article "utterly repudiate[d] all spirit of communism." This disclaimer coincided with months of statements from party leaders. The WPC clearly believed in the unity of capital and labor, in the underlying unity of society and its classes. As early as November 16, just a few months after the founding of the party, vice president William Wellock declared that "capital is not the enemy of labor." Rather, capital and labor were "dependent on each other for existence." It was "the brawny enduring muscle of the laborer" that gave life to capital, and capital renewed itself by being paid out in wages. A few weeks later, Wellock expressed the same sentiment in different words. This time he said that capital itself was not wrong; instead, the improper use of capital produced evil. If used properly, capital created jobs, enhanced property values, and built industries. Labor could "do as well without capital as the hand . . . without the head."[19]

H. L. Knight, the party's secretary, concurred when he claimed that the WPC had no objection to the rich per se, to people who were "honestly rich" and who spent their money "properly." It was only when the rich foisted "enormous and tyrannical monopolies" upon the people, enacted "injurious and oppressive laws," stole the public lands, and committed similar crimes that "they should be pulled down."[20]

The WPC expressed its harmonious social philosophy most clearly when it defined the term *workingman*. He was simply someone who was "not a millionaire." Storekeepers worked as hard as other workingmen, although their labor was "of the brain and not the hands." But "the brain of the merchant" was "useless without hands to help it, and the hands of the workingmen" were "helpless without the assistance of the brain" so that the middle classes had common cause with more traditionally defined workingmen. Therefore, party leaders invited the middle class to join; in fact, they invited everyone who worked, whether with his hand or with his brain, to become a member.[21]

If the Workingmen rejected theories of class conflict, how did they explain the problems confronting California in 1877? They did so by developing their own understanding of the state's history, based partly on fact and partly on their historical perceptions. According to Denis Kearney, the dream of California had once been reality. The state had been an Eden of bountiful fields and countless animals. Its climate had favored the products of every country, and its land and mineral wealth had "justified her proud name as the El Dorado of the world." California presented itself to citizens of other lands as "pre-eminent in resources." But a monstrous conspiracy developed. A few selfish people, not content to be part of an economy and society in which everyone could prosper, had established an aristocracy and carefully laid plans to destroy freedom. The crisis began, argued the WPC, when this small group seized the wealth of California by monopolizing the land of the state.[22]

The Workingmen explicitly denied any animosity toward capital or wealth. They could hardly have done otherwise, desiring to succeed as they did. They accepted the existence of a basic relationship between capital and labor, and they argued that everyone had the right to possess what he earned. They simply wanted a piece of the action and believed they could not get it because land monopolists had seized all the wealth for themselves. These California land-grabbers seemed stronger, more grasping, and more destructive than monopolists else-where. In their greedy struggle for gain, they had "fastened upon every industry, levied tribute upon every element of prosperity, and made all classes of labor subservient to the machinations of their rapacity." By capturing control of the land, a handful of men had despoiled Califor-nia's greatness.[23]

Even though the great fortunes of San Francisco derived from new types of commercial, industrial, and manufacturing enterprises, the Workingmen still associated wealth with land. According to them, it was not the Central Pacific that made the big four so fabulously rich; it was their land. These great landholders, "bedecked with diamonds and living in luxury," had become "the curse of the country" by trying to make homesteads "a luxury almost unattainable by a man who earns his daily bread by his daily labor."[24]

This view of the relationship between land and wealth reflected eighty years of federal land policy as well as general American atti-tudes toward wealth. Since the Land Act of 1796, the federal govern-ment had been selling the public domain at low prices. Only fifteen years before, the Homestead Act of 1862 theoretically made it possible for any American to acquire 160 acres free. Americans firmly believed that land was the source of wealth, that it should be available to all citizens, and that independent farmers were the backbone of a free so-ciety. The Workingmen themselves called land "the heritage of the people" and insisted that it must not be owned by a favored few. They wanted land not being used for pasture, cultivation, or homesteads to be redistributed to actual settlers.[25]

Their intense desire for land heightened in the 1870s as govern-ment reports detailed the increased concentration of landholdings in the state. Board of Equalization figures showed that the 122 largest farms in the state exceeded the other 23,515 in aggregate size, and the federal censuses of 1870 and 1880 echoed the point.[26]

At the same time, to explain conditions in San Francisco, Work-ingmen drew on the historical experience of Europe, where land was the traditional source of wealth, where men with land were rich—those without, poor. Many Workingmen were Irish immigrants whose centuries-old conflict with English landlords had imbued them with an overwhelming desire to own property. Although it may seem contradictory for the overwhelmingly rural and agricultural Irish peasantry to have settled in American cities and then bemoaned land concentration in this country, it was not. In cities, immigrants could communicate and interact with their own countrymen; they were not culturally isolated as they would have been in rural regions. Moreover, most Irish immigrants had few resources when they arrived in America, and they had neither the capital nor the skills to practice large-scale farming in the United States. When they arrived, most Irish immigrants were unskilled laborers, and it was the cities, with their factories, mills, and waterfronts, where they could find work—even if they would have preferred an agricultural existence, a preference reflected in their bitterness about land-grabbers and land concentration.[27]

They also feared land concentration because of the historic meaning of land in Europe. There, great landowners had belonged to a separate class, an aristocracy. Previously, such a class had never damned California; society had been open and egalitarian. Now, as the Workingmen looked around, it seemed that land concentration had spawned a California nobility. The residents of Nob Hill had achieved their object all too well while creating a life-style all too reminiscent of the European upper class. The Workingmen observed the nabobs and *did* equate them with Old World noblemen. The Workingmen sincerely believed that Flood and Fair, Stanford and Crocker wanted to wear coronets and tiaras.

Instead of honoring and respecting these would-be aristocrats, the Workingmen scorned and reviled them. The posturing of the nouveaux riches had backfired, and the Workingmen cursed them as "a class foreign to our institutions." America was no longer a nation with "none so rich and powerful and unscrupulous as to oppress his neighbors." Life in the United States had become "infinitely worse" than in the monarchies of Europe, worse even than in "the Dark Ages, when iron-clad robbers rode forth from their keeps and robbed their victims." Half a dozen Sacramento shopkeepers had accumulated millions while "thousands and thousands of workingmen, more able in bodies and brains and common morality, did not have a crust to eat after a lifetime of toil." In the eyes of the Workingmen, these millionaires surpassed the grandees of Europe in "supercilious pride and extravagance and vice." They built "colossal houses with skyscraper

tops" that were "vulgar imitations of the castles of the Old World."
Workingmen imagined millionaires sleeping in French beds, "soaked
to their underclothing with Oregon cider labelled champagne and
with stomachs distended with boned turkey." The residents of Nob
Hill were a "shoddy aristocracy" in a country dedicated to the principles of equality.[28]

Once the Workingmen had combined the ideas of land monopoly
and landed aristocracy, they used their theory to explain political
corruption, political repression, and Chinese immigration to San
Francisco. All these phenomena, according to the WPC, were tightly
linked to one another and to the eventual overthrow of the American
republic. As the Workingmen saw it, the rich had once been patriotic
citizens who served their country well. Now they thought only of
themselves while they used their power for personal advantage—to
subvert the American economic, political, and social systems.

In the 1870s, a series of scandals lent support to these claims. Brokers sold positions on the police force, and candidates for teaching
jobs bought examination questions. The new city hall was a colossal
boondoggle, and serious defalcations occurred in municipal government. The mint, customs' house, and post office all benefited a band
of politicians called the federal ring. In 1877, a United States senator
from California, the secretary of the Senate, and the superintendent
of the mint had used the naval pay office to embezzle thousands of dollars. When three municipal officials committed suicide, it seemed as if
the exposures had only begun.[29]

The WPC blamed San Francisco's wealthiest people for rampant
graft, corruption, and plunder. In every department of the federal government, they had established "a confirmed system of fraud and robbery." The army had become "effete and miserable," the navy "rotten
with stealing." In the public offices of San Francisco, "fraud stalked
triumphant." Bribery, forgery, and perjury had "debauched the public
conscience, destroyed the moral sense, and imperiled the honor of the
nation." In procuring their wealth, according to the Workingmen,
leading citizens had "endangered the existence of governmental structure" and "undermined the foundations of the social system."[30]

Finally, the theory continued, the conspirators planned to import
Chinese labor as a way to reestablish slavery. As the Workingmen saw

it, the Chinese were subservient pawns of the nobility and posed an economic and moral threat to the city. The party claimed that they were the lowest form of humanity, knowing nothing of family, having no conception of property, and practicing loathsome habits. Workingmen attacked the Chinese for refusing to accept American customs, wear American clothes, speak English, and worship in Christian churches. The WPC loudly proclaimed that Chinatown housed every conceivable vice: prostitution was rampant, gambling was uncontrolled, lotteries were ruining the youth of the city and swallowing up hard-earned savings. "Effusions" from opium dens were polluting the atmosphere, filth abounded in the streets, and the cubic air ordinance was openly scorned.[31]

Paradoxically, the workingmen probably recognized similarities between Chinatown and South of Market. They saw the maldistribution of property and the noxious physical environment in both regions. But, instead of thinking that the Chinese had also been victimized, the Workingmen believed that the Chinese were satisfied. Because the Chinese spoke a different language, followed different customs, and looked different, the Workingmen believed that they had different needs, desires, and values. As the Workingmen saw it, they themselves wanted land, the Chinese had no conception of property; they desired wives, the Chinese were satisfied with whores; they were free and honest laborers, the Chinese were foreign slaves. More than that, the WPC asserted that the nature of Asians was to live in poverty. And, on the basis of that simple contention, the party tried to explain unemployment in San Francisco. Since the Chinese accepted poverty, they worked for wages too low to support honest white men.[32]

At this point in their argument, the Workingmen tied the Chinese to the land-grabbers and aristocrats. Because the nobles cared more about profits than opportunity and the dream, they preferred Chinese labor. The Workingmen feared that this competition would make it increasingly difficult for white men to support themselves. They would eventually be forced out of the economy altogether, leaving no one except the aristocrats and their Chinese slaves. Free labor would disappear, and the American republic would vanish.[33]

In evaluating the various political parties hoping to represent them, San Francisco's workingmen could choose between several that believed in the unity of society (the Workingmen's Party of San Francisco, the Workingmen's Party of California, and the National Labor Party) and one that believed in the existence of an inevitable class conflict (the Workingmen's Party of the United States). Of the three non-Marxist parties, only the WPC survived long enough to formulate and articulate a coherent explanation for conditions in San Francisco and for the seeming failure of the California dream. That explanation, wrongheaded as it was, made sense within the history of the United States, California, San Francisco, and the lives of the Workingmen. However, to understand the appeal of the WPC and to differentiate it from rival parties in the city, we also must examine the specific programs of each party and see how each intended to reconstruct the city.

9. Platforms and Programs

Between late July and the end of 1877, each of the four parties presented a platform and a series of proposals to end the social, economic, and political problems facing San Francisco's workingmen. Although these platforms resembled one another in many ways, they differed significantly, and the differences suggest what workingmen wanted, what they did not want, and what policies they thought would restore the city.

In these platforms, three kinds of planks existed: those appearing in several documents including that of the WPC, those appearing only in platforms other than that of the WPC, and those appearing only in the platform of the WPC. The first sort of plank (that appearing in several platforms) suggests desires that were commonly accepted. Such a plank was of primary importance to the entire working class, but, at the same time, not very useful in helping people decide whether to support the WPC or one of the other parties. If parties other than the WPC advocated a particular policy, the advocacy of that policy could not have helped people choose one party rather than another.

Planks that appeared only in the platforms other than the WPC's reveal policies—given the WPC's electoral successes—that were not of primary importance to workingmen. If workingmen had considered a policy crucial, and if a party other than the WPC had advocated such a policy, one can assume that workingmen would have supported the other party. By the same logic, planks appearing only in the WPC's platform must have been extremely important to workingmen since advocacy of those policies distinguished the WPC. Thus, careful analysis of the different platforms allows us to understand the nature of the parties themselves, the differences among them, and why people supported the WPC rather than another party.

Of all the policies advocated in San Francisco during the summer and fall of 1877, the most widely known, and the one for which the Workingmen's Party of California is most famous, was opposition to Chinese immigration and employment of Chinese labor. At every WPC mass meeting, Denis Kearney trumpeted his clarion call, "The Chinese Must Go!" Historians of the party have never been able to explain its existence without extensive reference to this demand.

The constitution adopted at the first convention of the WPC declared, in its second plank, that cheap Chinese labor was "a curse to our land, a menace to our liberties and the institutions of our country, and should therefore be restricted and forever abolished." Its next formal platform asserted that Chinese labor was "a curse to our land, degrading to our morals, a menace to our liberties, and should be restricted, and forever abolished; and 'the Chinese must go.'" The document went on to demand that California corporations be legally prohibited from employing Chinese labor.[1]

Nevertheless, the WPC was not alone in making anti-Chinese demands, either before, during, or after that crucial summer. As Alexander Saxton has pointed out, the Chinese were "the indispensable enemy" of the state's working class. No California labor movement could succeed during the late nineteenth century without a commitment to anti-Chinese policies and programs.[2]

This realization explains one reason for the failure of the Workingmen's Party of the United States to appeal to the city's workingmen. It was the only workingmen's party in the city *not* to criticize Chinese immigration. In trying to attract the support of San Francisco's workingmen, the WPUS made a fatal tactical error in refusing to adopt an anti-Chinese stance. Even before the July riots, the party had made its position known. In early June, its official newspaper, the *Labor Standard*, published an editorial entitled "Don't Kill the Coolie" and urged workingmen to fight for "the abolition of the coolie system." After that, workingmen should struggle to abolish capitalism itself. The coolie was a slave, the wage laborer was a slave, and the capitalist was a slaveowner. "Organize, organize, organize; but *don't kill the coolie!*"[3]

The party's California branch concurred and made its attitude known at the mass meeting on July 23. That night the meeting's organizer told his audience that they had not assembled to discuss the Chinese question but to give moral support to their fellow workingmen in the East. But the crowd did not want to hear about the eight-hour day; it wanted to discuss the coolie question. Again and again it interrupted speakers with cries of "Tell us how to drive out the Chinamen!" and "What do we care for ballots? It's the Chinamen we're after!" When the speakers refused to change the tone or content of their speeches, part of the crowd broke away and headed for Chinatown, thus beginning the riots. That night the WPUS almost certainly lost its chance to win the hearts of San Francisco's workingmen, even as it expressed a much more honorable social, ideological, and philosophical position.[4]

Other workingmen's parties were more sympathetic to the demands of their hoped-for constituents. Both the Workingmen's Party of San Francisco and the National Labor Party espoused anti-Chinese positions, although with differing degrees of intensity. The WPSF took a relatively mild stand. Although it regretted the presence of the Chinese in the city and claimed that they had "a tendency to degrade labor and to depreciate wages," it refused to blame them for conditions in San Francisco. It preferred directing its energies to "the destruction of that political and capitalistic power that has steadily encouraged their presence and continued emigration."[5]

Of all the workingmen's parties that sprang up in 1877, the National Labor Party took the strongest anti-Chinese stand. Not only did it demand the immediate prohibition of Chinese immigration, but it also demanded the removal of all impediments to Chinese *emigration* from California. At the time, every Chinese who left the state by steamship (presumably to return to China) was required to obtain a permit from the Chinese company to which he belonged. This permit cost $25 and was considered a substantial deterrent to Chinese re-migration. The NLP demanded a law making it a felony to require, issue, or charge for permits to leave the state. Finally, the NLP opposed the employment of Chinese labor in preference to white labor or citizens of the United States.[6]

Thus, in the fall of 1877, the Workingmen's Party of California was not alone in attacking the Chinese. The recognition that the Workingmen's Party of San Francisco and the National Labor Party also attacked the Chinese forces us to seek other explanations for the appeal of the WPC. In order to understand its appeal to the workingmen of the city, in contrast to what it stood for, we must understand its other positions as well as those of the other workingmen's parties.

Three categories of demands—social, political, and economic—are significant. The analysis of social issues is more interesting for what is missing than for what is present. Other than the expression of anti-Chinese sentiments, the platforms are remarkably devoid of social concerns. Except for the anti-Chinese plank, only one social issue appeared in more than one platform: the demand for free, compulsory public education. The National Labor Party, the Workingmen's Party of the United States, and the Workingmen's Party of California all made this demand. The National Labor Party also advocated that schools be nonsectarian, that technical and labor schools be established, and that the state found an asylum for orphans and waifs. The Workingmen's Party of the United States—not surprisingly, given its class orientation—made demands about the condition of life among the working class: sanitary inspection of all factories and dwellings, and free courts of law. Neither the Workingmen's Party of California nor the Workingmen's Party of San Francisco made a single additional demand primarily meant to modify social as opposed to economic or political conditions.[7]

Also not surprisingly, given the desperate economic conditions prevailing in California, several platforms concentrated on economic issues. And yet the analysis of economic issues contains a major surprise. With several minor exceptions, the platform of the Workingmen's Party of California was amazingly devoid of economic considerations.

To begin with, only five economic demands were common to more than one platform, including that of the WPC. The first concerned land. Both the Workingmen's Party of California and the National Labor Party wanted to limit the disposition of government-owned land to actual settlers and to limit new grants to 160 acres. Moreover, both wanted to limit the maximum amount of land that any individual could own. If someone already owned more than the specified maximum, the excess should be confiscated and redistributed. In view of the WPC's theory about the decline of California and its concern about land-grabbers and land monopoly, this emphasis is not unexpected. Nevertheless, the duplication of policies between the WPC and the NLP meant that land policy did not provide a useful discriminant for workingmen trying to decide which party to support.

Neither did the issues of subsidies to corporations, prison labor, the eight-hour day, or work performed for the government. Both the NLP and the WPC demanded that government stop assisting corporations. Three parties, the WPC, NLP, and WPSF, demanded that all labor done for the government be paid by the day and not by contract; and two parties, the WPC and the WPUS, wanted to prohibit private employers from using prisoners in competition with free labor. The only economic demand common to all four platforms was the implementation of an eight-hour workday. Other than this last demand, then, there was little agreement among the workingmen's parties on economic policy.

In fact, the National Labor Party espoused a broader range of economic policies than any of the other parties and also advocated a series of measures that foreshadowed Populism and Progressivism. It demanded the revision of tax laws to aid farmers, the abolition of national banks, and the unlimited monetization of silver. The party wanted government to establish savings banks and a bureau of commerce. It thought that California should create a bureau of mines and limit the ownership of mineral lands to citizens. It also demanded the prohibition of corporations except under tight regulation, and high protective tariffs to safeguard the jobs of the working class. In making all these demands, the NLP stood alone.

The Workingmen's Party of San Francisco joined the NLP in advocating that government set freight and utility rates, and the WPUS joined in suggesting the creation of a bureau of labor statistics. All three parties, the NLP, WPUS, and WPSF, demanded that the national government acquire the country's railroad and telegraph lines and that state or local governments take over the water and gas companies. The Workingmen's Party of the United States made several unique economic demands: the abolition of the wage-labor system, organization of trades unions, prohibition of child labor, and liability of employers for job-related accidents.

But the Workingmen's Party of California, the party that won the allegiance of the city's working class, made none of the demands so common to reform parties, especially labor parties, in the late nineteenth and early twentieth centuries. It actually set itself apart from the other workingmen's parties in the city by not advocating economic policies that were becoming increasingly accepted in the city and in the nation.

This is not to say that the WPC did not make any economic demands in addition to land regulation and the others previously mentioned. But they seem relatively minor in comparison to the lengthy list advocated by the NLP and the major reforms suggested by the WPUS. In its first platform only, the WPC demanded reform of the national financial system. In the second, it "utterly repudiated" the spirit of communism, advocated equal pay for women, demanded government limits on interest rates, and called for major reforms of the federal tax system. Given the history of the party, its well-known rhetoric, and the ideas for which its leaders are most famous, one has difficulty concluding that San Francisco's working class signed up on the basis of these few proposals. Such a conclusion suggests that the major appeal of the party, and what separated it from other workingmen's parties in the city, was not economic issues at all.

Thus, in order to distinguish the WPC from the Workingmen's Party of the United States, the Workingmen's Party of San Francisco, and the National Labor Party, it is necessary to consider those platform sections that concerned the political system. Once again, we find a remarkable occurrence. The WPC platform emphasized political institutions much more than that of any other party. The WPC, along with the National Labor Party, advocated the direct election of the president, vice president, and senators of the United States; and both also demanded that no one be allowed to hold more than one office concurrently. The WPSF joined these two parties in suggesting that all government officials be paid by salary and not be allowed to keep any of the fees they collected. However, other than these few planks, not the Workingmen's Party of San Francisco, the Workingmen's Party of the United States, or the National Labor Party made a single demand for reform of the political system.

In contrast, the Workingmen's Party of California made a number of political demands. On two occasions, it insisted that officials who violated the public trust be declared felons. The party's first platform declared that "malfeasance in public office should be punishable by imprisonment . . . for life, without intervention of the pardoning power." Some months later it demanded that "the legislator who violates the pledges given to secure his election should be punished as a felon." In addition, the WPC demanded abrogation of the power to pardon; both its first and second platforms advocated the abolition of the executive right to pardon at all levels of government. The WPC platform also contained clauses sharply limiting the power of the legislature and special interests. It demanded that "there should be no special legislation [passed] by the State Legislature, and the Legislature should not meet more often than once in four years. All laws before taking effect should be submitted to the people for ratification." In another plank, the WPC demanded a state constitutional provision "forever prohibiting lobbying around the State Capital during the sessions of the Legislature."

These provisions demanding the limitation of governmental powers and the reduction of special interest influence are the major elements distinguishing the WPC platform from those of the other workingmen's parties. Therefore, unless we are willing to argue that workingmen supported the WPC, rather than one of the other new parties, for reasons entirely separate from its stated positions, we need to understand the significance of these demands.

The party's two earliest platforms contained an important clue: direct and indirect references to the Constitution of the United States. The first section of the party's second platform resolved

> that we recognize the Constitution of the United States of America as the great charter of our liberties and the paramount law of the land, and the system of government thereby inaugurated by its framers as the only true, wise, free, just, and equal government that has ever existed—the last, best, and only hope of man for self-government.

The constitutional reference in the earlier platform was more obscure but still hard to overlook.

> The Workingmen of California desire to unite with those of other States in effecting such reforms in our General Government as may be necessary to secure the rights of the people as against capital, to maintain life, liberty,

and happiness against land and money monopoly. Only in the people, the honest workingmen, can we hope to find a remedy.

This clause suggests that the WPC saw itself as something more than a party, and the preamble to the first platform reinforces this suspicion.

> Whereas, the Government of the United States has fallen into the hands of capitalists and their willing instruments; the rights of the people, their comfort and happiness are wholly ignored, and the vested rights of capital are alone considered and guarded, both in the State and Nation: the land is fast passing into the hands of the rich few. Great money monopolies control Congress, purchase the State Legislation, rule the Courts, influence all public officers and have perverted the great Republic of our fathers into a den of dishonest manipulators. This concentration and control of wealth has impoverished the people producing crime and discontent, and retarded the settlement and civilization of the country. In California a slave labor has been introduced, to still further aggrandize the rich and degrade the poor. The whole tendency of this class legislation has been to undermine the foundations of the Republic, and pave the way for anarchy and misrule.

Simply put, the WPC wanted to restore the Union. It considered itself a movement dedicated to destroying the nefarious plot of land-grabbers and the Chinese. It intended to maintain traditional American institutions and to revitalize the American republic itself. If we examine speeches, poems, and songs, in addition to formal party statements, we find an extraordinary self-vision. The WPC considered itself a holy crusade dedicated to preserving and reinvigorating the Republic of the founding fathers.

In this regard, San Francisco's Workingmen resembled their counterparts in other American cities. Workingmen in Cincinnati (at a comparable stage of that city's development) also espoused a republican ideology. There, workers saw themselves possessing two identities, "workers who operated in a highly stratified economic sphere and citizens who participated in what they believed was an egalitarian political sphere." They were convinced that government acted as "a neutral arbiter between labor and capital and would act to correct the inequities of economic life." In Cincinnati, as in San Francisco, workers saw "their economic interests as consistent with republican obligations" and frequently argued that they were attempting to defend the republic by restoring the commonwealth that had previously existed. "It was almost as if ideology alone could restore the venerated republican community that no longer existed, if indeed it ever had."[8]

In thinking about itself, the WPC and its members used a wide variety of similes and metaphors. In order to express their goals and their visions, the Workingmen conjured up analogies from sources as disparate as the Bible and the French Revolution. They drew on every historical era for appropriate images to describe themselves and their mission, but the one common theme was the struggle to preserve freedom and liberty. They compared Denis Kearney to American freedom-fighters like George Washington and John Adams, Andrew Jackson and Abraham Lincoln. They likened him to such biblical insurgents as Esther's Mordecai and Jesus. The current struggle was equated with the Pilgrim fathers, the American Revolution, and the Civil War.[9]

References to the American Revolution pervaded their thought. A hundred years ago, according to one party spokesman, George Washington had planted the tree of liberty in America, but now it had begun to wilt, to droop, and to fall. Seeing the danger, Denis Kearney had braced the tree with his back and called for help. His followers were propping it up, and they would not allow a single leaf to fall. The WPC's great parade through the streets of San Francisco on Thanksgiving Day 1877 was filled with references to the Revolution. One banner read "The sons of liberty, still alive"; another, "United we stand, divided we fall." Voltaire's axiom "The pen is mightier than the sword" was resurrected; and the "right of revolution" was proclaimed "sacred." A huge centennial picture portrayed a boy beating a drum to the music of fifes played by American patriots. In the background, Continentals stormed Bunker Hill, and the caption blazed "What our fathers gained, we will preserve."[10]

Of all the historical parallels drawn by the party, none captured its imagination or had the same significance as the Civil War, the most recent battle for liberty. One Workingman said that he had shouldered a gun for four years to liberate mental and physical slaves. Now he was ready to free enslaved workingmen. Another had stormed Lookout Mountain, now he was ready to battle up Nob Hill. In addition to being the Grand Army of the Republic, the Workingmen's Party of California was the Anti-Slavery Society; in addition to being Old

Abe, Denis Kearney was John Brown. One of the party's hymns, "The Song of the Sand Lot," was sung to the tune of "John Brown's Body," which was, of course, sung to the same tune as "The Battle Hymn of the Republic." In it, the "Citizens 'Two Hundred'" were compared to "the Southern Chivalry," but a new day was dawning. "The bugle blast of freedom" was "sounding through the land . . . to call the sons of toil of high and low degree . . . to rally to the standard of a higher freedom's cause." Workingmen were warned, "Make ready for the battle and arm you for the fray" because "this war will be a long one, for the enemy is rich." Nonetheless, there was no cause for fear.

> The God of battle's with us, and will give us victory
> The God of battle's with us, and will give us victory
> The God of battle's with us, and will give us victory
> The cause of a higher liberty.[11]

The party's songs and poems teemed with images that suggested the resurrection, rebirth, and renewal of freedom; the death and destruction of slavery. In "The Song of the Sand Lot," Denis Kearney was "resurrected." In the grand, triumphal march, "We the Workingmen are Coming!"

> Long and hard have white men suffered
>   'Neath the cruel yoke
> But at last the bonds we've severed
>   Labor has awoke
>
> Brighter days will shine upon us
>   When our coast is free![12]

"Appeal to Californians" told "Freeman" to arouse himself and defend the nation from "swarming serfs."

> No feudal lords, no foreign slaves
> Shall live where freedom's banner waves.
> No castles, no serfs, no scheming foe
> Shall doom our state to want and woe. . . .
>
> There is no peace, the conflict's nigh.
> Rally, heroes, in legions strong.
> Form martial ranks, ye veteran throng,
> Freeman, forward in freedom's fight,
> Strike for liberty, life and light.[13]

"Vote for the New Constitution" and "The Heathen Chinee" iterated the same vision of a great battle in which the forces of good and freedom would confront the minions of evil and slavery. According to the former verse,

It is the freemen of this land of ours
They are marshalling their forces
To battle for their rights
And by the God of battles
They mean to make a glorious fight,
To save our noble Golden State
From the slavery of Asia, in its filth and crime,
From the cormorants of greed and lust,
From the devouring Molochs of corporation power,
And from the land monopolists that claim this fair land of ours.[14]

The latter poem urges Workingmen to

fill up your pouch,
And fill up your can,
Shoulder your musket
And call out your man;
For our sons and our daughters
We'll fight till we're free,
For we're bound to be rid
Of the heathen Chinee.[15]

All these sentiments, goals, and feelings were wrapped up in the final verse of "To the Workingmen."

Workingmen of California
Your's the task to renovate,
And to purify the records
Of our grand and noble State.[16]

Thus, the Workingmen's Party of California differed from other workingmen's parties because of its larger vision and its sense of mission. Neither the Workingmen's Party of San Francisco nor the National Labor Party developed or expressed a coherent world view. Although their platforms resembled that of the WPC in many ways, they did not enunciate an overall interpretation that explained the historical evolution of conditions in San Francisco, in California, or in the

United States. Lacking that coherent exegesis, they created no context to provide meaning for their proposals, no sense of mission to energize and arouse their audience.

The only other party presenting such a view was the Workingmen's Party of the United States. However, it had almost certainly lost legitimacy and credibility when it failed to espouse an anti-Chinese position. Moreover, its basic world view contradicted that of San Francisco's workingmen. They, after all, were men who had traveled thousands of miles in search of a dream. Most had crossed a continent, and tens of thousands had crossed an ocean as well. They had come to California because they wanted to succeed and because they believed that they could in the Golden State. For many, it had not happened; for others, it had not happened to the degree anticipated; for still others, there was a fear that success had ended. There was a gap between reality and expectation. But the WPC promised that it could still happen; that California was indeed the land of opportunity, that the long journey had been worthwhile, and that a person could still make it. All that was necessary was to purge the system of those individuals who had perverted it.

By way of contrast, the Workingmen's Party of the United States, with its socialist interpretation, implicitly suggested that the dream was a nightmare, that the trip had been a waste of time, that the California of their minds was a fantasy, and that individual fortunes were not even desirable. Frank Roney put it slightly differently. According to him, the hope of San Francisco's workingman, "the fellow without property, . . . was to be a small property holder at some time in the near future; consequently, his sympathies were with the class to which he later hoped to belong."[17] In other words, despite their actual class, if there is such a thing, San Francisco's workingmen saw themselves not as part of the working class but as part of the future middle (or even upper) class. As with mobility, what mattered was not reality, but perception. Thus, San Francisco's workingmen were willing to fight, not to destroy an unjust system, but to preserve and protect a system that had been perverted. The WPC allowed them to maintain their illusions and their view of the world, things that socialism precluded.

10. The Rhetoric of Riot

Fully understanding the WPC's appeal and the preference of San Francisco's workingmen for it rather than other parties requires more than an analysis of party principles. It does not explain how a man like Denis Kearney developed his ideas or how he came to establish a political party. Limiting the analysis to goals and objectives reveals nothing about the emotional psychology of participation while implying that people join political movements only because of objective issues and concerns. But other factors including race, religion, socioeconomic status, and family history dispose people to prefer one party to another. In the case of the WPC, its appeal also depended heavily on the character of its leader, Denis Kearney, and on the relationship between Kearney and his followers.

As we have already seen, Denis Kearney wanted to succeed, had already achieved some success, and would ultimately be more successful. In July 1877, he so identified with the established classes that he joined the Committee of Safety to help quell the riots at the end of the month. But two weeks later, he had an experience that changed his life and San Francisco's history.

Along with a group of other draymen, he called on Senator A. A. Sargent to discuss the hauling business of the federal customs house. According to a newspaper report, the senator received them "with manifest contempt" and paid them "not the slightest heed." Within two weeks, Kearney was addressing public crowds, and the first object of his wrath was Sargent. Kearney sponsored a resolution that confidence in Sargent "as a conscientious and impartial representative of the people" was "irreparably destroyed," and that his conduct toward constituents had demonstrated an "utter lack of dignity and spirit that should invest his high position." Shortly thereafter, in explaining his reasons for establishing a new political party, Kearney attacked the existing ones and called Sargent a politician who put his own interests ahead of the people's. The basis for his view of California's downfall had been established.[1]

Within a short time, Kearney was including the Committee of Safety in his panoply of evils. At an organizational meeting of the WPC, Kearney used sweeping invective to denounce the committee and its leader, William T. Coleman. He said they had usurped the power of the mayor and the Board of Supervisors, and he wondered what right the city had to arm them. At another meeting, he labeled the committeemen "cowards," and his audience issued "three groans" for them. On yet another occasion, he lambasted the committee as "a mob of the damnedest cutthroats that ever disgraced a city." Kearney had come to see the Committee of Safety as an organization meant to quell working-class protest in the city.[2]

Kearney's understanding of what had happened to city, state, and nation emerged from his experiences in San Francisco, including current economic difficulties, his encounter with Senator Sargent, and his participation in the Committee of Safety. It also developed from widely held views about the Chinese, land monopoly, and the arrogance of wealth in the city. But what gave him control of workingmen and secured him their affection was style. Contemporaries and historians alike have called Kearney a demagogue, "a leader who obtains power by means of impassioned appeals to the emotions and prejudices of the populace." But this definition hardly differs from that of charisma, and, by extension, a charismatic leader, "a rare quality or power attributed to those persons who have demonstrated exceptional ability for leadership and for securing the devotion of large numbers of people."[3] One man's demagogue can be another's charismatic leader, and Kearney could be called either or both, depending on one's point of view.

San Franciscans recognized Kearney's enormous power over his followers and understood that it emanated from his persona as much as from his words and ideas. The *Post* suggested that his intellect was not brilliant but implied that his temperament let him utilize his faculties to the utmost. "Whatever he attacks he seems to project himself upon as if shot out of a cannon, and grapples it like a bulldog." The *Chronicle* noted that "he is a ready and forcible speaker" but that his speeches were "more remarkable for vigor than for anything else," and frequently profane.[4]

Henry George believed that Kearney's power derived from an emotional quality. He compared Kearney to the Roman Cincinnatus, who led the people but would accept no office; Kearney wore rough work clothes and planned to return to his dray after he led the people to victory. "These things, the style of his oratory, the prominence he had attained, his energy, tact, and temperance, gave him command." When Kearney denounced politicians and struck down rivals, George suggested that he appealed not only to prejudice and jealousy but also to the personal interest and ambition of his followers. "The political hewers of wood and drawers of water, who made up the [WPC] clubs, flattered themselves with the idea that *they* were the men of whom sheriffs, and supervisors, and school-directors, and senators, and assemblymen were to be made, and they brought to the new party and to the support of Kearney all the enthusiasm which such a hope called forth."[5]

Several events occurred in July 1878 that illustrate Kearney's hold over the Workingmen and the depth of their feelings for him. He was about to depart San Francisco for Boston, and the WPC sponsored a fund-raising benefit. An estimated thirty-five hundred people attended, and "the hall was filled as it never filled except on St. Patrick's Day." When Kearney arrived, he received an ovation worthy of the saint himself. Although he was ill and could barely speak, the crowd refused to leave him alone. At every interval in the program, cries of "Kearney, Kearney" became more and more strident until they were all but irrepressible. At last, he made his way to the stage. "The moment he became visible, the whole house rose to its feet and saluted him, the men with wild volleys of cheers and the ladies with showers of bouquets." When the ovation finally subsided, Kearney "loaded himself . . . with flowers till he was an invisible moving vase and bowed himself away amid another cyclone of cheers." On the day of Kearney's departure, an enormous gathering saw him off. Bands, military companies, and orators all participated in a tremendous demonstration of loyalty and affection. "The scene was not dissimilar to that witnessed on the departure of General [Ulysses S.] Grant on his European tour."[6]

What caused these feelings? What earned Kearney this devotion and affection? In short, Kearney understood the psychology of his followers, and thus he understood their needs. There was an extraordinary interaction in San Francisco that summer and fall, an interaction among Denis Kearney, the Workingmen of the city, and the city's formal leaders. In late July, workingmen had formed a crowd, but officials and civic leaders had crushed it. Consequently, workingmen could no longer act like a crowd. But psychologically, they were still one and did not know another way to protest.

Kearney taught them. He told them how to behave under the new circumstances. At the same time, he spoke in familiar ways, in a language that they could understand. But in shepherding his flock, he himself followed a path mapped out by the leaders of the city—political, religious, and economic. Without realizing precisely what they were doing, they taught Kearney and the Workingmen the new boundaries of acceptable political behavior.

Between early September and late December, Kearney used this information to transform the crowd into a nascent party. He did so by speaking the language of the crowd to advocate the means of the party. As a result, the WPC bridged the gap between crowd and party, helping the city's workingmen abandon one form of political behavior and adopt another. They accepted the WPC, and they followed Kearney precisely because it and he were not yet so socialized and so acculturated to the new form of political action, the party, that they had become incomprehensible.

The crucial mode of discourse, and what shaped the interactions among Kearney, workingmen, and city officials, was "the rhetoric of riot." After the last night of violence in July, there was no further rioting in San Francisco. No person was injured, and no property was damaged. Peace settled on the city. And yet the speeches of Kearney and his fellows are better denoted as harangues, diatribes, or tirades than orations. They were inflammatory at least, incendiary at most. In one of his more famous speeches, Kearney declared that the Workingmen could solve California's problems quickly. Every freeman had the right to a musket and ammunition. In a year, twenty thousand men would have joined the party, and twenty thousand muskets would be in their hands.

> Then, let them bring on the regular army to put us down. Let them bring on their police, their Committee of Safety. . . . We don't want to send little boys out to burn Chinese wash-houses; no, we want organization to resist the regular army and the gray coats and the Committee of Safety when the time comes. . . . A little judicious hanging right here and now will be the best course to pursue with these capitalists and stock sharps who are all the time robbing us.[7]

In response to this speech, John G. Day claimed that it was a desperate time and that desperate means had to be used. Every citizen had the right to a musket, and there would soon be "a social revolution" that would "convulse the country."[8]

A few weeks later, Kearney attacked the enemies of the party, but especially the Nob Hill millionaires. He told his followers:

> When we issue a call, we want you to act promptly. We want to know the man who will discharge any workingmen who turn out to attend these meetings. We will brand him so that every workingman in the city shall know him. . . . I tell you, and I want Stanford and the press to understand, that if I give an order to hang [Charles] Crocker, it will be done; and if I give an order to pull down that fence, it will be done. The dignity of labor must be sustained, even if we have to kill every wretch that opposes it.[9]

A few days later, Kearney was arrested. Charged with using language that tended to incite violence and riot, he was accused of having said:

> The Central Pacific Railroad men are thieves, and will soon feel the power of the workingmen. When I have thoroughly organized my party, we will march through the city and compel the thieves to give up their plunder. I will lead you to the City Hall, clean out the police force, hang the prosecuting attorney, burn every book that has a particle of law in it, and then enact new laws for the workingmen. I will give the Central Pacific just three months to discharge their Chinamen, and if that is not done, Stanford and his crowd will have to take the consequences. I will give Crocker until November 30 to take down the fence around Yung's house, and if he does not do it, I will lead the workingmen up there, and give Crocker the worst beating with the sticks that a man ever got.[10]

The other statement for which Kearney was charged had the same tenor.

> The man who claims to be a leader, the first man who flags in interest in this movement, I want to make a motion that he be hung up to a lamppost, by the eternal we will take them by the throat and choke them until their life's blood ceases to beat, and then run them into the sea. . . . Recollect Judge Lynch, and that is the judge that the workingmen will want in California, if the condition of things is not ameliorated. I advise every man within the sound of my voice, if he is able to, to own a musket and a hundred rounds of ammunition.[11]

What was the meaning of this violent rhetoric? Why did Kearney address his followers in this way? How do we balance the fury of Kearney's speech against the peacefulness of his, and their, actions? Was Kearney serious and did he really want the Workingmen to use the full force of their numbers against their enemies? The answer to the last question seems the easiest to deduce. Had Kearney wanted his men to attack any person or any property, they would have. The fervor of their allegiance to him makes any other answer unthinkable. But then, why did he address the city in this fashion?

To begin with, the Workingmen enjoyed the strength and vitality of his language. It was the language of the crowd, the traditional language of political protest, the language they knew. Newspapers regularly commented on audience response to his hard-hitting talk. At one meeting, "the superheated enthusiasm of the masses occasionally ebulliated in exclamations of indignation" against their foes. At another, many "seemed ripe for hostility to commence, and asked . . . volunteers to lead them on to Chinatown." Fortunately, good counsel prevailed, and the gathering dispersed peacefully.[12]

At still another meeting, the more incendiary the speeches, the more delighted the audience seemed. "For any particularly bloody remark, it would yell delightedly." When Denis Kearney screamed that the Workingmen should arm themselves and then let the city bring on the army, the police, and the Committee of Safety, "uproarious applause" filled the room. When he shouted that he wanted to organize to resist the army and the committee, applause and "cries of derision against the Committee" split the air. When John Healy asked the Workingmen what to do with Stanford, Crocker, and other millionaires, "the audience roared, 'Hang 'em! Hang 'em!'"[13]

But no one ever dangled. No lamppost ever bent under the weight of a body; no tree limb ever snapped under the force of a deadweight. And the explanation, once again, has to do with Kearney's language. For all the invective, for all the vituperation, he never once counseled an overt act of violence. Every call to action was a noncall. Every exhortation was carefully qualified by time, place, or circumstance—if this happened, at that time, in such a place, THEN you should and we will. . . . He never issued a single call for direct, immediate action.

Consider the selections from Kearney's speeches previously quoted. In each, the dominant tense is future, and the dominant mood is conditional. In the first, he implied a desire for battle only after the party had organized and its men had been armed. *Then* he looked forward to confrontation and urged the city to bring on its forces. He did not say that hanging *was* the best course to pursue; he said that hanging *will be* the best course to pursue. In the next extract, Kearney did not order his followers to act now; he ordered them to act promptly *when* he issued a call. He did not tell his followers to hang Charles Crocker or to pull down his fence. He told his followers that *if* he gave an order to hang Crocker, and *if* he gave an order to pull down his fence, *it would be done*, at that time. Kearney was urging nothing now; he was making a statement of fact about future action under specified future conditions.

All the statements that produced Kearney's first arrest in early November were phrased in precisely the same way: descriptions of situations as they would exist in the future, generally after another situation had come into existence. Reading the verbs and their qualifiers, omitting the inflammatory nouns, the statements have a different tone and feeling.

> are . . . will soon feel. . . . When I have thoroughly organized . . . we will march . . . and compel. . . . I will lead . . . clean out . . . hang . . . burn . . . and then enact. . . . I will give . . . and if that is not done. . . . I will give . . . and if he does not do it, I will lead . . . and give.[14]

The statement that produced the second charge was phrased in the same way:

> the first man who flags . . . I want to make a motion that he be hung up . . . we will take them and choke them . . . and then run them into the sea. . . . Recollect Judge Lynch, and that is the judge that the work-

ingmen will want . . . if the condition of things is not ameliorated. I advise every man . . . if he is able . . . to own a musket.[15]

All Kearney's rantings were structured similarly. First, consider the
stripped down version of a speech delivered at the end of the year, a
version showing only tense and mood. Then analyze the entire text.

> We intend . . . and if this won't do, we will . . . and when [it] comes, we
> won't. . . . We are going to . . . and if [they] . . . we will . . . too. . . .
> You must be. . . . [They] must . . . if. . . . We want to . . . and
> thereby. . . . We have the numbers to . . . but you will be. . . . If they
> . . . as I know they will, [then]. . . . You must be ready. . . . We
> will. . . . [16]

Now the complete selection.

> We intend to try and vote the Chinamen out, to frighten him out, and if
> this won't do, to kill him out, and when the blow comes, we won't leave a
> fragment for the thieves to pick up. We are going to arm ourselves to the
> teeth, and if these land-grabbers and thieves go outside the Constitution,
> we will go outside the Constitution, too, and woe be to them. You must be
> prepared. The heathen slaves must leave this coast, if it cost 10,000 lives.
> We want to frighten capital and thereby starve the white men so that they
> will be exasperated and do their duty. This is the last chance the white
> slaves will ever have to gain their liberty. . . . We have the numbers to
> win at the ballot box, but you will be cheated out of the result, and all
> history shows that oppressed labor has always to get its right at the point of
> the sword. If the Republican robber and the Democratic thief cheat you at
> the election, as I know they will, shoot them down like rats. You must be
> ready with your bullets. We will go to Sacramento and surround the Legis-
> lature with bayonets and compel them to enact such laws as we wish.[17]

In addition to qualifying his harangues and placing his calls for violence at some unspecified future time, Kearney counseled another
kind of action—institutional politics. He told his followers to use ballots, not bullets. Nearly every one of his speeches contained a call to
use formal political processes. At one of his earliest public appear-
ances, even before the WPC had been organized, Kearney proposed to
settle the labor question "right here and now by flying to the ballot
box." He told his audience that they could "revolutionize this vast
country" and that there could be "a workingman in the Presidential
chair."[18]

In an interview, Kearney said that his sole object was to organize oppressed labor into a political party to obtain "through the ballot box a redress of the wrongs which had afflicted the downtrodden laborer." The WPC did not hold meetings for incendiary purposes but to form a political party and drive thieves and corrupt rascals from power. In his most interesting and provocative statement on the subject, Kearney told his partisans that organization was "the only way to success." He averred that "by organizing they were endeavoring to prevent any riots from growing out of the movement." [19]

What do we make of all this, of the phrasing of Kearney's speeches and of the contradictory statements he made, advocating indefinite violence on the one hand, formal political action on the other? How do we draw a larger picture to illustrate not only Kearney's speeches but also the attitude of the Workingmen toward Kearney? What can we infer from the fact that Workingmen never rioted after the WPC had been formed? One possible explanation is that Kearney did not understand what he was doing, did not choose his words or phrase his thoughts so carefully that they can be subjected to grammatical and syntactical scrutiny. After all, he was a relatively uneducated man, an Irish immigrant of no particular training, a drayman. But other evidence suggests that this explanation will not do. Kearney claimed that he was misquoted in the press, that newspapers did not print exactly what he said, that they omitted all his qualifications. In an interview he accorded one journalist, Kearney claimed that his words had been seriously misinterpreted. He "did not threaten to hang Mr. Crocker. I said he would be hanged if I gave an order to hang him, but I meant to have him hanged in a legal way if he deserved it." [20] Kearney's first reading of the statement is certainly correct, and even his second construction can be justified. Kearney seems to have chosen his words carefully and understood precisely what they meant. Then just what was he doing?

Just what he said he was doing. Telling the crowd not to rise up— yet. To wait and see. To bide their time. His followers were men whose traditional form of political protest was the crowd. But they had tried crowd action and been crushed. So now they were trying something new, a political party; but they had no certainty that it would be any more successful than riot. Kearney was just as unsure. He, and they, knew only that violence had recently failed. But the new kind of protest was totally untried. It might work, and it might not. Kearney told his men to give it a shot. If it worked, well and good; they would have a powerful new tool. If it failed, they were no worse off than before, and he gave them permission to form another crowd and riot.

Kearney filled his speeches with warnings about what would happen if he and his troops did not get their way. Late in August, several weeks before he and Day organized the WPC, he told a gathering of workingmen that they needed a new political party to effect a new deal in politics. He wanted the people to own the offices and elect new officials. Then, if officials did not do their duty, they would hang from the nearest lamppost. Several weeks later, he told another assemblage that they should not use violence unless it was necessary to enforce their rights. Two weeks later, he claimed that he preferred workingmen to use legitimate means to gain their rights. But, if everything else failed, he favored powder and bullets, and he advised every man to sharpen his saber, have a musket, and prepare ammunition.[21] In mid-October, he expressed this in a letter to the *Chronicle*:

> We can organize. We can vote our friends into all the offices of the State. We can send our Representatives to Washington. We can use all legitimate means to convince our countrymen of our misfortunes and ask them to vote the moon-eyed nuisance out of the country. But this may fail. . . . We call upon our fellow Workingmen to show their hands, to cast their ballots right, and to elect the men of their choice. We declare that when they have shown their will . . . and that will be thwarted by fraud or cash, by bribery and corruption, it will be right for them to take their own affairs into their own hands and meet fraud with force.[22]

The party understood Kearney. After he and other party captains were arrested in early November, the executive committee issued orders repeating what its leader had been commanding.

> Do not commit any deeds of violence; do not in any way harass the officers of the law. Await a full and impartial expression of the law. It is the wish of the imprisoned; it is the programme of the WPofC that they be arrested, tried, and if not convicted, then you will know that it is lawful for a speaker to express his opinion in this boasted free country. If the law says they are not guilty, then, having committed no offense against the law, they are entitled to speak and be protected, forcibly if necessary in that

right. But until the law passes on that right, you have no right to object, in any way, to the arrest of any of us.[23]

Kearney and the Workingmen did not consider political protest to be a process in which differing ideas competed and in which the majority dominated. They thought of it as a process by which they would get what they wanted, just as the traditional crowd rioted until constituted authority negotiated and a satisfied mob dispersed. The Workingmen were willing to use formal political institutions as long as they succeeded in producing the desired result; if they failed, it was back to the barricades.

Kearney's view of negotiations with city authorities reflected this attitude. He would make his demands, and they would submit. A demand had to be respected, and he implied that if it was not, riot would ensue.

> We will claim our right as American citizens to stop before the City Hall and send a committee of three to the major and demand of him the repeal of the gag law. We shall also claim the right to march down in a body near the mail dock and demand of the company that they bring no more Chinamen here. In England you can make a demand, and it will be respected; in free America, you are arrested for it.[24]

He said the same thing slightly differently a few days later, and the difference in phrasing emphasizes his concept of "the right to have demands met."

> I consulted lawyers today about making demands. They told me I could make demands as an American citizen. On the 29th therefore, we mean to demand of the Supervisors the repeal of the gag law. . . . We propose to appoint a committee to wait on the Pacific Mail Steamship Company and demand that they bring no more Chinese to our shores, and next to expel the thieves, the political bummers, the vagabonds that now infest our country.[25]

In one of his early speeches, John G. Day discussed demands in a way that clearly reflected the mentality of European grain rioters and expressed their expectation of official submission. More than any other statement, this smoking gun links San Francisco's crowd/Workingmen to the traditional European preindustrial crowd. "When the organization is sufficiently powerful it will visit the municipal authorities and demand that the capitalists throw open the doors of their storehouses to feed the starving poor, and charge the cost thereof to the state."[26]

Kearney, Day, and the Workingmen were grafting the rhetoric, goals, and mentality of the crowd onto the political party. They were using a new (at least to them) kind of institution to gain their objectives, but they still interpreted the world in the old way—they would achieve their will by making demands. They were willing to give the party a chance, but if it failed, they would fall back on the way of the past—they reserved the right to revolt.

Such violent declamations dismayed San Franciscans of a more tranquil temper, and as a result, many turned against Kearney and the WPC. Some opponents of his style came from within the party itself, some from competing parties, and some from outside the working class, but altogether, many denounced Kearney and the WPC over the issue of rant and bombast. At one WPC meeting, shortly after Denis Kearney had burst onto the scene, Patrick J. Healy deprecated both his methods and his motto. According to Healy, his "violent and incendiary speeches had perhaps done more to bring reproach upon the cause of labor reform in this city" than anything else. "His wild talk," as reported in the newspapers, had been taken to represent the spirit of the labor reformers, whereas "nothing was more repulsive to them." No bloated capitalist or railroad magnate was doing half as much against the cause of labor as men of his stripe. Several weeks later, T. J. Day, another party leader, also dissociated himself from Kearney's rhetorical style. He told his audience that he wanted their meetings to "be of such a character that I will not have to apologize for any incendiary remarks uttered by any of the speakers." When Day had finished his remarks and Kearney began to orate in his usual manner, Day objected, and a fight seemed imminent. Only the appearance of armed police restored order.[27]

Opposition from within the party was more than matched by hostility from without, and both the Workingmen's Party of the United States and the National Labor Party criticized Kearney. On November 3, several newspapers reported the formation of the NLP and details of its platform. According to the *Chronicle*, the party had actually written its platform several months before but had decided not to an-

nounce it publicly. Now, however, the situation had changed. A fa-
natical excitement fired labor, and the city trembled. The party hoped
that by issuing its platform, "it could draw from Kearney the best and
most intelligent of his followers and array them on the side of law and
order." The *Bulletin* emphasized that organizers of the NLP "bitterly
opposed" the incendiary speeches of Kearney and his friends. At a
meeting a week later, one speaker implicitly compared the NLP to the
WPC. The former party was

> not gotten up by demagogues for the purpose of opposition, but for the
> only purpose of ameliorating the condition of the workingmen and form-
> ing a party which would meet the wants of the masses. The present agita-
> tion [the WPC] was seeking to bring about the same result as the NLP, the
> amelioration and elevation of labor, but the men who are leading this agi-
> tation are misguided and radical in their method of procedure.[28]

The WPUS also separated itself from Kearney and his mode of discourse. In general, the party did not think that Kearney understood
the cause or the remedy for current labor problems. But it also objected to violent speech or action.[29] This crucial difference distinguished the WPC from other workingmen's parties.

If some workingmen, and some workingmen's parties, objected to
Kearney's vituperation, how much more so did San Franciscans of another status. While the Workingmen attempted to learn a new mode
of political action and protest, other San Franciscans watched and
tried to figure out what they were doing. Most residents of the city,
especially the more affluent and established members of the community, imagined only two kinds of political activity, the mob and the
party, and they had difficulty conceptualizing the sort of transition
that the WPC represented. As they observed the party, all their evidence suggested that it was an incipient mob, not a nascent party. It
was composed of people they did not know, people who lived South of
Market, in sections of the city not usually familiar to the middle and
upper classes. Party members tended to be poor immigrants with
strange and confusing patterns of manner, behavior, and speech. In
July, workingmen had actually emerged and threatened the security of
the city. Now, in September and October, the city heard Kearney's
bluster and feared for its future.

Most San Franciscans were unable to distinguish between rhetoric and behavior; they did not listen carefully to what Kearney said, and they believed that the party was attempting in the present what Kearney was threatening for the future if his demands remained unsatisfied. In a modern political system, statements of party leaders are generally taken at face value and accepted as party doctrine. What leaders advocate is understood to be what the party will try to accomplish if it gains power. Consequently, San Francisco listened to Kearney and trembled, not truly comprehending his message or understanding what it meant to his followers. The city did not appreciate the complexities of his language or its symbolic meaning to the city's workingmen. Therefore, the calls for repression that began to fill the air became more clamorous.

In fact, the city's first response to the WPC was neglect. Few of its early meetings were widely reported by the press, and the *Alta*, which generally spoke for the business and commercial community, hardly mentioned the party during September and October. But late in September, Denis Kearney, John G. Day, and several others wrote a letter to the mayor. Although newspapers did not print its text, it seems to have asked aid for the city's workingmen. Because the text has been lost, we cannot determine if its tone requested, pleaded, or demanded. In any case, the letter did not elicit a great deal of sympathy from the city administration. The mayor sent it to the Board of Supervisors, who referred it to the finance committee. More than two weeks later, this committee reported that it could do nothing. It had no power to appropriate money except for specific objects designated by the state legislature. However, it was going to order more street work than usual. Its only other action was to appeal to the "generous nature" of wealthy citizens and ask them to assist the unemployed. One supervisor introduced a resolution calling a meeting of influential citizens to devise measures to help, but the resolution was tabled.[30]

A week later, on October 15, perhaps because of the increasing stridency of Kearney's speeches, the board reversed itself and approved a resolution authorizing the mayor and finance committee to meet with leading citizens and work out a plan. Two weeks later, the meeting took place, and the upshot was still another committee to make recommendations to relieve the distress of the poor. The general tone of the meeting was quite clear; those in attendance opposed spending money on charity but favored expenditures in return for labor "in some line not determined." A few days later, now six weeks after Kearney and Day had sent their letter, still another meeting was held at the mayor's office to conclude arrangements to help the needy and the unemployed.[31] A committee was appointed to receive subscriptions to help the destitute and distribute the contributions. It also announced plans to establish a labor exchange to find jobs for the unemployed. It is worth noting that no workingman, no leader of the WPC, was asked to participate in any of these meetings or in the formulation of any of these plans. As a result, there was no dialogue between the party and the city and no possibility for the WPC to state its positions or its demands formally.

In the meantime, the attitude of the city's establishment toward the Workingmen was becoming clear. At the Board of Supervisors' meeting on October 22, several supervisors criticized the Workingmen and revealed an utter lack of compassion for them. Supervisor Gibbs avowed that he had no sympathy for demagoguery and claimed that the leaders of the WPC did not represent the workingmen. In fact, the self-proclaimed leaders of the party belonged in prison. Supervisor Hayes asserted that the board had done everything possible to provide work, and Supervisor Strother seemed astounded by the attitude of the Workingmen. According to him, the board had been "an exceedingly good friend" to the working class, and they had now shown themselves to be very ungrateful.[32]

While the city administration was spinning its wheels and sending the Workingmen's letter from one committee to another, Denis Kearney was becoming increasingly vociferous. In mid-October, the *Chronicle* commented on his style for the first time and chastised the party. Although the newspaper acknowledged the rights of speech and assembly, it also warned that men who "use indecent or vile language" were subject to arrest and punishment. If they incited "the people to acts of riot and violence," they could be "held to account in the Courts, and certainly ought to be put down by public opinion."[33] Official San Francisco had begun instructing the Workingmen in proper political behavior.

Lessons became more frequent at the end of the month, particularly after the meeting atop Nob Hill. The *Bulletin*, the *Chronicle*, and the *Examiner* all printed strong editorials attacking Kearney's speech and exhorting the Workingmen to behave. On October 30, both the *Chronicle* and the *Examiner* told the Workingmen to stay in their place. According to the former, the intent of the meeting was "mischievous," its location "inconvenient," and its purpose "intimidation." The newspaper recalled that it had "already advised the workingmen as to their proper course in securing justice. It can only be through legislation. Violence of any kind will not subserve their purpose." The *Examiner* concurred. The meeting of "so-called workingmen . . . at a place where no meeting of the kind ought ever to have been held" was more an act of defiance or threat than anything else. Although the newspaper claimed to have always supported workingmen, it would not "palliate or vindicate" violence or lawlessness. It warned the Workingmen that their worst enemies were those who advocated violence. From now on, it advised them to meet at suitable places where they would not be considered a menace.[34] In other words, they should stay where they belonged and behave peaceably.

During the next few days, the tone of the editorials themselves became menacing as they advised not only the Workingmen but also the city government. According to the *Bulletin*, the time had come when the city had to choose between the "reign of hoodlums, incendiaries, and murderers, and a government of order protected by law." It recommended that Kearney and his henchmen be arrested forthwith.

> The sooner the hand of authority is laid upon them the better. They have done their best to encourage incendiarism and riot. As far as was possible, they have put in jeopardy the peace of the entire city. The conduct of these men is not only dangerous, but it is criminal in this, that it openly encourages defiance of authority and law. The attempt to organize the vicious elements of the city into an open warfare against property and personal safety ought to be arrested at once.[35]

The *Chronicle* seconded these sentiments, proclaiming that the

> time has arrived to interpose a barrier to the insolent progress of these would-be assassins, and prevent any dangers that might arise from a further extension of public leniency. The evil . . . has assumed such proportions as to seriously menace public safety, and fearless and decisive action on the part of our Municipal Authorities is now imperatively required. The in-

stant arrest of the leading agitators, their incarceration and their early trial and conviction for the gross offenses they have been guilty of, is what the peace-loving citizens of San Francisco demand.[36]

These demands for official action had an immediate effect. Mayor Bryant "sent for" Kearney, Day, and others "and treated them to some cool advice as to their incendiary utterances." Later the same day, the mayor met with city, municipal, criminal, police, and county judges along with the district attorney and chief of police—to plot strategy. Their game plan became clear a day or two later. On November 3, Kearney and other party leaders were arrested, charged with using language "having a tendency to cause a breach of peace."[37]

When Kearney was arraigned, he was in for a surprise. Bail was set at $12,000 even though the maximum fine, if he was convicted on all charges, was only $2,000. When his attorney asked for a reduction, the request was denied. Kearney sat in jail for five days, unable to post bond. Finally, on November 8, his supporters scraped together the required sum. But police authorities were on the alert. "No sooner were the four bonds prepared than three more warrants were served on him . . . with the bail fixed at $3,000 in each case."[38] Kearney was back in the slammer, needing another $9,000 to regain his freedom. The municipal authorities were sending a heavy-handed message about the kind of behavior they would tolerate.

The press exulted. The *Chronicle* believed that the arrests were having a positive effect on the city and restraining the level of protest. It hoped that "better and wiser men may eventually come to the front and convert what was originally intended as an incendiary crusade into an orderly and well-conducted political movement." The *Examiner* chimed in, asserting that the arrests had been made at a most opportune time and had broken the back of the movement. The police had swept boldly into meetings and fearlessly seized party leaders. Although the WPC claimed to have thousands of members, its leaders languished in prison, unable to raise bail. This was the proper "fate of those who play Jack Cade." It behooved all law-loving, peaceful, and orderly workingmen to cease attending. "The crisis has passed. The peace will be maintained."[39]

Now Archbishop Alemany added his voice to the chorus of teachers instructing the workingmen in what they should, and should not, do.

He sent a circular letter to every priest in the city and ordered them to read it from the pulpit on the following Sunday. It was, he said, "our duty to keep away from secret organizations calculated to endanger the peace of society." Many had allowed themselves "to be misguided and enrolled in associations led by irresponsible men for evil purposes— the disturbance of the peace, the destruction of property and life, and the establishing of anarchy." This kind of behavior would "entail much suffering and misery, violent deaths and a train of grievous ca-lamities." It was "a grievous sin against God to countenance such dis-turbances of the peace," and the good archbishop requested his flock "to join no secret societies, *and to abstain from meetings incentive to dis-turbance,* bearing in mind that God is a God of peace and not of anar-chy and sedition."[40]

For two months, Kearney and the other WPC leaders had been counseling San Francisco's Workingmen not to use violence, to be-have peacefully, and to form a political party. The men had listened, difficult as it must have been, and had discarded traditional modes of action, always keeping riot in reserve if their demands were not met. But city officials had not understood what was happening, and so they now intervened, throwing party leaders in prison and setting unrea-sonable bail. The archbishop had loudly seconded newspaper attacks. Surely this was the time for Workingmen to act, to throw down their placards and raise up their rifles. They did neither.

They did not resume rioting because Denis Kearney and other WPC leaders commanded them not to, and their failure to return to the barricades indicates how far Kearney had taken them down the road leading away from crowd to party. An extraordinary scene played itself out the night of his arrest. That afternoon, the police had come to Kearney's house to apprehend him, but they inadvertently nabbed his brother Daniel. Consequently, Kearney expected his arrest, and he told a crowd of followers what was going to happen. More important, he also told them what to do. Each newspaper gave a slightly different account of what ensued, but they all agreed on the outcome. The Workingmen accepted Kearney's arrest with no attempt at violence, no thought of a heroic rescue. The version in the *Examiner* had Kear-ney telling his men that if he was arrested, they should "do nothing rash, but hear me out, and I'll stand trial, and see whether these bloodhounds can drag the workingmen down." When the police came, he submitted quietly, the Workingmen obeyed him, and the officers led him away.[41]

The *Bulletin*'s account resembled the *Examiner*'s. Kearney told his followers to commit no overt act when he was arrested, and they complied. There was "no sign of any desire to do violence to anyone." Day mounted the podium, and he told the men "to sustain the laws of the country." He assumed a style of rhetoric similar to that of Kearney, telling the men that it was not yet time to explode.

> Truly it has been said that we are on a volcano. Its craters are in every city of the United States, and when one breaks out, all will burst forth. The capitalists want to be secure; let them have some feeling for the workingman. If not, this great social fabric will fail. . . . Unless we have redress, this warfare will grow hotter and hotter, until the people resort to the last means of sustaining their rights. We will stop this agitation only when we no longer have breath to utter our feelings.[42]

Of all the accounts of Kearney's arrest, the *Chronicle*'s was the most dramatic (and perhaps the most dramatized). Maybe the *Chronicle* was playing to the passions of the crowd, and maybe it was the most accurate. On several occasions, Kearney claimed that it alone printed his speeches accurately. In any event, the basic story is the same, even if the details differ in intensity. It reported that the agitator told his audience to "do nothing outside the law" if he was arrested. If he was bailed out, he wanted them to put him "at the head of 50,000 men," and they would "astonish these aristocrats" with their "brilliant parade." By this account, the crowd rushed to his rescue when the police arrived, but Kearney exhorted them, "Back, back, boys, back and keep cool! Let the law take its course. Don't fear for me. I am all right." Total calm prevailed.[43]

A similar situation developed when John G. Day and H. L. Knight were arrested the next night. Day's arrest occurred at the start of a meeting and apparently caused little uproar, although the assembly was meeting under unusually difficult circumstances. Later on, when the police returned for Knight, the response was different. According to the *Bulletin*, the crowd roared and hissed. The *Examiner* characterized the mood as "pandemonium." Both newspapers agreed that another party leader, Thomas Bates, restored order. He commanded the crowd to sit down and obey the law, and they complied. Like Kearney and Day, Bates understood the way to choose and use his words. The next night, he delivered two speeches, and they contained the same message; obey the law now, then we'll see. In his first appearance, he attacked incendiarism and said he would kill any man who threatened his property. He told his audience that many members of the party had property worth $10,000 to $50,000, and if anyone started talking about the destruction of property, these men would turn against them. It was essential to respect the law. Later, he himself was arrested, and the officer charged him with saying: "We have a law—a system of laws—brought about by corruption, and we want a change. I say we can have it, and I say by the great God we will have it. We will have it if we have to fight until h—l freezes over."[44]

When the cases against party leaders reached court, Judge Robert Ferral dismissed them on a technicality. He ruled that the Board of Supervisors had not properly passed the law under which the men were arrested because it had not been published the requisite number of days before the final vote was taken.[45]

But the police immediately arrested the defendants again, and a hearing was held to determine if there was sufficient evidence to bind them over to a grand jury on a charge of riot. In summing up his case, prosecuting attorney Delos Lake called Kearney a "second Rienzi" and asked, "What despotism would be worse than that in which an ill-educated fellow like Kearney was the moving power?" He read long sections from *Henry VI* and compared Kearney to Jack Cade. Finally, he proclaimed Kearney mad and declared that his "species of insanity" would be "better cured in the County Jail than in a lunatic asylum."[46]

Judge Ferral took the case under advisement and then issued his opinion. He began by quoting the definition of riot: "Any use of force or violence, disturbing the public peace, or any threat to use such force or violence, if accompanied by immediate power of execution, by two or more persons acting together, and without authority of law, is a riot." He continued by saying that he had investigated all the legal authorities to the best of his ability but that he had "been unable to find any authority which goes so far as to say that a public meeting at any particular place, unaccompanied by the display of weapons, where neither life nor property is immediately assailed, and where the only noises are the cheers of the audience in approval of the speakers, would be a riot either at common law or under the statute." Therefore, he was dismissing the charge.[47]

Now, he too lectured the defendants and explained the limits of acceptable legal behavior. He wanted them to understand that free speech was not "a license to say whatever one pleases, regardless of the rights and feelings of others." No one had the right to advise the commission of a crime or to incite riot and bloodshed. Anyone who did would be punished.

> High-handed violence in this country is a crime against free government and a reproach to a self-governing people. It appeals to the basest passions and the worst elements in the community, and robs the cause itself of the respect and sympathy of the law-abiding citizens. United action, intelligent co-operation, strong arguments, and dispassionate language, on the other hand, never fail in a good cause.[48]

Kearney and his colleagues were free, and the judge had tried to delimit the boundaries of proper behavior. Unfortunately, the Board of Supervisors was not satisfied with these judicial proceedings. They enacted the infamous gag law, which made it

> unlawful for any person, by word, or act, or deed, or by word, language, or expression, oral, written, or printed, to advise, advocate, encourage, incite, ask, order, request, counsel, solicit, endeavor to induce or persuade, state, suggest, or propose to another or others, or commit or cause to be committed, any felony, misdemeanor or crime, or public offense whatsoever, then or at any future time, or indefinite time, or upon the occurrence or non-occurrence of any event or fact, or upon the compliance or non-compliance by any person or persons, or associations or corporations with any term or condition, or upon the performance of any act or deed.[49]

The Workingmen saw Kearney's arrest, his subsequent trial and acquittal, and the passage of the gag law as susceptible of two contradictory interpretations. The events associated with the trial seemed to suggest that there was no grand conspiracy to destroy freedom and liberty, that formal institutions were functioning properly, and that people could be confident that governmental processes had not been compromised. But the enactment of a law abridging freedom of speech indicated just the opposite, that there was in fact a great assault on liberty and that freedom had to be resurrected and secured. The cavalier treatment of the party and its members convinced many San Franciscans that WPC theories were correct, and citizens flocked to join in record numbers. Frank Roney claimed that he signed up to protest the denial of fundamental liberties.[50] The party had now become a movement to protect the civil rights of all Americans.

But the Board of Supervisors' attack on basic liberties also suggested that the new methods of political behavior might not be enough and that a reversion to crowd tactics might be in order. Immediately after the release of Kearney and company from jail, the WPC entered a new phase of its history; it ceased to talk and began to act. And the variety and nature of its actions most clearly reveal its transition between crowd and party, its movement from bullets to ballots.

11. From Crowd . . .

Between Kearney's release from jail and the party's demise less than three years later, the WPC displayed a fascinating duality of behavior. In some ways, its conduct and tactics resembled the traditional crowd. It held mass meetings and demonstrations; its leaders delivered fiery harangues. The party paraded through the streets of San Francisco. Perhaps most important, it attempted to recreate those horizontal and vertical linkages that had characterized preindustrial society, linkages that were quickly becoming outmoded in the modern industrial world. Therefore, it simultaneously served as a church, lodge, fraternal organization, and mutual aid association. At the same time that the WPC wanted to reconstruct a sense of community among the working class, it also hoped to restore the easy feeling of camaraderie that had once existed between the people and their leaders.

Meanwhile, the WPC behaved in ways that were indistinguishable from the popular political parties of the day. The WPC created a hierarchical organization, campaigned for support, and urged its adherents to become naturalized and register to vote. It participated in electoral politics, elected municipal and state officials, and worked to revise California's constitution.

The Workingmen's Party of California was a transitional form of political protest, helping its members abandon older, no longer acceptable ways of expressing dissatisfaction and begin to use newer, institutional politics. The crowd, as a form of political behavior, had ceased to exist when its members were allowed, encouraged, and finally forced to participate in electoral politics in order to protest. If it stretches the point to say that political parties evolved from the crowd (after all, organized parties existed before the demise of the crowd), it is not too much to say that the crowd led its members into and merged them with the party.

One of the WPC's most important crowd-like activities was its great parade on Thanksgiving Day 1877, less than two weeks after Kearney and his fellows were released from jail. According to Rudé, parading was as typical of preindustrial crowds as "the resort to natural justice," and Susan Davis has shown that nineteenth-century American urban parades were "political acts" meant to build, maintain, and confront power relations. "In the nineteenth-century city, parades were used to define what society was or might be."[1]

The Workingmen began to think about a tremendous procession through the city shortly after they had established the WPC. As early as mid-September, the party was considering a demonstration of workingmen and trades organizations, and it planned to take "every precaution . . . to prevent the participation of disorderly disposed persons." This prospect so terrified the Chronicle that it attacked the proposal and recommended that every thinking person reject it. "No possible good" could come from the demonstration, and it might incite the "vicious element" of the city to attack Chinese laundries once again. Nevertheless, a month later Kearney announced that the party would definitely parade through downtown on Thanksgiving.[2]

No one laid any concrete plans until after Kearney's release from jail, and then the entire party turned its attention to the project. For days, the party and its leaders prepared. Each ward club planned to march separately, and many made elaborate arrangements. They appointed committees to supervise banners, music, and mottoes. They hired bands and constructed floats. But making these plans raised important questions. Should the aides of grand marshal Kearney walk or ride on horseback? The party decided that only Kearney should ride and that other men "should not spend their hard-earned savings to ride like aristocrats." Should there be bands in the parade? If there were, would they diminish the complaint of poverty? The response was clear; bands were in. Should flags and drums be draped in mourning to symbolize the death of freedom, as Kearney suggested? The answer was a resounding no. After all, the Workingmen bore no responsibility for the crisis in the country.[3]

On the eve of the parade, the party's executive committee took care of last-minute details. Aides and assistants besieged Kearney with questions and suggestions. Notices urging decorum were sent to all divisions, and every man was appointed a committee of one to preserve order. After a mild disagreement, it was decided that Kearney should wear a white rosette faced in scarlet. Other marshals and aides would simply have badges bearing their respective titles.[4]

The day of the parade was crisp and clear, and a huge throng of Workingmen gathered in the early hours of the morning. The procession began at the corner of Tenth and Brannan streets at precisely ten o'clock. Thousands of marchers advanced briskly and orderly through the streets, singing songs, bearing banners, and waving flags. Among the delegations, the Eleventh Ward Club was especially visible, and its contingent provided rare evidence that children were involved in WPC activities. Four hundred men marched, and forty of their sons accompanied them, carrying pickets, signs, and banners. "We Want a Press Free and Honest" and "We Want a New Deal All Around" typified the slogans. A squadron of boys preceded the club members and supported an immense, painted transparency. One side showed the factories, workshops, and products of the Pacific Coast. On a wharf in front of one factory, a knot of Workingmen bade farewell to the last Orientals in California. Laden with luggage, the coolies embarked for China. The other side of the transparency bore a picture of George Washington and was emblazoned with the rallying cries "We Uphold the Dignity of Labor" and "Workingmen to the Front! In Your Hands Rests the Future." After a march of several miles, the cavalcade arrived at the sandlots, where the paraders listened to addresses, heard poems, and sang songs.[5] Days of fevered planning had culminated in a great parade, and San Francisco's Workingmen, once a mass of faceless men, had emerged from anonymity to proclaim themselves an integral part of the city's life.

The parade forced the strength and power of the Workingmen on the city, but it also revealed the dual nature of the party to astute observers. H. L. Knight, the party's vice president, understood that the WPC could act like a crowd or act like a party depending on its mood and the needs of the moment. Just after the parade, he explained the party's precise character to the rest of the city. As he put it, the parade demonstrated that the Workingmen could be orderly when they chose but that they could take it "rough-and-tumble" with anybody in the world.[6]

The party's mass public meetings, held every Sunday afternoon on the vacant sandlots across from the new city hall, demonstrated the same duality. On the one hand, they became gay and festive, with the atmosphere of a carnival. The large crowds attracted refreshment booths that created "the atmosphere of a Centennial exhibition." A cartoon in San Francisco's weekly *Wasp* depicting one of the party's mass meetings was entitled "The Latest Phase of American Politics— A Sunday Matinee on the Sand-Lot," as if the meeting were political theater. Among the enormous throng listening to Kearney, the drawing depicted hucksters of fruits and vegetables, and men selling cigars, much like candy-choppers in a theater. But the most fascinating aspect of the scene was the social mix. Intermingled with Workingmen were ladies with parasols. Next to laborers wearing broad-brimmed slouch hats or billycocks stood gentlemen in frock coats and derbies. At the back of the multitude, swells in top hats smoked cigars and escorted finely gowned ladies. One elegant couple sat in a buggy, he with topper and cigar, she with parasol and chapeau.[7]

On the other hand, party leaders used these gatherings as a forum for bombastic declamations. In early December, William Wellock advised the Workingmen to learn to shoot quail, a seemingly innocuous suggestion but one with hidden meanings. Two days later, he repeated his advice, explaining "to a constantly cheering and laughing audience" his tactics for encounters with "flocks of quail which are so abundant in this state. This bird is a good one to make war on being a greedy and voracious one, eating more than it can digest." At another meeting the same day, he "did not think it necessary to explain his meaning about killing quail; the men probably saw it for themselves." It should have been obvious. "Some birds . . . had short tails, and some long, and it was for the Workingman to choose his own game."[8]

Kearney wasn't as subtle as Wellock, but he did continue to choose his tenses and his moods carefully. On one occasion, he declared that "when the Chinese question is settled, we can discuss whether it would be better to hang, shoot, or cut the capitalists to pieces." On another, he declared that "if the ballot fails, the bullet. That 'if' must come in. If the ballot fails, we are ready to use the bullet." On still another occasion, newspapers reported him asking his followers how many of them had muskets and urging them to arm themselves. Things had "gotten too hot." There was "a white heat" in San Francisco, and the men had to be ready when Kearney issued the call. "Learn to put a cartridge in, and learn to shoot it off. Let them interfere with us!"[9]

As usual, the city failed to recognize Kearney's use of the future and the conditional, despite his deliberate emphasis—and description became reality. On January 5, 1878, Kearney and other party leaders were indicted for rioting. Several days later, after posting bond, they were arrested again, this time for using language tending to cause a breach of the peace. By now, Kearney was correct. The city was in a white heat. Three regiments of the national guard were summoned to the armory and put on ready alert. A deputation of supervisors headed for Sacramento to persuade the state legislature to pass its own gag law.[10] Meanwhile, Mayor Bryant took matters into his own hands and forbade public assemblies.

> Whereas, persons assemble in this city and county and threaten to commit offenses against the property and lives of the inhabitants, and such assemblies are not held for any lawful purpose, but to create disturbances, in which public offenses may be committed:
>
> Now . . . I do hereby declare that such assemblies are unlawful and will not be permitted, but will be dispersed, and all persons composing them and taking part in their proceedings will be arrested. And I advise all persons to stay away from such meetings and not be present as spectators from curiosity or any other idle motive, for such attendance encourages those engaged in promoting disturbances, interferes with the operations of those who seek to keep the peace, and may result in harm to the innocent as well as the guilty.
>
> I trust that the men who guide these assemblies will not compel the use of force in securing obedience to law. But I shall not shrink from using all the power at my command to preserve the peace of the city and county. Such assemblies, wherever held, in halls, upon the streets, or on sand-lots, will be suppressed, and the supremacy of law and order resolutely maintained.[11]

The city's continued hysterical reaction to the bluster of Kearney and company may have resulted, at least partly, from another of the party's activities—the formation of military companies. To the city, these companies posed a clear threat to peace and safety. To Wellock, their sponsor, the companies would create a sense of fellowship and community. To him, uniforms, rifle practice, and precision drill would be visible symbols of membership in the WPC and a source of pride. Wellock initially proposed that each ward club appoint a drill sergeant to teach the men to march properly, look sharp on ceremonial occasions, and provide a bodyguard for Kearney, but this simple idea soon evolved into the complex project of organizing military companies in each ward. By January, three wards had set up squadrons, and several others had begun to plan. Kearney became commander-in-chief of all the companies and bore the impressive title, lieutenant-general. His staff contained an adjutant and three other officers. Each individual squad had a captain, first and second lieutenants, sergeant, and corporal. The various platoons were lettered according to a complicated system but were commonly referred to by nicknames. One was known as the True Blues and another as the Independent Rifles.[12]

Properly equipping these irregulars presented serious financial problems. Many men had been out of work for so long that they could barely afford necessities, and belonging to a military company took money. One needed the official uniform of jet black pants, powder blue shirt, and fatigue cap. Arms cost even more. Springfield rifles with bayonets were the most desired weapon, but several companies had only muskets. Others satisfied themselves with broomsticks. The president of one club asked the entire group to subsidize the militiamen, but the Committee on Processions decided that each man had to provide for himself. The military companies therefore remained an elite to which every man aspired: the Praetorian Guard of the WPC.[13]

Despite the city's fear, there is another way of conceiving the military companies. They fit into a well-established tradition in the city. In 1876, San Francisco had fifteen independent military organizations with more than a thousand members. The most famous was the Sumner Light Guard, particularly noted for its crack rifle team. The Sumners were also a popular social organization, with many prominent members who gave frequent parties. They were said to be "young, buoyant of spirit, and nothing was more enjoyable to them than a mirthful frolic." San Franciscans considered it "a mark of distinction to receive an invitation to a ball or party conducted under [its] auspices."[14]

One crucial difference distinguished the military companies of the WPC from organizations like the Sumner Light Guard—their institutional context. The guard was almost certainly an independent organization whose membership did not significantly overlap with that of any other group. To the contrary, the military companies of the WPC were part of an entire community that the larger organization was attempting to create. John Bohstedt has argued that crowds developed in societies characterized by tight vertical and horizontal social linkages, linkages that had weakened and broken in the modern industrial city. According to Bohstedt, the breaking of those bonds had substantially contributed to the decline of the crowd.[15] In San Francisco, the WPC was trying to restore those bonds, to forge tighter links among its members, as well as between its members and the city's official leaders. It was trying to restore the kind of traditional society that many of its members wanted.

In doing so, the WPC performed the roles of a multitude of organizations that were becoming differentiated in modern society. It served as a social network and a church. It functioned as a voluntary organization and a mutual aid society. It looked out for the economic needs of its members. Military companies were only one aspect of a community structure meant to encompass the lives of the Workingmen. The significance of these organizations resulted as much from the community structure they were meant to create as from their overt objects. The key to understanding this aspect of the WPC is to recognize that, unlike voluntary associations in a modern society, the WPC did not confine itself to a single aspect of life. It tried to look after every phase of its members' world. Once again, it straddled the boundary between preindustrial and modern.

In this regard, the WPC was not unique and resembled movements in other cities. The United Labor Party in Cincinnati enabled people to be part of a larger organization, provided an outlet for religious energies, looked after the obligations of citizenship, and afforded opportunities for leisure. Likewise, Detroit's Independent Labor Party meant to do more than change the terms of employment and alter the relationships between employers and employees. It meant to produce political changes and reform society as a whole. It provided an entire community subculture that offered the services of a union, saloons, the press, and leisure-time activities.[16]

Those who joined the WPC entered an active and vital world. If a man desired, he could literally allow the party to dominate his life. Between September 1877 and June 1878, various affiliates held more than five hundred meetings.[17] Attendance ranged from a handful to thousands, and a member could attend several gatherings a week. He could spend Sunday afternoons at the mass meetings and go to his weekly ward club meeting one night. If he wanted to be more active, he could become an officer or serve on a committee. Each ward club boasted permanent officers and an executive council, and nearly every club created smaller groups to manage its internal affairs. It might set up membership, music, or social committees. Maybe the members wanted a committee to publish lists of everyone in the ward who employed Chinese. In some wards, committee proliferation necessitated a committee to decide which new committees to appoint![18]

These business meetings were only a small part of the organization's activities; and it also conducted a vigorous social life. Ward clubs sponsored entertainments, balls, and picnics such as an excursion to the Cremorne Gardens in Martinez. The guests took a steamer from the Clay Street wharf early in the morning and enjoyed dancing and other amusements on board. At the park, they enjoyed a full program of games and contests for which they could win prizes. The second-best woman round-dancer received a three-dollar French corset, and a meerschaum pipe went to the best ticket seller. There were several gold pieces, perfume, pillows, buttons, and hose. Tickets, including roundtrip transportation and admission, were one dollar. Children under twelve were admitted free.[19]

Various ward clubs also sponsored "entertainments." One such affair attracted nearly a thousand guests to Union Hall and was termed a "dignified" and "stimulating" evening. After short speeches by party leaders, the performance began. One man rendered a solo basso, and a woman presented a comic number. Then Flora Neal sang, and Tom Bates's rendition of "Shamus O'Brien" brought tears to the eyes of all.

The highlight of the evening was "a laughable farce entitled 'The Workingmen's Riot on Nob Hill,'" in which the Crocker family was "burlesqued." The event raised $350 and was described as a "great success."[20]

At the same time that the WPC looked out for its members' social lives, it also cared for their economic well-being. Perhaps the most critical problems in San Francisco were poverty and unemployment, so the WPC attempted to solve the economic crisis. One of its programs was establishing independent businesses. The idea of setting up laundries particularly appealed to party members as a way of simultaneously creating jobs and attacking the Chinese. In 1878, the WPC founded several laundries on a cooperative basis. One club sold 1,500 shares of stock in a washhouse at one dollar a share. Another formed a White Laundrymen's Association, leased a lot, and put up a building. The business became a going concern and quickly showed a profit. The enterprises did so well that Kearney (unsuccessfully) asked James Flood for $100,000 to establish cooperative laundries throughout the city.[21]

Of course, the Workingmen's Party knew that a few laundries could not end unemployment in San Francisco, so it tried other tactics as well. It sent delegations to the mayor and Board of Supervisors asking them to create public works projects such as spending $75,000 to fill Mission Creek. Other groups requested businessmen to discharge their Chinese employees. At every sandlot meeting, the party posted a list of firms that hired Chinese workers and asked its members to boycott them. Each issue of The Open Letter, the party's newspaper, published the names of blacklisted companies. The party also tried to help its members help themselves. In December 1877 it established a free labor exchange to help unemployed white men and women locate jobs. The party also recognized that some San Franciscans needed immediate assistance, and it raised money for the benefit of impoverished members and their families. One club donated $54 to a destitute widow, and another woman received $65 to open a business.[22]

These charitable activities show that the Workingmen no longer felt confident about the ability of organized religion to provide benevolence. If they had, there would have been no need for the WPC to dispense it. But traditional churches had generally ceased to provide adequately for the spiritual needs of Workingmen, who increasingly relied on the WPC for services customarily provided by churches. As early as November 1877, party leaders, especially William Wellock, were making anticlerical speeches, and on the fifth of that month he proclaimed the church and the press responsible for the Workingmen's troubles. He declared Christianity "a cloak" for any man who wanted to become a thief.[23]

An incident in April 1878 reveals the growing estrangement between Irish Workingmen and the Catholic church. Joseph Sadoc Alemany, the archbishop of San Francisco, who had previously denounced the July rioters and Denis Kearney, publicly attacked the WPC and urged all Catholics to withdraw from the party. His pastoral letter outraged WPC members. One club passed a resolution requesting the "Reverend Archbishop to look after his spiritual affairs and not this movement of ours." Kearney was especially incensed and announced that he never permitted bishops or priests to interfere in his politics. The WPC was not a religious movement, a German movement, or a Catholic movement. It was, he stressed, a movement of honest American workingmen. In the end, Alemany's pressure had no noticeable effect.[24]

Because so many workingmen no longer found traditional religious institutions meaningful, many of them turned to the WPC for spiritual guidance. They found more satisfaction in the teachings of two party leaders, Wellock and Isaac Kalloch, than they did in those of orthodox ministers. By 1878 the WPC began developing religious overtones.

Wellock, the party's vice president, claimed to have been an itinerant preacher in England and now styled himself an expounder of the gospel. He became known as Parson Wellock and delivered sermons rather than speeches.[25] He began his lessons with biblical quotations and interpreted Scripture according to the needs of the Workingmen. When Wellock read in the Bible, "Whatsoever riches a man has got, that shall he be answerable for, as he himself is only a steward," he interpreted it to mean that selfish men would have to answer to God. God would bring the rich to judgment "before this great reckoning to which the mass of people belong." On another occasion, Wellock used the text, "The earth is the Lord's and the fullness thereof." He continued by quoting the biblical punishment for men who defiled the earth and trod upon the good, the true, the pure, and the beautiful— their heads would be taken off and placed before the sun. Yet another time, he asked the biblical question, "Ye serpents, ye generation of vipers, how shall ye escape the damnation of Hell?" His answers made it quite clear that land-grabbers would not.[26]

The press severely criticized Wellock's interpretation of the Bible, and the WPC replied by indicting organized religion. Workingmen were not interested in hearing San Francisco ministers unless they "purged their societies from the old leaven of slavery, pride, hypocrisy, and deceit." Until then, Denis Kearney would "draw onto the Sand Lots five times the number on the Sabbath that the most eloquent clergyman could call into . . . church." As long as the ministers preached politics against the Workingmen, their leaders planned to deliver "frequent political sermons in the Sand Lots on Sunday."[27]

The religious aspect of the WPC intensified dramatically on July 4, 1878, when Isaac Kalloch, one of San Francisco's most prominent ministers, suddenly announced his support for the party. Kalloch had arrived in the city three years before as spiritual leader of Metropolitan Temple, the largest Baptist church in America. Located at Fifth and Jessie streets, its main auditorium had three thousand seats, and a smaller hall upstairs could accommodate another thousand. However, Metropolitan Temple differed from other churches in the city, and Kalloch's beliefs diverged radically from those of most other San Francisco clergymen. He installed libraries, reading rooms, gymnasiums, day nurseries, and sewing and manual-training courses. His church acquired a modern, liberal reputation, as Kalloch accepted Darwinian theories and questioned the infallibility of Scripture. Several years before, Kalloch had expressed his ideas about contemporary religion when he "inveighed against fashionable churches" and called them "toys for grown-up people as much as a carriage or a box at the opera." He also criticized the "false system of respecting persons in a church for the sake of their wealth, position, or good clothes," and he deplored "the various methods adopted to exclude the poor from the churches." He believed that there should be "free churches for poor and rich alike" where they could meet on the same footing.[28]

Now Kalloch announced his conversion to Kearneyism. In his Independence Day sermon, he prayed "that capital may respect the rights of labor . . . that the Chinese may go . . . that the grasping spirit of remorseless monopoly may be stayed." As a result, Workingmen began flocking to his church, and its halls became packed as never before. Kalloch became one of the party's most powerful leaders, and a year later the WPC nominated and elected him mayor of San Francisco.[29]

The extraordinary range of WPC activities made it desirable for the party to have a permanent home, a place where all these activities could be conducted and the members gather. One Sunday in December 1877, Wellock announced plans for a Workingmen's Temple. An anonymous benefactor had donated the land, another had volunteered to do the plumbing and gasfitting free, and the United Carpenters had offered to construct the building gratis. Sixteen thousand tickets would be sold to raise money for materials, and a five-man committee was appointed to oversee the project. Ten days later, its chairman proudly announced that the building would be completed by Washington's birthday and that a grand ball was being planned to celebrate the event.[30]

Wellock and the Workingmen had several reasons for wanting their own building. For one thing, they could never find enough meeting places; their many gatherings created a real space problem. Furthermore, many halls and rooms were unavailable because proprietors feared the party. Wellock thought that a temple would alleviate the shortage of meeting space, but he also viewed the structure as a clubhouse where members could improve themselves. Wellock thought that having their own building would enable the Workingmen to exercise the right of free speech and "elevate the character." He argued that people who think, reason, and present their thoughts to others improve their mental capacity and benefit their associates. Therefore, he presented the proposal.[31]

The WPC wanted to restore the bonds of preindustrial society, to recreate the holistic, organic sense that had been lost during urbanization and industrialization. It wanted to make its members into a community. In order to do so, it formed military companies, created a rich social life, looked out for the economic well-being of Workingmen, took on the character of a church, and made plans to construct a temple.

But the party hoped to do more than recreate the ties that had historically united the lower classes internally. It also hoped to restore the vertical ties that had linked the lower and upper classes. On November 16, Wellock asserted the unity of society and denied the existence of class conflict. Capital and labor were dependent on each other for their existence, and consequently the workingmen's movement would not include just "workingmen." Storekeepers worked just as hard, although their labor was of the brain and not the hands. "But the brain of the merchant" was "useless without hands to help it, and the hands of the workingmen" were "alike useless without the assistance of the brain, so that the middle classes . . . have common cause with us." He invited the middle classes to join the party and urged storekeepers, college graduates, and people of refinement to aid the party and bring true liberty to all American citizens. "If such men proved worthier of the trust, then the present leaders would step down but not out, would fall into the ranks, and, throwing away narrow prejudices, would conquer or die in the strife."[32]

The Workingmen actually wanted to be led by society's traditional leaders, wanted them to assume their historic role. Kearney and Knight made this abundantly clear when they planned the Thanksgiving Day parade. Kearney invited the governor, the mayor, all city officials, the pulpit, and the press to march at the head of the parade. Knight sent a letter to the Board of Supervisors inviting them to march with the Workingmen.[33] The party did not want to destroy traditional society, it wanted to return to a form of society that it knew and understood. The problem was not with the structure of society, it was with the perversion of society by evildoers, and the party wanted to cleanse and purify it. To do so, it adopted many forms of action characteristic of the crowd, and it also tried to recreate the social structure that it knew and accepted. But it used other means as well.

12. . . . to Party

The Workingmen's Party of California was not just a crowd, it was also a political party composed of men not used to participating in formal institutional politics, of men more familiar with the barricade than the ballot box. But they were slowly moving out of the crowd and into the convention. They were being pushed by a society that no longer accepted the crowd, and they were being pulled by Denis Kearney, who could lead the crowd and determine its direction.

Kearney was a bridge crossing the gap between crowd and party, providing followers a passage from one kind of activity to another. But Kearney did not act alone. The WPC had other leaders, who had already crossed to the other side. Frank Roney represented those Workingmen who identified with organized labor and wanted the WPC to seek basic union goals. Before coming to San Francisco, he had been active in the iron molders' local in Omaha, and when he reached San Francisco in 1875 he joined the local and sent for his card. In later years, he helped organize the Seamen's Protective Union and the Trades Assembly of San Francisco. In 1885, he persuaded all the iron workers' organizations in the city to join the Federated Iron Trades Council and then became first president of the Trades and Labor Federation of the Pacific Coast. When the WPC established its own newspaper, Roney wanted it to support the union movement, and he headed a delegation that met with the directors of the newspaper. The editor agreed to go along philosophically but refused to pay union scale. The foreman "positively declined to have anything whatever to do with the union," and Denis Kearney declared himself "flatly opposed" to unions. In part, this conflict over unionism explains Roney's bitter fights with Kearney and his later attempt to organize a rival Workingmen's Party. In fact, Roney had little or no sympathy with Kearney or the principles of the WPC. He later wrote that he joined the party primarily as a means of protesting the denial of basic constitutional rights by the city's administration, and he claimed that many others joined for the same reason.[1]

Charles J. Beerstecher, not one of the party's best-known figures, differed from both Kearney and Roney. His father had participated in the German revolutions of 1848 and seems to have taught him the principles of socialism. In 1877 Beerstecher headed the German-speaking section of the Workingmen's Party of the United States in San Francisco. Like "practically all the members" of this organization, he soon allied himself with the WPC. In May 1878 at the party's state convention, he introduced a resolution recognizing "the Socialistic Workingmen's Party of the United States as a kindred organization, having for its purpose and end the emancipation of the Workingmen" and declaring "our brotherhood" with it. The party adopted the resolution, and that fall it elected Beerstecher a delegate to the state constitutional convention. A year later, its votes propelled him into the state Railroad Commission.[2]

Although most of San Francisco's workingmen were not ready for trades unionists like Roney or socialists like Beerstecher and felt more comfortable with Kearney and Wellock, they were prepared to hear them and include them in their movement, further indicating the organization's transitional nature. But the most important evidence that the WPC stood precisely at the point where crowd and party intersected was its political activity, contemporaneous with its crowd-like behavior. The party quickly turned its tremendous energy to electoral politics as well as mass demonstrations and meetings. Within a few months of its founding, it elected local officials in Alameda, Berkeley, San Leandro, and Redwood City, as well as in Nevada and Santa Cruz counties. However, none of these early victories compared in importance with the party's stunning success in electing delegates to the California Constitutional Convention of 1878.

In preparation for this election, the party began a naturalization and registration drive. It urged every immigrant to become a citizen and every member to register. In May 1878, when the party nominated candidates, it involved individual members as much as possible. Every branch club made nominations, which it submitted to the voters of the whole ward. They then chose a number of candidates proportional to the number of party members in the ward. The entire party ratified the selections at a mass meeting. Its intent was to "go back to the primitive simplicity of the founders of the government of the people, for the people, and by the people." [3]

A few months before the election of delegates, California's conservative press proclaimed that there would be only one issue in the election: Kearney and the WPC. Newspapers throughout the state called for the rejection of party labels and recommended the selection of a nonpartisan ticket to defeat the Workingmen. The *Alta* repeatedly urged a "Citizen's ticket, on which everybody opposed to the reign of Kearney could unite." The pressure for unity became so intense that it alarmed the Workingmen. One of their leaders warned that, unless they awoke, the constitutional convention would be "packed . . . by property-holders," and there would be a property qualification for voting. In May, after much squabbling, the Republicans and Democrats did unite to choose a nonpartisan slate. The lines were now clearly drawn. The election was to be a contest between the Workingmen on one side and everybody else on the other. [4]

After a heated campaign, election day finally arrived. In the end, the WPC carried San Francisco but not the state. Its candidates swept all ten of the city's senatorial districts for a total of thirty delegates, and its members elected twenty-two others throughout California. Altogether its fifty-two seats were about one-third of the convention, and the party's representatives played a major role in writing the new state constitution. [5]

In 1879 the WPC led the drive to ratify the new constitution, and it also elected a number of officials. Statewide, the party voted in eleven senators, seventeen assemblymen, and a railroad commissioner. Only Republicans outnumbered Workingmen in the legislature. In San Francisco itself, voters chose Workingmen to be mayor, sheriff, auditor, tax collector, treasurer, and district attorney. Party members also became attorney and counselor, public administrator, and surveyor. Moreover, the party elected several judges and a number of school directors. The WPC had become a major force in state and municipal politics. [6]

The provisions of the California constitution of 1879 also reveal the inherent duality of the WPC. On the face of it, this constitution seems to have embodied very little of the Workingmen's program. According to Henry George, "it was totally without any shadow of reform" that would "lessen social inequalities or purify politics." He could see little difference between it and the newer constitutions of other states. It was "anything but . . . communistic, for it entrenched vested rights—especially in land—more thoroughly than before." It levied a poll tax, disenfranchised many laborers, and introduced a property qualification to vote. It even prohibited public works as a way of providing employment. All-in-all, George thought that it "sacrificed the interests of the laboring classes . . . to what the land-owners regarded as their interests, while in other respects its changes . . . were out of the line of true reform." In short, the new constitution was "anything but a workingman's Constitution."[7]

Ever since, historians have concurred with George, and tried to explain why the Workingmen were so ineffective in the convention and why they achieved so few of their goals. The reply has generally been political naiveté and inability. The Workingmen's delegates were unfamiliar with politics and without any special ability, such as legal training, which qualified them to lead the convention. On the other hand, the "non-partisan group contained many of the best lawyers and shrewdest politicians in the state, and had . . . a high degree of ability in political engineering." Therefore, they dominated the meeting and blocked the Workingmen.[8]

However, this argument ignores the basic fact that Workingmen provided the major organized support for the new constitution and led the fight for ratification. They did so because the new constitution embodied the same mixture of forward- and backward-looking goals that they had been pursuing all along. At its heart, the California constitution of 1879 contained a commitment to property. The first section of the first article reiterated the inalienable rights of all men including "acquiring, possessing, and protecting property." The provisions in regard to land reflected almost perfectly the beliefs of the Workingmen: that everyone should own property and that property rights are sacred. This article, passed by a coalition of Workingmen and Grangers, ordered the legislature to "protect by law, from forced sale, a certain portion of the homestead and other property of all heads of families."

Then it declared that great landholders were against the public interest and should be discouraged. However, only "means not inconsistent with the rights of private property" should be used. Finally, the article declared that state lands suitable for farming should be distributed only to actual settlers in parcels not exceeding 320 acres.[9]

The new constitution, like the Workingmen, also opposed Chinese immigration. It forbade corporations and government agencies to employ Chinese and ordered the legislature "to discourage their immigration by all means within its power . . . and provide the necessary legislation to prohibit the introduction into this state of Chinese."

In general, California's new constitution preserved those political values and institutions that had been sanctified since the Revolution. The "Declaration of Rights" guaranteed, once again, religious freedom, the right of habeas corpus, and trial by jury. It promised freedom of the press and public assembly as well as protection from unjust search, unsubstantiated charges of treason, and ex post facto laws. In other words, many of the rights guaranteed by the federal Constitution were repeated. The structure of state government also followed that of the national: three branches, separation of powers, checks and balances.

In addition to all these provisions designed to preserve and protect the republic, the constitution of 1879 foreshadowed a new era, particularly in regard to corporations, railroads, and public utilities. The legislature was obligated to regulate and limit the prices charged by telegraph and gas corporations as well as the fees set for storage and wharfage. No corporation could issue stocks or bonds "except for money paid, labor done, or property actually received." Fictitious increases of stock or bonded indebtedness were prohibited, and new stocks or bonds could not be issued without shareholders' permission given publicly. All transportation companies were declared "subject to legislative control," and the constitution forbade such common practices as company officers supplying materials, issuing passes to state officials, and granting rebates and discounts to favored places and persons.

The Workingmen supported the constitution of 1879 because, like themselves, it looked into both the past and the future. After the document was ratified, the WPC praised itself. It had created an organization of "honest men, the most powerful . . . party . . . ever established in any state of the union." The WPC had won each of its fights while contending with "the power of wealth and unprincipled politicians." Nowhere in the world had "labor ever gained such a fight over tyrants and the oppression of the people." To Denis Kearney, ratification represented "a grand victory of the people." Every man who voted for the constitution was equally entitled to credit and deserved the gratitude of every Californian and every American. The supporters had recognized that "the new instrument . . . contained the seeds of prosperity for the state." They understood that "its acts . . . would bring justice, equality, and prosperity to the state, and peace, plenty, and sunshine to the firesides of the people."[10]

Two days later, the *Chronicle*, now supporting the WPC, explained how the constitution would benefit the state. It claimed that the "new Constitution . . . laid the foundation for a grand and glorious commonwealth." No longer would privileged classes exact unrestrained tribute from the people. Everyone would be "equal before the law" and receive "the full fruits of his industry." Equal taxation and freedom from monopoly meant "more room for expansion, better opportunities for growth, and brighter prospects to all honest people." The state's enormous resources would soon open "vast avenues to the workingman and capitalist, increasing the volume of trade for the common carrier and the merchant, yielding interest for the banker, making new homes for the people, and filling the land with happy hearts and smiling faces." The future of California was "grand and glorious."[11]

But the WPC did not survive to enjoy the future; it disappeared almost as rapidly as it arose. Never again did it achieve the electoral success of 1879, and by 1881 it had all but vanished. Very early, Lord Bryce argued that the party's demise was simply a swing of the political pendulum. Throughout the world the WPC was interpreted as a movement to destroy property rights and overturn the social order. At last, the people of California and San Francisco had become ashamed of themselves and returned to the traditional parties.[12]

Other historians have emphasized internal conflicts within the WPC rather than changed attitudes on the part of the electorate. In the winter of 1880, Denis Kearney went east on a political trip, and new leaders appeared in his absence. When Kearney returned, "he felt immediately obliged to enter into competition" with them. The resultant political jockeying and infighting contributed in large measure to the collapse of the party.[13]

Still other explanations of the party's disintegration emphasize external politics. Although the Workingmen had elected the mayor of San Francisco and many other city officials, not one of their candidates was elected to the Board of Supervisors. Frank Roney charged that a deal had been made to deny the party effective control of the city, though no proof has ever been offered.[14] In any event, the party now had to confront the realities of administering, rather than criticizing, the government. As difficult as this would have been under the best of circumstances, a divided administration in this context produced a powerless, paralyzed government. Ultimately, the council instituted impeachment proceedings against Mayor Isaac Kalloch. Although charges of malfeasance could not be proved, Kalloch's reputation and effectiveness were severely damaged.

The point is, once the Workingmen did gain power, they found it hard to use their positions effectively. Kalloch and the other WPC officeholders had no practical experience in politics and could not exercise effective control over the city. At the same time, they could be manipulated by other, shrewder politicians. Years later, Chris Buckley, who rebuilt the Democratic Party on the ruins of the WPC and became boss of the city, recalled how he had taken advantage of Kearney's ineptitude. In 1879 he struck a bargain with Denis whereby the WPC could support the Democratic candidates for national offices. In return, the Democrats would support WPC candidates for state and municipal posts. What Buckley realized, and Kearney did not, was that no municipal elections would be held in 1880 because of provisions in the new constitution. As a result, Workingmen went to the polls that fall and voted the Democratic ticket. They never returned to the WPC fold.[15]

All these accounts of the demise of the WPC contain some truth. But each of them overlooks a crucial fact: the nature of the Workingmen and the special set of social, political, and economic circumstances that produced the WPC. The Workingmen hung on the edge of the transition between one kind of political activity and another. Therefore, they acted in ways characteristic of both—like a crowd in some ways, a political party in others. Like the crowd, the WPC existed only to accomplish specific goals. Like the crowd, once it got what it wanted, it went home. After its members believed their work done, the WPC had no further purpose and disappeared.

Denis Kearney's address to the party when the constitution was ratified reveals this clearly. In his speech Kearney became nostalgic and sentimental, comparing the darkness of the past with the brilliance of the future. He told the newly elected delegates that they were the "ripe fruit of a great political harvest." The Workingmen had "sowed good seed and . . . reaped a bountiful harvest." They had "trusted God . . . would reward truth and honesty, and He . . . had not disappointed."[16]

Kearney asked his audience to think about the state of affairs when they began their agitation. He asked what their hopes had been, what their condition. "Darkness behind, blackness before and a growing misery" was the "actual condition" of the Workingmen. "No silver lining" shielded "the cloud of misery." The WPC emerged "in those stormy times" and held its first meetings "under the guns of assassins, led on by the police, officered by the servile tools of unscrupulous scoundrels." However, the party had forbearance and an admirable temper. It had prevailed and adopted a platform that was "the shibboleth of labor all over the world." It was the "Magna Charta of emancipated manhood."[17]

According to Kearney, the Workingmen had molded the constitutional convention "to their will." They deserved credit for all its good points and also for its ratification. Now, they were gathering to select candidates for office. Kearney cautioned the delegates to "deliberate . . . calmly and with fairness, but . . . fearlessly also." They had already "achieved undying renown," and Kearney charged them to complete their "heaven-born task." He commissioned them to "seize the entire government . . . in every department and throughout its various ramifications." If they did, "a new departure" would have been taken.[18]

Ten years later, Kearney explained very clearly why the WPC disappeared so quickly. He had just read *The American Commonwealth* by Lord Bryce and took issue with several points made there. He wrote the author to express his displeasure, and he challenged many comments including "since 1880 he [Kearney] has played no part in California politics" and "the movement fell as quickly as it rose." Kearney explained to Bryce that he had "stopped agitating after having shown the people their immense power and how it could be used." He said that the movement "stopped when I stopped, that was after accomplishing what we desired." Like so many other social and political coalitions, the WPC's very success finished it off. Once it had accomplished its primary goal, it could no longer hang together.[19]

In this regard, as in so many others, the WPC must be recognized as a clear transition between the crowd and the party, between two forms of political action rarely related to each other by historians. During the nineteenth century, as a democratic ideology became widespread in the United States, and as that ideology allowed political institutions to incorporate a larger proportion of the population, old forms of political behavior ceased to be acceptable. As people were expected, and allowed, to express political discontent through the formal institutions of organized politics, they were no longer permitted to form crowds. But they had yet to learn the ways of the party. They could not simply cease to behave as they always had. They could not simply leave the crowd and create the party. Therefore, they formed organizations that shared characteristics of both kinds of institutions. The WPC disappeared when it had completed its final task: politicizing its members into the culture of the party. When the WPC had trained its followers to act as members of a political party and not as members of a crowd, they had no further need of it, and the party collapsed.

Of course, the WPC is only a single example of this phenomenon, and to support these generalizations more fully, it would be desirable to have other instances. But we now know where to find them. To locate other examples of transitional crowd/parties, the search needs to center on the last crowd in a particular place. To find out what happened to the crowd, and especially how it flowed into the party, we need to study final crowds, their members, and their successive forms of political behavior.

Conclusion

Traditionally, when historians have studied civilization and its discontents, they have focused on three questions: the reasons for discontent, the demands made for recourse, and the degree of the protesters' success. But with few exceptions, they have not studied the forms of expression given to dissatisfaction. They have not typically asked why protesters behave in a certain way and express themselves in a particular fashion. Historians have frequently taken the behavior of the dissatisfied for granted. The major exception to these generalizations is the school of crowd historians exemplified in the first generation by George Rudé, Eric Hobsbawm, and Charles Tilly, and more recently by a group of younger historians too numerous to mention. In addition, there have been a few others who have analyzed a particular kind of protest behavior, such as Susan Davis, who has studied parades in an exemplary fashion. These, however, are the exceptions.

It is in this context that studying the Workingmen's Party of California increases our historical knowledge most fully. The reasons for discontent in San Francisco during the 1870s, although certainly worth studying for their own sake, parallel many of the reasons for discontent throughout the country in the nineteenth century—depression, economic change, racism, maldistribution of wealth, and frustrated ambitions. The demands of the WPC, although certainly important to its members and to a greater understanding of the history of San Francisco, resemble demands made by other popular movements late in the nineteenth century, including the Populists and the Progressives. Finally, in terms of success, the party's activities brought no long-lasting fundamental change to the social, political, or economic order of California, much less the United States.

But what the WPC does reveal clearly is the changing nature of the expression of discontent during the nineteenth century: the transition from crowd action and riot to formal institutional parties and politics. In July 1877, San Franciscans erupted into three nights of violence to express their dissatisfaction with conditions in the city; and less than two months later they formed a new organization to voice their discontent. The transition from bullets to ballots in San Francisco that year tells us much about how dissatisfied Americans expressed themselves in the nineteenth century.

It also raises a new set of questions for political historians. Usually, when they study the development of political institutions in the nineteenth century, especially democratic political institutions, they study ideology and its acceptance. When they study parties and politics, they tend to study leadership and structure, not mobilization, recruitment, and socialization. Rarely do they analyze how people learned to accept and use new political institutions.[1]

When placed in this context, the WPC also links two historical schools that are not often associated with each other—the crowd and the political party. Because historians tend to study subjects, such as crowds and parties, rather than concepts, such as the expression of dissatisfaction, they have not seen that the crowd and the party can be two different ways of accomplishing the same end, the voicing of political opinions, especially dissatisfaction. Moreover, analyzing the WPC reveals how and why the transition between crowd and party occurred, and how and why people ceased to express themselves in one way and began to do so in another. Therefore, considering the WPC raises, and begins to answer, at least one fundamental historical question—how people have expressed dissatisfaction—and joins two subjects of historical investigation—crowds and parties. However, these insights seem to contain an inherent contradiction that must be resolved.

The July riots were neither the last appearance of a crowd nor the last riot in San Francisco, much less the United States. How then is it possible to claim that the evolution of the July riots into the Workingmen's Party of California represents the transformation of bullets into ballots? The resolution of the contradiction requires considera-tion of several factors and conditions. First, the population of the United States, and San Francisco, was constantly changing for the next half century. Massive European immigration continued almost unabated until passage of the Immigration Acts of 1917, 1921, and 1924. Moreover, the majority of later immigrants came from South-ern, Eastern, and Central Europe, those parts of the Continent least characterized by democratic political institutions. Consequently, the newcomers needed constantly to be socialized and taught to abandon the crowd and embrace the ballot box. Although it would take statis-tical analysis of successive crowds to determine if they were, in fact, composed of recent immigrants who had not yet learned these skills, the experience in San Francisco in 1877, in which members of the WPC were much more likely to be newly arrived in the United States and newly registered to vote, strongly suggests that this was the case. So the crowd continued to exist but with a constantly shifting com-position, and it was the changing population of the country that kept the crowd alive.

A second issue that needs to be remembered is success or failure. Denis Kearney never proclaimed the death of the crowd. Rather, he continued to use the language of the crowd and constantly threatened crowd tactics if institutional politics did not accomplish the goals of his followers. Thus, in examining later crowds, we can hypothesize that they emerged if formal politics did not satisfy the demands of those who joined them. If people achieved their goals through formal political structures, they remained quiescent. If they did not, it was back to the barricades.

The third point (and this is obvious but might tend to be over-looked) is that many Americans have not had access to formal politi-cal institutions. Women and African Americans are perhaps the two most noticeable instances, and they have repeatedly used crowds to express their demands in the twentieth century. Although it would be almost impossible to prove, it seems safe to say that the group that has formed crowds less than any other in twentieth-century America is also the group with the greatest access to the political process—the white male middle class.

Thus, for the crowd to disappear entirely, two conditions must be satisfied. First, there must be universal access to democratic political institutions without regard to such factors as sex, race, religion, age, class, or sexual preference. And second, access must be real and not just a front. Groups must believe that their interests are being legitimately represented and that they are receiving a satisfactory response from the government. They must be convinced that their needs are being met. If these two conditions are satisfied, they will rely on formal political institutions to express their grievances; if these conditions are not met, they will resort to the crowd.

Perhaps the clearest example of these ideas is the most noticeable instance in which the white middle class resorted to crowd action in recent American history, the antiwar movement of the 1960s and 1970s. When those in the white middle class became convinced that government was unresponsive to their demands and that they were unable to make themselves heard through the formal political process, they took to the streets, sometimes in demonstrations, sometimes in riots. And they remained there until the government responded. In more recent years, both the prochoice and the antiabortionist forces have formed crowds when they became persuaded that crowd action alone enabled them to make themselves heard.

In other words, people retain the option of going from ballots to bullets if government does not listen. Thomas Jefferson expressed this in his first inaugural address when he listed "the essential principles of our government":

> a jealous care of the right of election by the people—a mild and safe corrective of abuses which are lopped by the sword of the revolution where peaceable remedies are unprovided;
>
> absolute acquiescence in the decisions of the majority—the vital principle of republics, from which there is no appeal but to force, the vital principle and immediate parent of despotism.[2]

Appendix

TABLES OF CORRELATION COEFFICIENTS
(Pearson Product-Moment Correlations [r])

Expressing the measure of association between the percentage of registered voters in each of San Francisco's 136 voting precincts who possessed a particular socio-economic characteristic (the independent variable) and the percentage of votes cast in each of the precincts for the candidates of the Workingmen's Party of California in the election of delegates to the California Constitutional Convention of 1878 (the dependent variable).

TABLE A.1   AGE

Age	r
21–44	.4847
21–24	−.0059
25–29	.2197
30–34	.0774
35–39	.3491
40–44	.1194
45–82	−.4947
45–49	−.2697
50–54	−.3161
55–59	−.1874
60–64	−.1048
65–69	−.0788
70–74	−.0748
Over 74	−.1139

TABLE A.2 NATIVITY

Nativity	r
USA	−.8165
New England	−.5804
Mid-Atlantic	−.6486
South Atlantic	−.3812
Old Northwest	−.2871
Old Southwest	−.5303
Trans-Mississippi	−.3598
FOREIGN	.8200
Europe	.8278
Great Britain[1]	.1994
Ireland	.7707
Western[2]	.0262
Central/Southern	.0920
Germany	−.2140
Austria	−.0070
Hungary/Balkans	−.1141
Russia	−.0017
Scandinavia	.2794
Americas[3]	−.1424

[1] England, Scotland, Wales.
[2] Iberia, France, and the Low Countries.
[3] Excluding Canada and the United States.

TABLE A.3 OCCUPATION

Occupation	r
Professional/Technical	−.6877
Managerial/Proprietary	−.6494
White Collar	−.8359
Sales	−.3984
Clerical	−.7939
Service	.1477
Blue Collar	.8550
Craftsmen	.5435
Operatives	.4727
Common Laborers	.7561

TABLE A.4   YEAR OF REGISTRATION TO VOTE

Year	r
Pre−1870	−.5000
Pre−1866	−.0715
1866	−.5457
1867	−.0469
1868	−.0362
1869	−.3015
1870−75	−.5025
1870	−.1156
1871	−.0583
1872	−.0683
1873	.0248
1874	−.1542
1875	−.0680
1876−78	.4606
1876	.0227
1877	.1114
1878	.4595

TABLE A.5   YEAR CITIZENSHIP OBTAINED

Year	r
Pre−1840	−.0388
1840−44	.1378
1845−49	.1202
1850−54	.0690
1855−59	.1112
1860−64	.2684
1865−69	.5128
1870−78	.7222
1870−74	.5709
1875−78	.6473
1875	.3299
1876	.5298
1877	.4036
1878	.3121

Appendix

TABLE A.6   ABILITY TO LOCATE
MEMBERS OF SAMPLE

Where Located	r
Not Able to Be Located	.5089
Not Located in City Directory	.2653
Not Located in Census of 1880	.2267
Located in Census of 1880	−.3792
At Same Address	−.2232
At New Address	−.3297

Notes

INTRODUCTION

1 Oscar Handlin, *Boston's Immigrants*, ix.
2 Lawson, *Black Ballots*, 345.
3 Lawson, *In Pursuit of Power*, xiii.
4 *Ibid.*, 11.

PROLOGUE

1 Ira B. Cross, *A History of the Labor Movement in California*, 89; San Francisco *Daily Morning Call*, July 24, 1877; San Francisco *Chronicle*, July 24, 1877; San Francisco *Evening Post*, July 24, 1877; San Francisco *Daily Evening Bulletin*, July 24, 1877; Philip Foner, ed., *The Formation of the Workingmen's Party of the United States*.
2 Cross, *Labor Movement*, 89; *Call*, July 25, 1877; *Post*, July 25, 1877; *Chronicle*, July 25, 1877; San Francisco *Daily Alta California*, July 25, 1877; *Bulletin*, July 25, 1877.
3 *Call*, July 26, 1877; *Chronicle*, July 26, 1877; *Post*, July 26, 1877; *Alta*, July 26, 1877; *Bulletin*, July 26, 1877.
4 *Call*, July 26, 1877; *Chronicle*, July 26, 1877; *Post*, July 26, 1877; *Alta*, July 26, 1877; *Bulletin*, July 26, 1877.
5 Hubert Howe Bancroft, *Chronicles of the Builders of the Commonwealth*, 1:362.
6 *Ibid.*; Henry George, "The Kearney Agitation in California," 437; Lucy Alice Harrison Pownall Senger to Joseph Pownall and Mary C. Harrison Newell Pownall, July 28, 1877: Pownall Family Papers.
7 *Alta*, July 24, 1877; *Bulletin*, July 25, 1877; *Call*, July 25, 1877; *Chronicle*, July 27, 1877.
8 *Alta*, July 24, 1877; *Bulletin*, July 26, 1877; *Call*, July 25, 1877; *Chronicle*, July 27, 1877.

9   Hubert Howe Bancroft, *Popular Tribunals*, 2:696–748.
10   Hubert Howe Bancroft, *The History of California*, 7:353–54.
11   Lucile Eaves, *A History of California Labor Legislation*, 28.
12   Cross, *Labor Movement*, 90–91.
13   Alexander P. Saxton, *The Indispensable Enemy*, 114–15.
14   Michael Kazin, "Prelude to Kearneyism: The 'July Days' in San Francisco, 1877," 9.
15   The use of the term *Workingmen* with a capital *W* refers to members of the Workingmen's Party of California. The same term with a lower-case *w* simply means members of the working class.
16   [California, Legislature, Joint Committee on Labor Investigation], *Reports*.

CHAPTER 1

1   Henry George, "The Kearney Agitation in California," 438.
2   Thomas Nast, "The Ides of March," *Harper's Weekly*, 24 (no. 1212), March 20, 1880, p. 1; *idem*, "Social Science Solved," *ibid.* (no. 1215), April 10, 1880, p. 1; *idem*, "Another Man Trembles for Our Republican Form of Government," *ibid.* (no. 1217), April 24, 1880, p. 1; James Bryce, *The American Commonwealth*, 2:425–48; Ira B. Cross, *A History of the Labor Movement in California*, 95; [J. C. Stedman and R. A. Leonard], *The Workingmen's Party of California*, 17–18; San Francisco *Chronicle*, September 14, 17, 1877; San Francisco *Examiner*, September 9–13, 1877.
3   Cross, *Labor Movement*, 95; [Stedman and Leonard], *Workingmen's Party of California*, 18–20; San Francisco *Daily Alta California*, September 22, 24, 1877; *Chronicle*, September 22, 24, 1877, June 24, 1878.
4   *Chronicle*, June 24, 1878; Cross, *Labor Movement*, 95–96; [Stedman and Leonard], *Workingmen's Party of California*, 19–20.
5   *Chronicle*, October 6, 1877; [Stedman and Leonard], *Workingmen's Party of California*, 20–22.
6   *Chronicle*, October 1, 1877; [Stedman and Leonard], *Workingmen's Party of California*, 20–22; Cross, *Labor Movement*, 96–97; Frank Roney, "History of the Workingmen's Party of California" (Frank Roney Papers).
7   Cross, *Labor Movement*, 96–97; [Stedman and Leonard], *Workingmen's Party of California*, 20–22.
8   *Chronicle*, October, November 1877, February 25, 1878; Cross, *Labor Movement*, 96; [Stedman and Leonard], *Workingmen's Party of California*, 22.
9   [California, Legislature, Joint Committee on Labor Investigation], *Reports*.

10 [Geo. W. Greene (pub.)], *The Labor Agitators; or, The Battle for Bread*, 24.
11 Ira B. Cross, ed., *Frank Roney, Irish Rebel and California Labor Leader*, 300.
12 [Stedman and Leonard], *Workingmen's Party of California.*
13 *Alta*, November 2, 1877.
14 San Francisco *Daily Evening Bulletin*, September 10, 1877; April 8, 1878; July 13, 1878.
15 San Francisco *Argonaut*, September 29, October 6, 1877.
16 *Ibid.*, November 17, 1877.
17 San Francisco *Illustrated Wasp*, October 20, 1877; January 26, February 2, 1878.
18 Hubert Howe Bancroft, *The History of California*, 7:351, 356.
19 John P. Young, *San Francisco*, 2:482, 532, 560, 608.
20 Alexander P. Saxton, *The Indispensable Enemy*, 125.
21 Carl Brent Swisher, *Motivation and Political Technique in the California Constitutional Convention*, 1878–79.
22 *Ibid.*; *Chronicle*, July 5, 1878.
23 [San Francisco, City and County, Registrar of Voters], *Great Register for 1878*; [United States, Bureau of the Census], Tenth Census of the United States: 1880; Manuscript Population Schedules, City and County of San Francisco.
24 For the correlation coefficients on which the following analysis is based, see the appendix.
25 It is beyond the scope of this work to account for this anomaly, but several explanations are possible. Perhaps there was ethnic conflict between the Eastern and Central Europeans on the one hand and the Northern and Western on the other. Perhaps Eastern and Central Europeans found conditions in San Francisco much more acceptable than did Northerners and Westerners, and they were therefore less likely to participate in a protest movement. Or, finally, perhaps immigrants from the autocracies, especially Germany, were dissatisfied with the WPC itself, particularly its lack of class consciousness, and believed that a different kind of movement would have been more appropriate.

CHAPTER 2

1 [United States, Bureau of the Census], *Statistics of the Population of the United States in 1870*, 347; idem, *Statistics of the Population of the United States at the Tenth Census*, 498.
2 Gunther Barth, *Instant Cities*, 129, 133.
3 Irving McKee, ed., *Alonzo Delano's California Correspondence*, 53; Anna Paschal Hannum, ed., *A Quaker Forty-Niner*, 302; Richard A. Dwyer and Richard E. Lingenfelter, eds., *The Songs of the Gold Rush*, 17–18.

4   I. J. Benjamin, *Three Years in America, 1859–1862*, 1:298–99.
5   Horace Bushnell, *Characteristics and Prospects of California*, 21; Ernest Seyd, *California and Its Resources*, 64; James Crapper, *A Month in California*, 18; Thomas Woodbine Hinchcliff, *Over the Sea and Far Away*, 196–97; Henry Morford, *Morford's Scenery and Sensation Hand-Book of the Pacific Railroads of California*; Charles Carleton Coffin, *Our New Way Round the World*, 474–75.
6   California Immigrant Union, *Memorial and Report*.
7   Immigrant Association of California, *[Second] Annual Report*.
8   [John S. Hittell], *All About California and the Inducements to Settle There*, 18–26.
9   Charles Victor Hall, *California*, 1–12.
10 W. G. Marshall, *Through America, or, Nine Months in the United States*, 270; Lady Duffus Hardy, *Through Cities and Prairie Lands*, 144; W. F. Ross, *Westward by Rail*, 318.
11 San Francisco *Daily Morning Call*, July 5, 1872.
12 *Ibid.*, August 9, 1872. The classic account of the diamond hoax is contained in Asbury Harpending, *The Great Diamond Hoax and Other Stirring Incidents*. See also Bruce A. Woodard, *Diamonds in the Sand*, and Richard A. Bartlett, "The Diamond Hoax." Barth, *Instant Cities*, 146–47, places the event in the context of speculation, gambling, and acquisitiveness in San Francisco.
13 *Call*, August 8, 1872.
14 San Francisco *Illustrated Wasp*, November 3, 1877. No account of San Francisco was considered complete without a description of the frenzy in the gambling palaces and stock exchanges. See, e.g., B[enjamin] E. Lloyd, *Lights and Shades in San Francisco*, 33–45, 203–07. Butterfield's raffle is mentioned in Neil L. Shumsky, ed., "Frank Roney's San Francisco—His Diary: April, 1875–March, 1876," 258. On the general propensity to gamble in the city, see Barth, *Instant Cities*, 144–48.
15 Harriet Lane Levy, *920 O'Farrell Street*, 15–16, 160–62.
16 Mrs. Fremont Older, *The Socialist and the Prince*, 1.
17 R. H. Conwell, *Acres of Diamonds* (New York, 1915), 17–21, reprinted in Oscar Handlin, ed., *Readings in American History*, 453–54.
18 James D. Hart, *The Popular Book*, 161–62.
19 Frances Trollope, *Domestic Manners of the Americans*, 258–59; Charles Dickens, *The Life and Adventures of Martin Chuzzlewit*, 272–73.
20 James Fenimore Cooper, *Home as Found*, 103.
21 Henry George, "What the Railroad Will Bring Us."
22 Rodman W. Paul, *California Gold*, 40–42.
23 *Ibid.*, 39–49; Rodman W. Paul, *Mining Frontiers of the Far West, 1848–1880*, 18–21; John W. Caughey, *Gold is the Cornerstone*, 159–66; Hubert Howe Bancroft, *The History of California*, 6:409–11.

24 John S. Hittell, *A History of San Francisco, and Incidentally of the State of California*, 210–12.

25 *Ibid.*, 212–13; Bancroft, *History of California*, 7:104, 107–11; John P. Young, *San Francisco*, 1:281; Frank Soulé, John H. Gihon, and James Nisbet, *The Annals of San Francisco*, 418–19.

26 David Hawley, "Observations Recorded for H. H. Bancroft"; San Francisco *Daily Alta California*, November 13, 1867.

27 [United States, Bureau of the Census], *Compendium of the Ninth Census*, 596; [United States, Bureau of the Census], *Compendium of the Tenth Census*, 1:380–81; 2:1356.

28 [United States, Bureau of the Census], *Productions of Agriculture at the Tenth Census*, 25.

29 Samuel L. Bell, "Annual Address to the California State Agricultural Society."

30 Bancroft, *History of California*, 7:110; Caughey, *Gold is the Cornerstone*, 349–52.

31 Dale L. Morgan, ed., *In Pursuit of the Golden Dream*, by Howard Calhoun Gardiner.

32 Clarence D. Long, *Wages and Earnings in the United States, 1860–1890*, 84.

33 *Call*, August 6, 1871; *Bulletin*, July 21, 1877; unidentified article in Hubert Howe Bancroft, comp., Bancroft Scrapbooks, 30:14; Grant H. Smith, John Mackay, Grant H. Smith Papers; Hittell, *San Francisco*, 406; also see *Call*, September 27, December 23, 1874.

34 Charles Crocker, Crocker's statement, prepared for H. H. Bancroft, Charles Crocker Papers; David S. Lavender, *The Great Persuader*, 2, 48.

35 Lavender, *Great Persuader*, 2–3; Crocker's statement, Crocker Papers; Collis P. Huntington, Huntington's statement prepared for H. H. Bancroft, Collis P. Huntington Papers; "Collis P. Huntington," *Dictionary of American Biography* (New York: Charles Scribner's Sons, 1928–36), 9:408–09.

36 Norman E. Tutorow, *Leland Stanford*, 4–8; George T. Clark, *Leland Stanford*, 13–35; [Edward Curtis], *Two California Sketches*, 3.

37 Tutorow, *Leland Stanford*, 8–15, 20; Clark, *Leland Stanford*, 35–46; Bertha Berner, *Mrs. Leland Stanford*, 6–7.

38 Crocker, Crocker's statement, Crocker Papers; "Charles Crocker," *DAB*, 4:352; David Warren Ryder, *Great Citizen*, 10; "Huntington," *DAB*, 9:408–09; Lavender, *Great Persuader*, 3–5.

39 Hugh Quigley, *The Irish Race in California and on the Pacific Coast*, 388; "William Shoney O'Brien," *DAB*, 13:612; James G. Fair, Fair's statement prepared for H. H. Bancroft, James G. Fair Papers; James C. Flood, Flood's statement prepared for H. H. Bancroft, James C. Flood Papers; Smith, John Mackay, Smith Papers.

40 Smith, John Mackay, Smith Papers; Flood, Flood's statement, Flood Papers; "John Mackay," *DAB*, 12:75–61; "O'Brien," *DAB*, 13:612; Fair, Fair's statement, Fair Papers.

CHAPTER 3

1 "Denis Kearney," *Dictionary of American Biography*, 11 vols. (New York: Charles Scribner's Sons, 1928–36), 5:269; Doyce B. Nunis, Jr., "The Demagogue and the Demographer; Correspondence of Denis Kearney and Lord Bryce," 274.

2 Henry George, "The Kearney Agitation in California," 438; Ira B. Cross, *A History of the Labor Movement in California*, 92–93; John P. Young, *San Francisco*, 2:518, 534.

3 San Francisco *Daily Morning Call*, April 25, 26, 1907; San Francisco *Chronicle*, April 26, 1907; David Warren Ryder, *Great Citizen*, 43; Jane Stanford to David Starr Jordan, May 9, 1900, Jane Stanford Papers; Denis Kearney to Leland Stanford, May 7, 1884, Leland Stanford Papers, Stanford Family Collection.

4 *Call*, April 26, 1907; George H. Tinkham, *California Men and Events; Time, 1769–1890*, 275.

5 Steven P. Erie, "Politics, the Public Sector and Irish Social Mobility: San Francisco, 1870–1900."

6 R. A. Burchell, *The San Francisco Irish, 1848–1880*, 54.

7 Peter R. Decker, *Fortunes and Failures*, 72.

8 Stephan Thernstrom, *The Other Bostonians*, 259. Steven J. Ross makes a similar point in his book about Cincinnati. "Whether the workers' standard of living was in fact declining as severely as they claimed—an issue still debated by economic historians—is less important than the workers' conviction that such was the case. *Workers on the Edge*, 43–44.

9 *Chronicle*, August 2, 1877, June 24, August 2, 1878; [Charles Allen Sumner], *Holding Down to the Main Question*; [J. C. Stedman and R. A. Leonard], *The Workingmen's Party of California*, 17.

10 San Francisco *Evening Post*, September 5, 1877; [Stedman and Leonard], *Workingmen's Party of California*, 38.

11 Frank Roney, [Diary of life in San Francisco during 1875 and 1876], Frank Roney Papers, reprinted in Neil L. Shumsky, "Frank Roney's San Francisco—His Diary: April, 1875—March, 1876," 250, 254; Mrs. Fremont Older, *The Socialist and the Prince*, 2–3.

12 [Geo. W. Greene (pub.)], *The Labor Agitators; or, The Battle for Bread*, 13.

13 [Stedman and Leonard], *Workingmen's Party of California*, 9, 13, 14.

14   B[enjamin] E. Lloyd, *Lights and Shades in San Francisco*, 132–33; Patricia
      E. Carr, "Emperor Norton I."
15   Mark Twain, *Sketches Old and New*, 54–59.
16   *Call*, May 15, 1870; Twain, *Sketches*, 60–67.
17   *Call*, May–August, 1875; Cecil G. Tilton, *William Chapman Ralston*,
      324–48.
18   San Francisco *Daily Alta California*, August 28–30, 1875; San Francisco
      Examiner, August 31, September 1, 1875.
19   *Call*, April 19, October 4, 1874; John S. Hittell, *A History of San
      Francisco, and Incidentally of the State of California*, 450–54.
20   Henry G. Langley, comp., *The San Francisco Directory* (1867–71); San
      Francisco *Daily Evening Bulletin*, January 17, 22, February 11, 24, 26,
      1870; *Chronicle*, January 20, 30, June 12, 1870; Hittell, *San Francisco*,
      373–75; Hubert Howe Bancroft, *The History of California*, 7:685.
21   Bancroft, *History of California*, 7:15, 119; Langley, comp., *City Direc-
      tory*, 1879, 35.
22   *Bulletin*, January 1, 3, 1871; Bancroft, *History of California*, 7:685; Hit-
      tell, *San Francisco*, 374–75; Young, *San Francisco*, 2:580–81.
23   Bancroft, *History of California*, 7:677; Hittell, *San Francisco*, 415;
      Tilton, *William Chapman Ralston*, 345–47.
24   Langley, comp., *City Directory*, 1877, 10; *idem, City Directory*, 1878,
      10; *idem, City Directory*, 1879, 35; Bancroft, *History of California*, 7:15;
      Hittell, *San Francisco*, 422; [San Francisco, Chamber of Commerce],
      Eleventh Annual Report (1879), 23; [San Francisco, City and County,
      assessor], *Annual Report . . . 1877* (1877).
25   Bancroft, *History of California*, 7:372; Hittell, *San Francisco*, 423–24.
26   Samuel Rezneck, "Distress, Relief and Discontent in the United States
      During the Depression of 1873–78"; O. V. Wells, "The Depression of
      1873–79"; E. Ray McCartney, *Crisis of 1873*.
27   Robert V. Bruce, *1877*, 19.
28   *Bulletin*, January 12, 22, 1870; *Alta*, March 23, 29, April 1, 5, 11, 1870;
      Cross, *Labor Movement*, 64.
29   Langley, comp., *City Directory*, 1872, 11; *idem, City Directory*, 1876, 12.
30   *Bulletin*, May 16, November 16, 1875, April 8, 1878; Bancroft, *History
      of California*, 7:352; San Francisco *Argonaut*, August 4, 1877; *Alta*,
      July 1, 1877.
31   *Chronicle*, February 1, 1878; *Call*, February 14, July 26, 1878; Cross, *La-
      bor Movement*, 71.
32   John A. Garraty, *Unemployment in History*, 108–09; Roney, [Diary of
      life in San Francisco during 1875 and 1876], Roney Papers.
33   [California, Bureau of Labor Statistics], *First Biennial Report*, 142–43.
34   [United States, Department of Labor], *Wages in the United States and
      Europe, 1870 to 1898*.

35 "Labor in America and Europe," *House Executive Document* 21, 807; [California, Bureau of Labor Statistics], *First Biennial Report*, 266–67; [United States, Senate, Committee on Finance], *Report on Wholesale Prices and Wages*, 1:60–66.

CHAPTER 4

1 Henry George, "What the Railroad Will Bring Us."
2 Rodman W. Paul, *California Gold*, 130–31, 144.
3 *Ibid.*, 130–46; Rodman W. Paul, *Mining Frontiers of the Far West, 1848–1880*, 30–33; John W. Caughey, *Gold is the Cornerstone*, 251–57.
4 Paul, *California Gold*, 182–83.
5 *Ibid.*, 152; Philip Ross May, *Origins of Hydraulic Mining in California*, 40–44, 55–57.
6 Paul, *California Gold*, 147–70; May, *Hydraulic Mining*; Caughey, *Gold is the Cornerstone*, 257–66; Robert L. Kelley, *Gold vs. Grain*, 21–56.
7 Carey McWilliams, *California*, 90.
8 Paul W. Gates, "California's Agricultural College Lands," 104; [California, Board of Equalization], *Report for 1872–73*, 22–24; [United States, Bureau of the Census], *Productions of Agriculture at the Tenth Census*, 34–35.
9 Gerald D. Nash, "Henry George Reappraised: William Chapman's Views on Land Speculation in Nineteenth Century California," 136; Joseph A. McGowan, *A History of the Sacramento Valley*, 1:160–61.
10 Nash, "Henry George Reappraised," 136; Gates, "California's Agricultural College Lands," 108.
11 Rodman Paul, "The Great California Grain War: the Grangers Challenge the Wheat King," 333; Horace Davis, *California Breadstuffs*, unidentified pamphlet bound in "Pamphlets on California Commerce."
12 Paul, "California Grain War," 332–33.
13 *Ibid.*, 338–40.
14 McGowan, *Sacramento Valley*, 1:259–60.
15 Hubert Howe Bancroft, *The History of California*, 7:113–14.
16 John S. Hittell, *A History of San Francisco, and Incidentally of the State of California*, 326.
17 *Ibid.*; Frank Soulé, John H. Gihon, and James Nisbet, *The Annals of San Francisco*, 626–29; B[enjamin] E. Lloyd, *Lights and Shades in San Francisco*, 519–23; John P. Young, *San Francisco*, 1:285.
18 San Francisco *Commerical Herald and Market Review*, December 17, 1869; January 13, 1871; January 12, 1872.
19 San Francisco *Daily Evening Bulletin*, December 2, 1869, August 6,

1870; San Francisco *Chronicle*, June 12, 1870; San Francisco *Daily Alta California*, August 19, 1870.

20 *Bulletin*, September 22, 1871.

21 Clarence D. Long, *Wages and Earnings in the United States, 1860–1890*, 84.

22 [United States, Department of Labor], *Wages in the United States and Europe, 1870 to 1898*.

23 [United States, Bureau of the Census], *Statistics of the Population of the United States at the Tenth Census*, 51, 382, 902; idem, *Statistics of the Population of the United States in 1870*, 749

24 *Bulletin*, January 10, 1876.

25 [United States, Bureau of the Census], "Ninth Census of the United States: 1870," Manuscript Schedules of Manufactures; idem, "Tenth Census of the United States: 1880," Manuscript Schedules of Manufactures.

26 *Ibid.*

27 *Ibid.*

28 William Laird MacGregor, *San Francisco, California in 1876*, 21–22.

29 *Alta*, November 1, 1874.

30 San Francisco *Evening Post*, July 25, 1877.

31 [United States, Bureau of the Census], *Statistics of the Population of the United States at the Tenth Census*, 539, 902; for information about the history of the shoemaking industry in the United States, see Paul G. Faler, *Mechanics and Manufacturers in the Early Industrial Revolution: Lynn, Massachusetts, 1780–1860*; for information about the cigar industry see Harold C. Livesay, *Samuel Gompers and Organized Labor in America*; also Patricia A. Cooper, *Once a Cigar Maker: Men, Women and Work Culture in American Cigar Factories, 1900–1919*. Cooper notes that the Chinese "dominated the trade in San Francisco" (p. 25).

32 [United States, Bureau of the Census], *Historical Statistics of the United States*, 409–10.

33 Robert Greenhalgh Albion, *The Rise of New York Port*.

34 Paul W. Gates, "Frontier Estate Builders and Farm Laborers."

CHAPTER 5

1 Alan Jay Lerner, *My Fair Lady* (New York: New American Library paperback, 1956), 97; George Bernard Shaw, *Pygmalion*, in *Bernard Shaw: Collected Plays with Their Prefaces* (New York: Dodd, Mead, 1972), 4:749.

2 Grant H. Smith, John Mackay, Grant H. Smith Papers; San Francisco *Examiner*, October 8, 1889.

3 Smith, John Mackay, Smith Papers; [United States, Pacific Railway Commission], *Report and Testimony*, 1:87–88; 5:2474.

4 Collis P. Huntington to Leland Stanford, April 10, 1871, April 6, 9, 1875; Collis P. Huntington to Mark Hopkins, November 4, December 1, 1871, May 7, September 13, 1875: Mark Hopkins Correspondence and Papers.

5 Charles Crocker to Collis P. Huntington, October 29, 1877: Hopkins Correspondence and Papers; statements of accounts, Collis P. Huntington Papers, box 235 (Syracuse University Library, Syracuse, N.Y.).

6 Assets of the Estate of Mark Hopkins, December 31, 1878, Huntington Papers, box 235.

7 Ledgers, January 1890 to December 1891, and January 1892 to December 1893: Huntington Papers, oversize packages 17 and 18; [California, Bureau of Labor Statistics], *First Biennial Report*, 135.

8 Smith, John Mackay, Smith Papers; Ellin Berlin, *Silver Platter*, 346.

9 Herbert Charles Nash, statement concerning Leland Stanford, Leland Stanford Papers, Bancroft Library; Moses Hopkins, statement concerning the life of Mark Hopkins, Mark Hopkins Papers; Grant H. Smith, *The History of the Comstock Lode, 1850–1920*, 263.

10 William D. Howells, *The Rise of Silas Lapham*, 25.

11 Mary Crocker to Hannah, March 12, 1881: Mary Crocker Correspondence.

12 John Walton Caughey, *Hubert Howe Bancroft*, 313–25.

13 George H. Morrison to Hubert Howe Bancroft [n.d.], James G. Fair Papers.

14 *Ibid.*

15 Smith, John Mackay, Smith Papers.

16 Oscar T. Shuck, *Sketches of Leading and Representative Men of San Francisco*, 962.

17 Quoted in Berlin, *Silver Platter*, 206.

18 Quoted in Gertrude Atherton, *My San Francisco*, 34.

19 *Ibid.*, 39.

20 Joseph Purtell, *The Tiffany Touch*, 121–22.

21 Bertha Berner, *Mrs. Leland Stanford*, 105; Astley D. M. Cooper, *Mrs. Stanford's Jewel Collection* (oil on canvas, 1898, Stanford Family Collection, Stanford University Museum of Art, Palo Alto).

22 Morrison to Bancroft [n.d.], Fair Papers.

23 Berlin, *Silver Platter*, 209.

24 Gunther Barth, "Metropolism and Urban Elites in the Far West," 160–72.

25 John P. Young, *San Francisco*, 2:603; Julia Cooley Altrocchi, *The Spectacular San Franciscans*, 169.

26 Gertrude Atherton, *Adventures of a Novelist*, 63–64.

27   Thorstein Veblen, *The Theory of the Leisure Class*, 63–64.

28   Henry G. Langley, comp., *The San Francisco Directory, 1875* (1875), 12; idem, *City Directory, 1877*, 9; B[enjamin] E. Lloyd, *Lights and Shades in San Francisco*, 31.

29   Harold Kirker, *California's Architectural Frontier*, 93.

30   San Francisco *Chronicle*, June 9, 1877; San Francisco *Newsletter and California Advertiser*, December 25, 1886, April 23, July 16, 1887; Amelia Ransome Neville, *The Fantastic City*, 178–79; San Francisco *Daily Morning Call*, July 18, 1875.

31   *Chronicle*, June 9, 1877; [San Francisco *Newsletter and California Advertiser*], *Artistic Homes of California* (San Francisco: Britton & Rey, [1887]); *Newsletter*, December 25, 1886.

32   *Chronicle*, July 15, 1878; Neville, *Fantastic City*, 178; Altrocchi, *Spectacular San Franciscans*, 175; Kirker, *California's Architectural Frontier*, 94; Oscar Lewis, *Here Lived the Californians*, 160.

33   Berner, *Mrs. Leland Stanford*, 21–23; Jessie Knight Jordan, recollections of the Stanfords, Jane Stanford Papers; Norman E. Tutorow, *Leland Stanford*, 210–11; Thomas Hill, *Palo Alto Spring* (oil on canvas, 1878, Stanford Family Collection, Stanford University Museum of Art, Palo Alto).

34   F. M. L. Thompson, *English Landed Society in the Nineteenth Century*, 25.

35   *Monterey, California: The Most Charming Winter Resort in the World* (Monterey, Calif. [?]: npub., 1881 [?]), 7–8; Altrocchi, *Spectacular San Franciscans*, 235–36; David Warren Ryder, *Great Citizen*, 4; Oscar Lewis, *The Big Four*, 87–88.

36   Berner, *Mrs. Leland Stanford*, 15.

37   See, e.g., accounts of Charles Crocker's funeral: *Chronicle*, August 21, 1888; *Call*, August 21, 1888; Lewis, *Big Four*, 101; H. L. Tevis to Louise Tevis Sharon, December 18, 18_, Sharon Family Papers; tomb of William Shoney O'Brien, Calvary Cemetery, San Francisco; Samuel Dickson, *Tales of San Francisco*, 604.

38   Neville, *Fantastic City*, 198, 208–09; Lewis, *Here Lived the Californians*, 167, 176; Altrocchi, *Spectacular San Franciscans*, 176; San Francisco *Daily Alta California*, March 19, 1876.

39   Lloyd, *Lights and Shades*, 355; *Newsletter*, December 26, 1896.

40   Lloyd, *Lights and Shades*, 356; San Francisco *Argonaut*, January 5, 1878.

41   Berner, *Mrs. Leland Stanford*, 160–79; George T. Clark, *Leland Stanford*; Hubert Howe Bancroft, *History of the Life of Leland Stanford*, 125–45.

42   Jackson Street Free Kindergarten Association, *Third Annual Report* (1882), 6, 15–16; idem, *Fifth Annual Report* (1884), 18–20; Tutorow, *Leland Stanford*, 284.

43   Oscar Handlin, "Comments on Mass and Popular Culture," in Norman Jacobs, *Culture for the Millions*, 64–65.

44   *Call*, November 14, 1910.
45   Berlin, *Silver Platter*, 291–93.
46   *Call*, June 10, 1878; D. O. Mills to [?], October 1882, Samuel L. Barlow Papers; Flora Apponyi, *The Libraries of California*; Tutorow, *Leland Stanford*, 211; [United States, Works Progress Administration, San Francisco Theatre Research Project], *History of Opera in San Francisco*, 1:99–102; Lloyd, *Lights and Shades*, 155–57.
47   Sam P. Davis, ed., *The History of Nevada*, 1:421–23; Russell R. Elliott, *History of Nevada*, 162–64; Gilman M. Ostrander, *Nevada*, 73; Oscar Lewis, *Silver Kings*, 167.
48   Tutorow, *Leland Stanford*, 251.
49   Elliott, *Nevada*, 164; Ostrander, *Nevada*, 94, 104.
50   Ostrander, *Nevada*, 105; James G. Fair to Johnson Camden, December 2, 1885, November 6, 1886, June 14, November 6, 1887, Johnson Camden Papers.
51   James G. Fair, Fair's statement prepared for H. H. Bancroft, Fair Papers.
52   Mrs. O. P. Jenkins, personal reminiscences of Mrs. Jane Lathrop Stanford, Jane Stanford Papers; Jessie Knight Jordan, recollections of the Stanfords, Jane Stanford Papers.

CHAPTER 6

1   [United States, Bureau of the Census], *Statistics of the Population of the United States at the Tenth Census*, 109; [Henry G. Langley], *Guidemap of the City of San Francisco*.
2   Alvin Averbach, "San Francisco's South of Market District, 1850–1950: The Emergence of a Skid Row," 200–01; San Francisco *Daily Morning Call*, April 28, 1872, February 22, 1874.
3   *Call*, February 22, 1874; [San Francisco, City and County, Health Officer], *Annual Report*, 392–93.
4   San Francisco *Chronicle*, 1870–80; *Call*, January 8, 1871.
5   [United States, Bureau of the Census], *Statistics of the Population at the Tenth Census*, 498; Henry G. Langley, comp., *The San Francisco Directory*, 1860–1880.
6   Robert Andrew Elgie, "The Development of San Francisco Manufacturing, 1848–1880: An Analysis of Regional Locational Factors and Urban Spatial Structure," 101, 115; B[enjamin] G. Lloyd, *Lights and Shades in San Francisco*, 175; John P. Young, *San Francisco*, 2:575; Langley, *City Directory, 1876*, 18; *idem, City Directory, 1880*, 20; [United States, Bureau of the Census], "Tenth Census of the United States: 1880," Manuscript Population Schedules; [San Francisco, City and County, Registrar of Voters], *Great Register for 1878*.
7   *Call*, May 29, 1870, May 7, 1871, February 22, 1874.

8 [United States, Bureau of the Census], *Statistics of the Population at the Tenth Census*, 649; [United States, Bureau of the Census], "Tenth Census of the United States," Manuscript Population Schedules; [San Francisco, City and County, Registrar of Voters], *Great Register*.

9 [San Francisco, City and County, Board of Supervisors], *Municipal Report . . for 1864–65* (1865), 119–20, 124; idem, *Municipal Report . . . for 1874–75* (1875), 83–84, 90; Lloyd, *Lights and Shades*, 380–83; Carroll D. Wright, *A Report on Marriage and Divorce in the United States, 1867 to 1886*, 456–57.

10 Frank Roney, [Diary of life in San Francisco during 1875 and 1876], Frank Roney Papers, reprinted in Neil L. Shumsky, "Frank Roney's San Francisco—His Diary: April, 1875—March, 1876," 262.

11 *Call*, May 7, 1870.

12 *Ibid.*, June 18, 1879.

13 San Francisco *Daily Alta California*, August 1, 2, 1874, March 13, August 20, 22, 31, 1876, August 13, 16, 1878; *Chronicle*, March 7, June 29, August 6, September 5, October 8, 1878; *Call*, April 11, May 13, 14, June 7, 9, 13, 15, 22, 1871; San Francisco *Evening Post*, March 24, July 13, 20, August 13, 20, 1877, January 12, 1878, June 19, 1879; Lloyd, *Lights and Shades*, 297–300; Langley, *City Directory*, 1880, 30–34; Herbert Asbury, *The Barbary Coast*, 150–64.

14 [San Francisco, City and County, Industrial School], *Annual Reports*, 1859–1879.

15 *Call*, February 21, 1871, October 10, 1872.

16 *Ibid.*, February 20, 1877.

17 *Post*, August 3, 6, 8, 10, 16, 20, 24, September 7, 1878.

18 Roney, [Diary of life in San Francisco during 1875 and 1876], Roney Papers.

19 *Ibid.*

20 *Call*, September 12, 1871, March 2, 1870.

21 *Ibid.*, January 7, April 7, 1870, October 5, 1874.

22 [San Francisco, City and County, Coroner], *Annual Report . . . 1878*; *Call*, April 9, 1871.

23 *Call*, February 24, 1871, March 12, 1872, January 4, 1879.

24 *Ibid.*, July 31, 1879.

25 *Post*, August 9, 1877.

26 San Francisco *Argonaut*, October 6, 1877.

27 William A. Bullough, *The Blind Boss and His City*, 28.

28 *Argonaut*, September 28, 1878.

29 *Argonaut*, March 30, 1878; Julia Cooley Altrocchi, *Spectacular San Franciscans*, 223; Amelia Ransome Neville, *Fantastic City*, 202.

30 Central Pacific Railroad Company vs. Cohen, Alfred A., *Answer*, 24, 48–49.

31 *Argonaut*, October 26, 1877.

32 *Ibid.*, May 5, 1877.

33 Hubert Howe Bancroft, *The History of California*, 7:601–06; John S. Hittell, *A History of San Francisco and Incidentally of the State of California*, 389–92; Young, *San Francisco*, 1:423–24; D. C. McRuer, *Summary of Objections to the "Goat Island Bill," Presented to the Senate Committee on Military Affairs*; [San Francisco, Chamber of Commerce], *Appeal to the California Delegation in Congress Upon the Goat Island Grant*.

34 *Call*, March 8, 17, April 4, May 15, 1872.

35 Eliot Lord, *Comstock Mining and Miners*, 309–14; William Wright, *The Big Bonanza*, 363–84, 488; Oscar Lewis, *Silver Kings*, 134, 139; [United States, Director of the Mint], *Annual Report . . . 1875*, 80–83.

36 *Chronicle*, February 1874 to December 1875; Lord, *Comstock Mining and Miners*, 315–16, 424–35; Joseph L. King, *History of the San Francisco Stock and Exchange Board*, 200.

37 *Call*, December 10, 12, 21, 30, 1874; *Chronicle*, January 27, 29, 1875; *Alta*, January 30, 1875.

38 J. F. Clark, *The Society in Search of Truth; or, Stock Gambling in San Francisco*, 43, 68–69, 80–81.

39 *Call*, August 6, 27, 1871, August 31, 1873, September 27, 1874.

PART III INTRODUCTION AND CHAPTER 7

1 Ira B. Cross, *A History of the Labor Movement in California*, 89.

2 George Rudé, *The Crowd in History, 1730–1848*; Eric Hobsbawm, *Primitive Rebels*; John Bohstedt, *Riots and Community Politics in England and Wales, 1790–1810*; William Reddy, *The Rise of Market Culture*; Charles Tilly, *The Contentious French*; Charles Tilly, Louise Tilly, and Richard Tilly, *The Rebellious Century, 1830–1930*.

3 Pauline Maier, *From Resistance to Revolution*; Dirk Hoerder, *Crowd Action in Revolutionary Massachusetts, 1765–1780*; Michael Feldberg, *The Turbulent Era*; Herbert G. Gutman, *Work, Culture & Society in Industrializing America*.

4 Rudé, *Crowd in History*, 5, 11; Hobsbawm, *Primitive Rebels*, 3, 110–13.

5 See chap. 1 for an explanation of these generalizations.

6 San Francisco *Examiner*, July 26, 1877; San Francisco *Chronicle*, July 26, 1877.

7 Michael Kazin, "Prelude to Kearneyism: The 'July Days' in San Francisco, 1877," 19–25; also see the description of the riots in the prologue.

8 San Francisco *Daily Evening Bulletin*, July 24, 25, 1877; *Examiner*, July 24, 25, 1877.

9 Donald C. Richter, *Riotous Victorians*.

10   Samuel Clark, *Social Origins of the Irish Land War*; Charles Townshend, *Political Violence in Ireland*, 1; Samuel Clark and James S. Donnelly, Jr., *Irish Peasants*, 25; Harvey J. Kaye, ed., *The Face of the Crowd: Studies in Revolution, Ideology, and Popular Protest: Selected Essays of George Rudé*, 168.

11   Adrian Cook, *The Armies of the Streets*, 27, 30, 197, 199.

12   Bohstedt, *Riots and Community Politics*.

13   Feldberg, *Turbulent Era*, 106–11, persuasively argues that education, temperance, and politics were all means of establishing order. Stanley K. Schultz, *The Culture Factory: Boston Public Schools, 1789–1860*, also claims that "education became a form of social insurance which protected society from serious consequences" (vii), and David Nasaw, *Schooled to Order: A Social History of Public Schooling in the United States*, demonstrates that "the common schools, the high schools, the colleges and universities . . . were expanded and transformed so that they might better maintain social order and increase material productivity" (4).

14   San Francisco *Daily Alta California*, July 24, 1877.

15   *Chronicle*, July 24, 1877; *Bulletin*, July 24, 1877.

16   *Bulletin*, July 25, 1877; *Chronicle*, July 25, 1877; *Examiner*, July 25, 26, 1877; *Alta*, July 25, 1877.

17   *Chronicle*, July 25, 26, 1877; *Bulletin*, July 25, 26, 1877; *Alta*, July 25, 26, 1877.

18   *Chronicle*, July 25, 1877; *Bulletin*, July 25, 1877; *Alta*, July 25, 1877.

19   *Chronicle*, July 26, 1877; *Bulletin*, July 26, 1877; *Examiner*, July 27, 1877.

20   *Chronicle*, July 27, 1877.

21   *Ibid.*; *Examiner*, July 27, 1877; *Alta*, July 27, 1877.

22   *Chronicle*, July 26, 1877; *Bulletin*, July 26, 1877.

23   *Alta*, July 27, 1877.

24   Robert J. Holton, "The Crowd in History: Some Problems of Theory and Method."

25   Michael E. McGerr, *The Decline of Popular Politics*, 3–11, esp. 5, 11.

26   *Bulletin*, July 24, 1877; *Chronicle*, July 24, 1877.

27   Alexander P. Saxton, *The Indispensable Enemy*, 21–30; Terrence J. McDonald, *The Parameters of Urban Fiscal Policy*, 132.

28   McDonald, *Urban Fiscal Policy*, 119.

29   [San Francisco, City and County, Registrar of Voters], *Annual Report . . . 1879*, in [San Francisco, City and County, Board of Supervisors], *Municipal Reports . . . 1879* (1879), 516.

30   [San Francisco, Registrar of Voters], *Annual Report . . . 1878*, in [San Francisco, Board of Supervisors], *Municipal Reports . . . 1878*, 323.

31   McDonald, *Urban Fiscal Policy*, 119–20.

CHAPTER 8

1 San Francisco *Examiner*, July 31, 1877.
2 *Ibid.*, September 3, 4, 1877; San Francisco *Chronicle*, August 26, 1877.
3 *Examiner*, July 25, August 21, 1877; San Francisco *Daily Evening Bulletin*, July 24, 1877.
4 *Examiner*, August 17, 1877; *Chronicle*, August 31, 1877; *Bulletin*, December 19, 1877.
5 *Examiner*, August 23, 1877; *Chronicle*, August 23, 1877; *Bulletin*, November 6, 1877.
6 Ira B. Cross, *A History of the Labor Movement in California*, 93–95; Hubert Howe Bancroft, *Popular Tribunals*, 2:708–09.
7 Because the July riots began after this meeting, historians have sometimes wondered if they (and the WPC) resembled the actions of rioting railroad workers in the East that same year. Were events in California a local variant of "The Great Uprising" during the "Year of Violence," or were they a unique phenomenon? Although historians of 1877 have found it difficult to ignore events in California totally, they have usually considered them only to a minimal degree. In *1877: Year of Violence*, Robert Bruce never mentioned Denis Kearney and the Workingmen's Party of California, and he discussed the July riots in only four out of nearly four hundred pages. A century ago, James Dabney McCabe took essentially the same tack. His attitude toward events in San Francisco is revealed by the subtitle of his *History of the Great Riots*, to wit, *Being a Full and Authentic Account of the Strikes and Riots on the Various Railroads of the United States and in the Mining Regions. Embracing Brilliant and Graphic Pen-Pictures of the Reign of Terror in Philadelphia, Baltimore, Chicago and Other Cities*. Nevertheless, the question of the relationship between events in San Francisco and events in the East has not been settled. Some years ago, Herbert Gutman called the national violence of 1877 "little understood" and suggested that the riots sprang out of "longstanding grievances that accompanied the transformation of Old [i.e., preindustrial] into New [i.e., industrial] America." He also argued that "characteristic European forms of 'premodern' artisan and lower-class protest" occurred in the United States before, during, and after industrialization, but he analyzed these forms of protest only "briefly": Herbert G. Gutman, *Work, Culture & Society in Industrializing America*, 54–55. What is really needed is a comprehensive study of the riots of 1877, both for its own sake and to resolve the question of any similarity between events in the East and events in the West. Until such a study appears, the question must remain unanswered.
8 *Examiner*, July 23, 1877; *Chronicle*, July 23, 24, 1877.
9 *Bulletin*, July 24, 1877.

10 Philip S. Foner, *The Workingmen's Party of the United States;* Philip S. Foner and Brewster Chamberlin, eds., *Friedrich A. Sorge's Labor Movement in the United States: A History of the American Working Class from Colonial Times to 1890.*

11 Foner, *Workingmen's Party,* 115.

12 *Chronicle,* July 24, 1877.

13 *Bulletin,* August 28, 1877.

14 *Examiner,* August 31, 1877.

15 *Chronicle,* November 3, 1877; *Bulletin,* November 3, 1877.

16 *Bulletin,* December 19, 20, 1877.

17 Hubert Howe Bancroft, *The History of California,* 7:335; Thomas Nast, "Social Science Solved," *Harper's Weekly,* 24 (no. 1215), April 10, 1880, p. 1.

18 Henry George, "The Kearney Agitation in California," 446–49.

19 [J. C. Stedman and R. A. Leonard], *The Workingmen's Party of California,* 72–86; *Chronicle,* November 17, December 6, 1877, May 16–21, 1878.

20 *Chronicle,* November 22, 1877.

21 *Chronicle,* November 17, December 27, 28, 1877.

22 [Stedman and Leonard], *Workingmen's Party of California,* 8–9, 12, 61; Workingmen's Party of California, Alameda County Executive Committee, *Denis Kearney and His Relations to the Workingmen's Party of California,* 18, 21–22; [Geo. W. Greene (pub.)], *The Labor Agitators; or, The Battle for Bread,* 4, 11; [Workingmen's Party of California], *To the People of California,* 3; Winfield J. Davis, *History of Political Conventions in California,* 1849–92, 366–69.

23 *Chronicle,* November 17, December 6, 19, 1877; [Stedman and Leonard], *Workingmen's Party of California,* 9; WPC, Alameda County Executive Committee, *Denis Kearney,* 31.

24 San Francisco *Daily Illustrated Open Letter,* February 3, 1878; *Chronicle,* November 17, December 6, 19, 1877, January 20, December 23, 1878; WPC, Alameda County Executive Committee, *Denis Kearney,* 31; [Stedman and Leonard], *Workingmen's Party of California,* 9.

25 [Stedman and Leonard], *Workingmen's Party of California,* 62; WPC, Alameda County Executive Committee, *Denis Kearney,* 18, 21–22; *Chronicle,* October 28, December 1, 1877, January 20, 25, 26, December 23, 1878; San Francisco *Daily Morning Call,* January 26, 1878; San Francisco *Daily Alta California,* January 25, 26, 1878; *Bulletin,* January 26, 1878.

26 [California, Board of Equalization], *Report for 1872–73,* 22–24; [United States, Bureau of the Census], *Wealth and Industry of the United States at the Ninth Census,* 346; [United States, Bureau of the Census], *Productions of Agriculture at the Tenth Census,* 34–35.

27 Arnold Schrier, *Ireland and the American Emigration,* 1850–1900, 6–7.

28   *Chronicle*, December 11, 1877, February 7, 1878; [Stedman and Leonard], *Workingmen's Party of California*, 12.

29   John P. Young, *San Francisco*, 2:516–23; George, "Kearney Agitation," 444–45.

30   *Chronicle*, December 3, 1877, February 6, 1878; *Open Letter*, June 2, 1878; WPC, Alameda County Executive Committee, *Denis Kearney*, 31; [Greene], *Labor Agitators*, 3; [Stedman and Leonard], *Workingmen's Party of California*, 14; [Charles Edward Pickett], *Philosopher Pickett's Anti-Plundercrat Pamphlet*, 12.

31   Cornel Lengyel, ed., *A San Francisco Songster*, 145; [Stedman and Leonard], *Workingmen's Party of California*, 7; San Francisco *Daily Sand Lot*, March 10, 1879; *Chronicle*, February 7, 1878; Workingmen's Party of California, Anti-Chinese Council, Investigating Committee, *Chinatown Declared a Nuisance!*

32   WPC, Anti-Chinese Council, *Chinatown Declared a Nuisance!*; [Greene], *Labor Agitators*, 9–10; [Stedman and Leonard], *Workingmen's Party of California*, 10–11, 14; *Chronicle*, September 22, 1877, January 7, 14, February 24, 1878; *Bulletin*, January 18, 24, February 4, 1878; *Call*, January 25, February 5, 11, 1878.

33   *Chronicle*, September 22, 1877, February 7, 24, 1878; [Stedman and Leonard], *Workingmen's Party of California*, 7; [Greene], *Labor Agitators*, 24–25; WPC, Anti-Chinese Council, *Chinatown Declared a Nuisance!*

CHAPTER 9

1   The platforms of the WPC referred to in this chapter can be found in [J. C. Stedman and R. A. Leonard], *The Workingmen's Party of California*, 61–63, 82–84.

2   In their ethnocentrism San Francisco's workingmen resembled the nativists of the 1840s and 1850s and particularly remind us of the relationship between nativism and radical republicanism. Another striking similarity is that many leaders of the earlier nativist movement were also of the petite bourgeoisie, like Denis Kearney, and attacked the elite and the poor with equal vigor. Nonetheless, the twenty- to thirty-year time lapse between the earlier nativist movement and the WPC, and the relatively young age of most Workingmen (see chap. 1) indicates that no causal link between the two movements can be forged, even recognizing the degree of Irish participation in both.

3   Philip S. Foner, *The Workingmen's Party of the United States*, 76.

4   San Francisco *Chronicle*, July 24, 1877; San Francisco *Daily Alta California*, July 24, 1877.

5   Descriptions of the platform of the Workingmen's Party of San Francisco can be found in the San Francisco *Daily Evening Bulletin*, August 28, 31,

1877; the San Francisco *Examiner*, August 31, 1877; and the *Chronicle*, August 31, 1877.

6 Accounts of the platform of the National Labor Party can be found in the *Chronicle*, November 3, 1877, and in the *Bulletin*, November 3 and December 10, 1877.

7 The declaration of principles of the Workingmen's Party of the United States is reprinted in Foner, *Workingmen's Party of the United States*, 115–16.

8 Steven J. Ross, *Workers on the Edge*, xix, 45–46, 56.

9 *Chronicle*, December 10, 28, 1877; Workingmen's Party of California, Alameda County Executive Committee, *Denis Kearney and His Relations to the Workingmen's Party of California*, 8, 13, 18, 20, 31.

10 *Chronicle*, November 30, December 10, 1877.

11 *Chronicle*, October 9, November 4, 1877; WPC, Alameda County Executive Committee, *Denis Kearney*, 20, 31; "The Song of the Sand Lot," unidentified broadside found in [Anonymous, (comp.)], Scrapbook of Ballots, Newspaper Clippings, etc., Pertaining to the Workingmen's Party of California.

12 Bertie Hale, "We the Workingmen are Coming!" unidentified broadside found in *ibid.*

13 D. W. C. Thompson, "Appeal to Californians," in San Francisco *Evening Post*, July 5, 1878.

14 Peter Bell, "Vote for the New Constitution," unidentified broadside found in [Anonymous], Scrapbook Pertaining to the Workingmen's Party of California.

15 James F. MacCaskie, "The Heathen Chinee," unidentified broadside found in *ibid.*

16 WPC, Alameda County Executive Committee, *Denis Kearney*, 34.

17 Ira B. Cross, ed., *Frank Roney, Irish Rebel and California Labor Leader*, 300.

CHAPTER 10

1 San Francisco *Chronicle*, August 12, 23, 1877.

2 *Ibid.*, September 24, October 9, November 22, 1877.

3 William Morris, ed., *The American Heritage Dictionary of the English Language* (Boston: American Heritage and Houghton Mifflin, 1969), 227, 350.

4 *Chronicle*, June 23, 1878; San Francisco *Evening Post*, March 29, 1878; Henry George, "The Kearney Agitation in California," 443–44.

5 George, "Kearney Agitation," 443–44.

6 *Chronicle*, July 16, 22, 1878.

7 *Ibid.*, September 22, 1877.

8 *Ibid.*

9   San Francisco *Daily Evening Bulletin*, November 1, 1877.

10   *Ibid.*, November 5, 1877.

11   *Ibid.*

12   *Chronicle*, October 12, 1877; San Francisco *Examiner*, September 22, 1877.

13   *Chronicle*, September 22, November 1, 1877.

14   *Bulletin*, November 5, 1877.

15   *Ibid.*

16   *Bulletin*, December 28, 1877.

17   *Ibid.*

18   *Chronicle*, August 19, September 2, 1877; *Examiner*, October 18, 1877.

19   *Chronicle*, December 28, 1877; *Bulletin*, October 1, November 6, 1877.

20   *Chronicle*, November 1, 1877; *Bulletin*, November 6, 1877.

21   *Chronicle*, October 8, 1877; *Examiner*, August 23, September 24, 1877.

22   *Chronicle*, November 16, 1877.

23   *Ibid.*, November 7, 1877.

24   *Ibid.*, November 18, 1877.

25   *Ibid.*, November 22, 1877.

26   *Ibid.*, November 10, 1877.

27   *Ibid.*, September 10, October 1, 1877.

28   *Ibid.*, November 3, 9, 1877; *Bulletin*, November 3, 1877.

29   *Chronicle*, November 13, 1877.

30   *Bulletin*, September 25, 1877; *Examiner*, September 25, October 9, 1877.

31   *Bulletin*, November 2, 1877; *Examiner*, October 16, 31, 1877.

32   *Examiner*, October 23, 1877.

33   *Chronicle*, October 13, 1877.

34   *Ibid.*, October 30, 1877; *Examiner*, October 30, November 3, 1877.

35   *Bulletin*, November 1, 1877.

36   *Chronicle*, November 3, 1877.

37   *Ibid.*, November 2, 3, 1877.

38   *Ibid.*, November 10, 1877; *Bulletin*, November 5, 1877; *Examiner*, November 5, 9, 1877.

39   *Chronicle*, November 8, 1877; *Examiner*, November 5, 1877.

40   *Examiner*, November 12, 1877; *Bulletin*, November 12, 1877.

41   *Examiner*, November 5, 1877.

42   *Bulletin*, November 5, 1877.

43   *Chronicle*, November 4, 1877.

44   *Bulletin*, November 5, 1877; *Examiner*, November 5, 1877.

45   *Bulletin*, November 14, 1877; *Examiner*, November 14, 1877; *Chronicle*, November 15, 1877.

46   San Francisco *Daily Morning Call*, November 16–18, 1877; *Bulletin*, November 16–18, 1877; *Alta*, November 16–18, 1877.

47 *Bulletin*, November 21, 1877; *Examiner*, November 21, 1877; *Chronicle*, November 22, 1877.
48 *Ibid.*
49 [San Francisco, City and County, Board of Supervisors], *Municipal Reports for . . . 1877–78* (1878), 904.
50 Ira B. Cross, ed., *Frank Roney, Irish Rebel and California Labor Leader*, 273–74.

CHAPTER 11

1 George Rudé, *The Crowd in History, 1730–1848*, 238; Susan Davis, *Parades and Power*, 5–6.
2 San Francisco *Chronicle*, September 18, 25, October 26, 1877.
3 *Ibid.*, November 26, 1877.
4 *Ibid.*, November 21–29, 1877.
5 *Ibid.*, November 30, 1877.
6 *Ibid.*, December 4, 1877.
7 "The Latest Phase of American Politics—A Sunday Matinee on the Sand-Lot," San Francisco *Illustrated Wasp* (July 24, 1880), 840–41.
8 *Chronicle*, December 5–7, 1877.
9 San Francisco *Daily Evening Bulletin*, January 16, 1878.
10 *Ibid.*, January 17, 1878; San Francisco *Daily Alta California*, January 17, 1878.
11 *Ibid.*
12 *Chronicle*, December 4, 1877, March 8, 12, June 7, 1878.
13 *Ibid.*, January 16, February 25, March 1, 8, June 8, 11, 1878; San Francisco *Daily Illustrated Open Letter*, February 11, 1878.
14 B[enjamin] E. Lloyd, *Lights and Shades in San Francisco*, 126–29.
15 John Bohstedt, *Riots and Community Politics in England and Wales, 1790–1810*.
16 Steven J. Ross, *Workers on the Edge*, 308–09; Richard Jules Oestreicher, *Solidarity and Fragmentation*, 128–32.
17 *Chronicle*, September 1877 to June 1878.
18 *Ibid.*, December 18, 19, 1877.
19 "Second Annual Picnic and Excursion of the Tenth Ward Indp't Rifles," broadside in [Anonymous, (comp.)], Scrapbook of Ballots, Newspaper Clippings, etc., Pertaining to the Workingmen's Party of California.
20 *Chronicle*, November 25, 1877.
21 *Ibid.*, February 21, March 9, May 20, 1878; "Another Disappointment of the Ass," *Wasp*, June 1, 1878.
22 San Francisco *Examiner*, December 19, 1877; *Chronicle*, January 16, February 2, 5, March 19, 26, 1878; *Open Letter*, 1877–78.
23 *Bulletin*, November 5, 1877.

24 *Chronicle,* April 8, 10, 12, 1878.
25 *Bulletin,* November 26, 1877
26 *Chronicle,* January 7, 14, 1878.
27 Workingmen's Party of California, Alameda County Executive Committee, *Denis Kearney and His Relations to the Workingmen's Party of California,* 19–20.
28 M. M. Marberry, *The Golden Voice,* 229–76; San Francisco *Evangel,* August 9, 1876.
29 *Evangel,* July 18, 1878.
30 *Chronicle,* December 10, 21, 1877.
31 *Ibid.,* December 10, 21, 29, 1877.
32 *Ibid.,* November 17, December 27, 28, 1877; *Bulletin,* December 28, 1877.
33 *Chronicle,* November 19, 25, 1877.

CHAPTER 12

1 Frank Roney, notes regarding *History of the Labor Movement in California,* Frank Roney Papers; Frank Roney, Diary of Life in San Francisco, 1875–1876, Frank Roney Papers; Ira B. Cross, ed., *Frank Roney, Irish Rebel and California Labor Leader,* 273–74; Alexander P. Saxton, *The Indispensable Enemy,* 121–27.
2 [J. C. Stedman and R. A. Leonard], *The Workingmen's Party of California,* 107–08.
3 San Francisco *Chronicle,* January 28, February 12, May 13, 1878.
4 Carl Brent Swisher, *Motivation and Political Technique in the California Constitutional Convention, 1878–79,* 19–24.
5 *Chronicle,* July 5, 1878; Swisher, *Motivation and Political Technique.*
6 *Chronicle,* September 3, 8, October 29, 1879; Hubert Howe Bancroft, *The History of California,* 7:411–12; Saxton, *Indispensable Enemy,* 141.
7 Henry George, "The Kearney Agitation in California," 446–49.
8 Swisher, *Motivation and Technique,* 27.
9 The California Constitution of 1879 is reprinted in William F. Swindler, ed., *Sources and Documents of United States Constitutions,* 1:469–508.
10 *Chronicle,* May 12, 14, 1879.
11 *Ibid.,* May 11, 1879.
12 James Bryce, *The American Commonwealth,* 1:443–46.
13 Saxton, *Indispensable Enemy,* 143–46.
14 Cross, *Frank Roney,* 302–04.
15 William A. Bullough, *The Blind Boss and His City,* 69.
16 *Chronicle,* June 3, 1879.
17 *Ibid.*
18 *Ibid.*

19   Doyce B. Nunis, Jr., "The Demagogue and the Demographer: Corre-
     spondence of Denis Kearney and Lord Bryce," 284, 286, 287.

CONCLUSION

1   One of the few exceptions to this generalization is Michael E. McGerr,
    The Decline of Popular Politics, but McGerr focuses more on de-mobiliza-
    tion, de-recruitment, and de-socialization and takes the prior stage
    somewhat for granted.
2   Saul K. Padover, ed., *Thomas Jefferson on Democracy* (New York: Men-
    tor paperback, 1953), 32.

Bibliography

PRIMARY SOURCES

Manuscript Collections

Baldwin, Elias J. Papers. Bancroft Library, University of California, Berkeley.

Barlow, Samuel L. Papers. Huntington Library, San Marino, California.

Camden, Johnson. Papers. West Virginia Collection, West Virginia University Library, Morgantown, West Virginia.

Crocker, Charles. Papers. Bancroft Library, University of California, Berkeley.

Crocker, Mary. Correspondence. California Historical Society Library, San Francisco.

Fair, James G. Papers. Bancroft Library, University of California, Berkeley.

Flood, James C. Papers. Bancroft Library, University of California, Berkeley.

Hawley, David. Observations Recorded for H. H. Bancroft. Bancroft Library, University of California, Berkeley.

Hopkins, Mark. Correspondence and Papers, 1861–78. Microfilm, Bancroft Library, University of California, Berkeley.

———. Papers. Bancroft Library, University of California, Berkeley.

Huntington, Collis P. Papers. Bancroft Library, University of California, Berkeley.

———. Papers. Syracuse University Library, Syracuse, New York.

Pownall Family. Papers. Huntington Libary, San Marino, California.

Roney, Frank. Papers, 1870–1925. Bancroft Library, University of California, Berkeley.

Sharon, Louise Tevis. Papers. Sharon Family Collection, Bancroft Library, University of California, Berkeley.

Smith, Grant H. Papers. Bancroft Library, University of California, Berkeley.

Stanford, Jane. Papers. Stanford Family Collection, Stanford University Library, Palo Alto, California.

Stanford, Leland. Papers. Bancroft Library, University of California, Berkeley.

———. Papers. Stanford Family Collection, Stanford University Library, Palo Alto, California.

Unpublished Manuscripts

Andrew, Bunyan Hadley. "Charles Crocker." M.A. Thesis, University of California, Berkeley, n.d.

Cioffi, Ralph Walter. "Mark Hopkins: Inside Man of the Big Four." M.A. Thesis, University of California, Berkeley, 1950.

Elgie, Robert Andrew. "The Development of San Francisco Manufacturing, 1848–1880: An Analysis of Regional Locational Factors and Urban Spatial Structure." M.A. Thesis, University of California, Berkeley, 1966.

Smith, Grant H., John Mackay. Grant Smith Papers. Bancroft Library, University of California, Berkeley.

Scrapbooks

[Anonymous, comp.]. Scrapbook of Ballots, Newspaper Clippings, etc., Pertaining to the Workingmen's Party of California. California Collection, California State Library, Sacramento.

Bancroft, Hubert Howe, comp. Bancroft Scrapbooks. 105 vols. Bancroft Library, University of California, Berkeley.

Fitzhamon, E. G., comp. The Streets of San Francisco. 4 vols. Bancroft Library, University of California, Berkeley.

Government Documents and Publications

Becker, George F. *Geology of the Comstock Lode and the Washoe District.* Washington: GPO, 1882.

[California, Board of Equalization]. *Report for 1872–73.* Sacramento: J. D. Young, 1873.

[California, Bureau of Labor Statistics]. *First Biennial Report.* Sacramento: J. D. Young, 1884.

[California, Legislature, Joint Committee on Labor Investigation]. *Reports.* In [California, Legislature], *Appendix to the Journals of the Senate and Assembly,* vol. 22, pt. 4 (1877/78). Sacramento: npub., 1878, pp. 1–9.

"Labor in America and Europe." *House Exec. Doc. 21,* 44th Cong., 1st Sess.

Lord, Eliot. *Comstock Mining and Miners.* Berkeley, California: Howell-North reprint, 1959.

Raymond, Rossiter W. *Mineral Resources of the United States and Territories West of the Rocky Mountains.* Washington: GPO, 1869.

"Report of the Joint Special Committee to Investigate Chinese Immigration." *Senate Report 689,* 44th Cong., 2d Sess.

[San Francisco, City and County, Assessor]. *Annual Report*. San Francisco: npub., 1864–81.

[San Francisco, City and County, Board of Supervisors]. *Municipal Reports*. San Francisco: W. M. Hinton, 1865–85.

[San Francisco, City and County, Coroner]. *Annual Report, 1878*. San Francisco: npub., 1878.

[San Francisco, City and County, Health Officer]. *Annual Report, 1877*. San Francisco: Spalding and Barto, 1878.

[San Francisco, City and County, Industrial School]. *Annual Report*. San Francisco: npub., 1859–79.

[San Francisco, City and County, Registrar of Voters]. *Annual Report, 1878*. San Francisco: npub. 1879.

———. *Great Register for 1878*. San Francisco: npub., 1878.

Swindler, William F., ed. *Sources and Documents of United States Constitutions*. Vol. 1. Dobbs Ferry, N.Y.: Oceana, 1973.

[United States, Bureau of the Census]. *Agriculture of the United States in 1860*. Washington: GPO, 1864.

———. *Compendium of the Ninth Census*. Washington: GPO, 1872.

———. *Compendium of the Tenth Census*. 2 vols. Washington: GPO, 1888.

———. *Historical Statistics of the United States: Colonial Times to 1957*. Washington: GPO, 1961.

———. *Manufactures of the United States in 1860*. Washington: GPO, 1865.

———. Ninth Census of the United States: 1870; Manuscript Schedules of Manufactures, City and County of San Francisco. Microfilm, Bancroft Library, University of California, Berkeley.

———. *Productions of Agriculture at the Tenth Census*. Washington: GPO, 1883.

———. *Statistics of Manufactures of the United States at the Tenth Census*. Washington: GPO, 1883.

———. *Statistics of the Population of the United States at the Tenth Census*. Washington: GPO, 1883.

———. *Statistics of the Population of the United States in 1870*. Washington: GPO, 1872.

———. *Statistics of the United States in 1860*. Washington: GPO, 1866.

———. Tenth Census of the United States: 1880; Manuscript Population Schedules, City and County of San Francisco. Microfilm, Bancroft Library, University of California, Berkeley.

———. Tenth Census of the United States: 1880; Manuscript Schedules of Manufactures, City and County of San Francisco. Microfilm, Bancroft Library, University of California, Berkeley.

———. *Wealth and Industry of the United States at the Ninth Census*. Washington: GPO, 1872.

[United States, Department of Labor]. *Wages in the United States and Europe, 1870 to 1898*. Washington: GPO, 1898.

[United States, Director of the Mint]. *Annual Report, 1875.* Washington: GPO, 1875.

[United States, Pacific Railway Commission]. *Report and Testimony.* 9 vols. Washington: GPO, 1887.

[United States, Senate, Committee on Finance]. *Report on Wholesale Prices and Wages.* 4 vols. Washington: GPO, 1893.

[United States, Works Projects Administration, San Francisco Theatre Research Project]. *History of Opera in San Francisco.* 2 vols. San Francisco: npub., 1938.

Willis, E. B., and P. K. Stockton, stenos. *Debates and Proceedings of the Constitutional Convention of the State of California, . . . 1878.* 3 vols. Sacramento: npub., 1880.

Wright, Carroll D. *A Report on Marriage and Divorce in the United States, 1867 to 1886.* Washington: GPO, 1889.

Directory and Map

Langley, Henry G., comp. *The San Francisco Directory.* San Francisco: Francis, Valentine, 1861–81.

[————]. *Guidemap of the City of San Francisco.* San Francisco: Francis, Valentine, 1880.

Printed Diaries, Reminiscences, and Letters

Atherton, Gertrude. *Adventures of a Novelist.* New York: Liveright, 1932.

Ayers, James J. *Gold and Sunshine: Reminiscences of Early California.* Boston: R. G. Badger, 1922.

Benjamin, I. J. *Three Years in America: 1859–1862.* 2 vols. Philadelphia: Jewish Publication Society of America, 1956.

Berner, Bertha. *Mrs. Leland Stanford: An Intimate Account.* Palo Alto, Calif.: Stanford University Press, 1934.

Burnett, Peter H. *Recollections and Opinions of an Old Pioneer.* New York: D. Appleton, 1880.

Chambliss, William H. *Chambliss Diary; or Society as It Really Is.* New York: Chambliss, 1895.

Cross, Ira B., ed. *Frank Roney, Irish Rebel and California Labor Leader: An Autobiography.* Berkeley: University of California Press, 1931.

Gardiner, Howard Calhoun. *In Pursuit of the Golden Dream.* Dale L. Morgan, ed. Staughton, Mass.: Western Hemisphere, 1970.

Gates, Paul W., ed. *California Ranchos and Farms, 1846–1862.* Madison: State Historical Society of Wisconsin, 1967.

Hannum, Anna Paschal, ed. *A Quaker Forty-Niner: The Adventures of Charles Edward Pancoast. . . .* Philadelphia: University of Pennsylvania Press, 1930.

Harpending, Asbury. *The Great Diamond Hoax and Other Stirring Incidents. . . .* Norman: University of Oklahoma Press, 1958.

Levy, Harriet Lane. *920 O'Farrell Street.* Garden City, N.Y.: Doubleday, 1947.

McKee, Irving, ed. *Alonzo Delano's California Correspondence.* Sacramento: Sacramento Book Collector's Club, 1952.

Neville, Amelia Ransome. *The Fantastic City.* Boston: Houghton, Mifflin, 1932.

Nunis, Doyce B., Jr. "The Demagogue and the Demographer; Correspondence of Denis Kearney and Lord Bryce." *Pacific Historical Review* 36 (1967), 269–88.

Shumsky, Neil Larry, ed. "Frank Roney's San Francisco—His Diary: April, 1875—March, 1876." *Labor History* 17 (Spring 1976), 245–64.

Tinkham, George H. *California Men and Events; Time, 1769–1890.* Stockton, Calif.: Record Publishing, 1915.

Descriptions, Travel Accounts, and Novels

Apponyi, Flora. *The Libraries of California.* San Francisco: A. L. Bancroft, 1878.

[Argonaut Publishing Company]. *The Elite Directory for San Francisco and Oakland.* San Francisco: Argonaut, 1879.

Bryce, James. *The American Commonwealth.* 2 vols., 3d ed. New York: Macmillan, 1909.

Bushnell, Horace. *Characteristics and Prospects of California.* San Francisco: Whitton, Townes, 1858.

Clark, J. F. *The Society in Search of Truth; or, Stock Gambling in San Francisco.* Oakland, Calif.: Pacific Press, 1878.

Coffin, Charles Carleton. *Our New Way Round the World.* Boston: Fields, Osgood, 1869.

Cooper, James Fenimore, *Home as Found.* New York: Capricorn Books paperback, 1961.

Crapper, James. *A Month in California.* London: Society for Promoting Christian Knowledge, 1873.

Dickens, Charles. *The Life and Adventures of Martin Chuzzlewit.* London: Oxford University Press, 1971.

Hardy, Lady Duffus. *Through Cities and Prairie Lands: Sketches of an American Tour.* New York: R. Worthington, 1881.

Hinchcliff, Thomas Woodbine. *Over the Sea and Far Away.* London: Longmans, Green, 1876.

Howells, William D. *The Rise of Silas Lapham.* Boston: Houghton Mifflin paperback, 1957.

Lloyd, B[enjamin] E. *Lights and Shades in San Francisco.* San Francisco: A. L. Bancroft, 1876.

MacGregor, William Laird. *Hotels and Hotel Life at San Francisco, California in 1876.* San Francisco News, 1877.

———. *San Francisco, California in 1876.* Edinburgh: T. Laurie, 1876.

Marshall, W. G. *Through America, or, Nine Months in the United States.* London: Sampson Low, Marston, Searle & Rivington, 1882.

Morford, Henry. *Morford's Scenery and Sensation Hand-book of the Pacific Railroads of California.* New York: Charles T. Dillingham, 1878.

Older, Mrs. Fremont. *The Socialist and the Prince.* New York and London: Funk & Wagnalls, 1903.

Ross, W. F. *Westward By Rail: The New Route to the East.* New York: D. Appleton, 1871.

Seyd, Ernest. *California and Its Resources.* London: Turner, 1858.

Trollope, Frances. *Domestic Manners of the Americans.* New York: Dodd, Mead, 1927.

Twain, Mark. *Sketches, Old and New.* New York and London: Harper & Brothers, 1875.

Watson, [Mary]. *San Francisco Society, Its Characters and Its Characteristics.* San Francisco: npub., 1887.

Newspapers

San Francisco *Chronicle* (1865–), 1870–80.

San Francisco *Commercial Herald and Market Review* (1867–1911), 1867–80.

San Francisco *Daily Alta California* (1849–91), 1860–80.

San Francisco *Daily Evening Bulletin* (1855–1929), 1877–80.

San Francisco *Daily Illustrated Open Letter* (1877–1878), 1878.

San Francisco *Daily Morning Call* (1856–1965), 1877–80.

San Francisco *Daily Sand Lot* (1879), 1879.

San Francisco *Evangel*, 1876–80.

San Francisco *Evening Post* (1871–1913), 1877–80.

San Francisco *Examiner* (1865–1976), 1877–80.

Contemporary Periodicals

Argonaut. San Francisco, 1877–80.

Illustrated Wasp. San Francisco, 1877–80.

Newsletter and California Advertiser. San Francisco, 1877–80.

Contemporary Pamphlets and Reports

California Immigrant Union. *Memorial and Report. . . .* Sacramento: T. A. Springer, 1872.

California Mining Company. *Annual Report.* San Francisco: Office of the Daily Stock Exchange, 1877–79.

Central Pacific Railroad Company vs. Cohen, Alfred A. *Answer: Alfred A. Cohen, Attorney Pro Se.* San Francisco: npub., 1876.

Conwell, R. H. "Acres of Diamonds." In Oscar Handlin, ed., *Readings in American History.* New York: Alfred A. Knopf, 1957.

Davis, Horace. *California Breadstuffs.* Unidentified pamphlet bound in "Pamphlets on California Commerce." Bancroft Library, University of California, Berkeley.

Dewey, Squire P. *The Bonanza Mines of Nevada.* San Francisco: npub., 1878.

[Greene, Geo. W. (publisher)]. *The Labor Agitators; or, The Battle for Bread.* San Francisco: Geo. W. Greene, n.d.

Hall, Charles Victor. *California: The Ideal Italy of the World; An Outline Mirror of the State for Health, Happiness, and Delightful Homes.* Philadelphia: npub., 1875.

[Hittell, John S.]. *All About California and the Inducements to Settle There.* San Francisco: California Immigrant Union, 1870.

Immigrant Association of California. *[Second] Annual Report.* San Francisco: Bacon, 1884.

Jackson Street Free Kindergarten Association. *Annual Report.* San Francisco: Dodge Brothers, 1882–86.

McRuer, D. C. *Summary of Objections to the "Goat Island Bill," Presented to the Senate Committee on Military Affairs. . . . .* San Francisco: npub., 1873.

Monterey, California: The Most Charming Winter Resort in the World. Monterey, Calif. (?): npub., 1881 (?).

[Pickett, Charles Edward]. *Philosopher Pickett's Anti-Plundercrat Pamphlet.* San Francisco: npub., 1879.

[San Francisco, Chamber of Commerce]. *Annual Report.* San Francisco: npub., 1878–80.

—————. *Appeal to the California Delegation in Congress Upon the Goat Island Grant.* San Francisco: *Alta California* Publishing House, 1872.

[San Francisco *Newsletter and California Advertiser*]. *Artistic Homes of California.* San Francisco: San Francisco *Newsletter*, 1887.

[Stedman, J. C., and R. A. Leonard]. *The Workingmen's Party of California: An Epitome of Its Rise and Progress.* San Francisco: Bacon, 1878.

[Sumner, Charles Allen]. *Holding Down to the Main Question.* San Francisco: npub., 1878.

[Workingmen's Party of California]. *To the People of California.* San Francisco: npub., 1878.

Workingmen's Party of California, Alameda County Executive Committee. *Denis Kearney and His Relations to the Workingmen's Party of California.* San Francisco: Faulkner & Fish, [1879?].

Workingmen's Party of California, Anti-Chinese Council, Investigating Committee. *Chinatown Declared a Nuisance!* San Francisco: npub., 1880.

Contemporary Articles and Speeches

Bell, Samuel L. "Annual Address to the California State Agricultural Society." *California Culturist* (San Francisco) 1 (September 1858), 149–58.

George, Henry. "The Kearney Agitation in California." *Popular Science Monthly* 17 (August 1880), 433–53.

———. "What the Railroad Will Bring Us." *Overland Monthly* 1 (July 1868), 297–306.

Huntington, Collis P. *California, Her Past, Present, and Future.* San Francisco: npub., 1900.

———. *The Future of the Negro.* San Francisco: npub., 1901.

SECONDARY SOURCES

Biographies

Bancroft, Hubert Howe. *Chronicles of the Builders of the Commonwealth.* 7 vols. San Francisco: History Company, 1891–92.

———. *History of the Life of Leland Stanford, a Character Study.* Oakland, Calif.: Biobooks, 1952.

Berlin, Ellin. *Silver Platter.* Garden City, N.Y.: Doubleday, 1957.

Caughey, John Walton. *Hubert Howe Bancroft.* Berkeley: University of California Press, 1946.

Clark, George T. *Leland Stanford.* Palo Alto, Calif.: Stanford University Press, 1931.

[Curtis, Edward]. *Two California Sketches.* San Francisco: Thomas Steam Printing House, 1880.

Evans, Cerinda W. *Collis Potter Huntington.* 2 vols. Newport News, Va.: Mariner's Museum, 1954.

Glasscock, C. B. *Lucky Baldwin.* New York: A. L. Burt, 1933.

Jordan, David Starr. "Jane Lathrop Stanford." *Popular Science Monthly* 75 (August 1909), 157–73.

Lavender, David S. *The Great Persuader.* Garden City, N.Y.: Doubleday, 1970.

Lewis, Oscar. *The Big Four.* New York: Knopf, 1966.

———. *Silver Kings.* New York: Knopf, 1964.

Livesay, Harold C. *Samuel Gompers and Organized Labor in America.* Boston: Little, Brown, 1978.

Lyman, George D. *Ralston's Ring.* New York: Ballantine, 1971.

Marberry, M. M. *The Golden Voice: a Biography of Isaac Kalloch.* New York: Farrar, Straus, 1947.

Redding, Benjamin Bernard. *A Sketch of the Life of Mark Hopkins of California.* San Francisco: A. L. Bancroft, 1881.

Ryder, David Warren. *Great Citizen: a Biography of William H. Crocker.* San Francisco: Historical Publications, 1962.

Shuck, Oscar T. *Sketches of Leading and Representative Men of San Francisco.* San Francisco: Bacon, 1875.

Tilton, Cecil G. *William Chapman Ralston: Courageous Builder.* Boston: Christopher, 1935.

Tutorow, Norman E. *Leland Stanford: Man of Many Careers.* Menlo Park, Calif.: Pacific Coast, 1971.

Articles

Averbach, Alvin. "San Francisco's South of Market District, 1850–1950: The Emergence of a Skid Row." *California Historical Quarterly* 52 (1973), 196–223.

Barth, Gunther. "Metropolism and Urban Elites in the Far West." In Frederic Cople Jaher, ed., *The Age of Industrialism in America.* New York: Free Press, 1968, pp. 158–87.

Bartlett, Richard A. "The Diamond Hoax." In *Great Surveys of the American West.* Norman: University of Oklahoma Press, 1967, pp. 187–205.

Carr, Patricia E. "Emperor Norton I." *American History Illustrated* 10 (July 1975), 14–20.

Coman, Edwin T., Jr. "Sidelights on the Investment Policies of Stanford, Huntington, Hopkins, and Crocker." *Bulletin of the Business History Society* 16 (November 1942), 85–89.

Dancis, Bruce. "Social Mobility and Class Consciousness: San Francisco's International Workingmen's Association in the 1880's." *Journal of Social History* 11 (Fall 1977), 75–98.

Erie, Steven P. "Politics, the Public Sector and Irish Social Mobility: San Francisco, 1870–1900." *Western Political Quarterly,* 31 (June 1978), 274–89.

Gates, Paul W. "California's Agricultural College Lands." *Pacific Historical Review* 30 (May 1961), 103–22.

———. "Frontier Estate Builders and Farm Laborers." In Walker D. Wyman and Clifton B. Kroeber, eds., *The Frontier in Perspective.* Madison: University of Wisconsin Press, 1957, pp. 144–63.

Handlin, Oscar. "Comments on Mass and Popular Culture." In Norman Jacobs, ed., *Culture for the Millions.* Princeton, N.J.: Van Nostrand, 1964.

Holton, Robert J. "The Crowd in History: Some Problems of Theory and Method." *Social History* 3 (May 1978), 219–33.

Kauer, Ralph. "The Workingmen's Party of California." *Pacific Historical Review* 13 (September 1944), 278–91.

Kazin, Michael. "Prelude to Kearneyism: The 'July Days' in San Francisco, 1877." *New Labor Review* 3 (1980), 5–47.

Nash, Gerald D. "Henry George Reappraised: William Chapman's Views on Land Speculation in Nineteenth Century California." *Agricultural History* 33 (September 1959), 133–37.

Paul, Rodman. "The Great California Grain War: The Grangers Challenge the Wheat King." *Pacific Historical Review* 27 (November 1958), 331–50.
———. "The Wheat Trade between California and the United Kingdom." *Mississippi Valley Historical Review* 45 (December 1958), 391–412.
Rezneck, Samuel. "Distress, Relief and Discontent in the United States During the Depression of 1873–78." *Journal of Political Economy* 58 (1950), 494–512.
Wells, O. V. "The Depression of 1873–79." *Agricultural History* 11 (1937), 237–51.

Dictionary

Johnson, Allen, and Dumas Malone, eds. *Dictionary of American Biography.* 20 vols. New York: Charles Scribner's Sons, 1928–36.

Monographs

Albion, Robert Greenhalgh. *The Rise of New York Port.* Newton Abbot: David & Charles reprint, 1970.
Armstrong, Leroy. *Financial California.* San Francisco: Coast Banker, 1916.
Asbury, Herbert. *The Barbary Coast.* New York: Alfred A. Knopf, 1933.
Austin, Barbara E. *A Story of Rancho del Paso.* Sacramento: Sacramento State College Alumni Association, 1962.
Bancroft, Hubert Howe. *Popular Tribunals.* 2 vols., San Francisco: History Company, 1890.
Barth, Gunther. *Instant Cities: Urbanization and the Rise of San Francisco and Denver.* New York: Oxford University Press, 1975.
Bohstedt, John. *Riots and Community Politics in England and Wales, 1790–1810.* Cambridge, Mass., and London: Harvard University Press, 1983.
Bruce, Robert V. *1877: Year of Violence.* Chicago: Quadrangle Books paperback, 1970.
Bullough, William A. *The Blind Boss and His City.* Berkeley, Los Angeles, London: University of California Press, 1979.
Burbank, David T. *Reign of the Rabble: The St. Louis General Strike of 1877.* New York: Augustus M. Kelley, 1966.
Burchell, R. A. *The San Francisco Irish, 1848–1880.* Berkeley and Los Angeles: University of California Press, 1980.
Calhoun, Craig. *The Question of Class Struggle: Social Foundations of Popular Radicalism during the Industrial Revolution.* Chicago: University of Chicago Press, 1982.
Caughey, John W. *Gold is the Cornerstone.* Berkeley: University of California Press, 1948.
Clark, Samuel. *Social Origins of the Irish Land War.* Princeton, N.J.: Princeton University Press, 1979.

Clark, Samuel, and James S. Donnelly, Jr. *Irish Peasants: Violence & Political Unrest, 1780–1914*. Madison: University of Wisconsin Press, 1983.

Cook, Adrian. *The Armies of the Streets: The New York City Draft Riots of 1863*. Lexington: University Press of Kentucky, 1974.

Cooper, Patricia. *Once a Cigar Maker: Men, Women and Work Culture in American Cigar Factories, 1900–1919*. Urbana: University of Illinois Press, 1987.

Cross, Ira B. *A History of the Labor Movement in California*. Berkeley: University of California Press, 1935.

Crothers, George Edward. *The Educational Ideals of Jane Lathrop Stanford*. Palo Alto, Calif.: Stanford University Press, 1933.

Dacus, J. A. *Annals of the Great Strikes*. New York: Arno and New York Times reprint, 1969.

Daggett, Stuart. *Chapters on the History of the Southern Pacific*. New York: Ronald, 1922.

Davis, Susan. *Parades and Power: Street Theatre in Nineteenth-Century Philadelphia*. Philadelphia: Temple University Press, 1986.

Davis, Winfield J. *History of Political Conventions in California, 1849–92*. Sacramento: California State Library, 1893.

Decker, Peter R. *Fortunes and Failures: White-Collar Mobility in Nineteenth-Century San Francisco*. Cambridge, Mass., and London: Harvard University Press, 1978.

Dickson, Samuel. *Tales of San Francisco*. Palo Alto, Calif.: Stanford University Press, 1947.

Dulles, Foster Rhea. *Labor in America: A History*. New York: Thomas Y. Crowell, 1960.

Dwyer, Richard A., and Richard E. Lingenfelter, eds. *The Songs of the Gold Rush*. Berkeley and Los Angeles: University of California Press, 1964.

Eaves, Lucile. *A History of California Labor Legislation, with an Introductory Sketch of the San Francisco Labor Movement*. Berkeley: University Press, 1910.

Elliott, Orrin Leslie. *Stanford University, the First Twenty-five Years*. Stanford, Calif.: Stanford University Press, 1937.

Fahler, Paul G. *Mechanics and Manufacturers in the Early Industrial Revolution: Lynn, Massachusetts, 1780–1860*. Albany: State University of New York Press, 1981.

Feldberg, Michael. *The Turbulent Era: Riot and Disorder in Jacksonian America*. New York: Oxford University Press, 1980.

Foner, Philip, ed. *The Formation of the Workingmen's Party of the United States: Proceedings of the Union Congress Held at Philadelphia, July 19–22, 1876*. New York: American Institute for Marxist Studies, Occasional Paper No. 18, 1976.

―――. *The Great Labor Uprising of 1877*. New York: Monad, 1977.

————. *The Workingmen's Party of the United States: A History of the First Marxist Party in the Americas.* Minneapolis: MEP, 1984.

Foner, Philip S., and Brewster Chamberlain, eds. *Friedrich A. Sorge's Labor Movement in the United States: A History of the American Working Class from Colonial Times to 1890.* Westport, Conn., and London: Greenwood Press, 1977.

Garraty, John A. *Unemployment in History: Economic Thought and Public Policy.* New York: Harper & Row, 1978.

Gutman, Herbert G. *Work, Culture & Society in Industrializing America.* New York: Vintage paperback, 1977.

Handlin, Oscar. *Boston's Immigrants: A Study in Acculturation.* New York: Atheneum paperback, 1968.

————. *The Uprooted.* Boston: Little, Brown, 1951.

Hart, James D. *The Popular Book.* Berkeley and Los Angeles: University of California Press, 1963.

Hobsbawm, Eric. *Primitive Rebels.* New York: W. W. Norton paperback, 1959.

Hoerder, Dirk. *Crowd Action in Revolutionary Massachusetts, 1765–1780.* New York: Academic Press, 1977.

Hofstadter, Richard, and Walter P. Metzger. *The Development of Academic Freedom in the United States.* New York: Columbia University Press, 1955.

Junior League of San Francisco. *Here Today.* San Francisco: Chronicle Books, 1968.

Kaye, Harvey J., ed. *The Face of the Crowd: Studies in Revolution, Ideology, and Popular Protest: Selected Essays of George Rudé.* Atlantic Highlands, N.J.: Humanities Press International, 1988.

Kelley, Robert L. *Gold vs. Grain: The Hydraulic Mining Controversy in California's Sacramento Valley.* Glendale, Calif.: Arthur H. Clarke, 1959.

King, Joseph L. *History of the San Francisco Stock and Exchange Board.* San Francisco: J. L. King, 1910.

Kirker, Harold. *California's Architectural Frontier.* San Marino, Calif.: Huntington Library, 1960.

Lawson, Steven F. *Black Ballots: Voting Rights in the South, 1944–1969.* New York: Columbia University Press, 1976.

————. *In Pursuit of Power: Southern Blacks and Electoral Politics, 1965–1982.* New York: Columbia University Press, 1985.

Lengyel, Cornel, ed. *A San Francisco Songster.* San Francisco: npub., 1939.

Lewis, Oscar. *Here Lived the Californians.* New York: Rinehart, 1957.

Lewis, Oscar, and Carroll D. Hall. *Bonanza Inn.* New York: Alfred A. Knopf, 1971.

Long, Clarence D. *Wages and Earnings in the United States, 1860–1890.* Princeton, N.J.: Princeton University Press, 1960.

Lotchin, Roger. *San Francisco, 1846–1856: From Hamlet to City.* New York: Oxford University Press, 1974.

McCabe, James Dabney. *The History of the Great Riots.* . . . New York: Augustus M. Kelley reprint, 1971.

McCartney, E. Ray. *Crisis of 1873.* Minneapolis: Burgess, 1935.

McDonald, Terrence J. *The Parameters of Urban Fiscal Policy: Socioeconomic Change and Political Culture in San Francisco, 1860–1906.* Berkeley and Los Angeles: University of California Press, 1986.

McGerr, Michael E. *The Decline of Popular Politics: The American North, 1865–1928.* New York and Oxford: Oxford University Press, 1986.

Maier, Pauline. *From Resistance to Revolution: Colonial Radicals and the Development of American Opposition to Britain, 1765–1776.* New York: Alfred A. Knopf, 1972.

May, Philip Ross. *Origins of Hydraulic Mining in California.* Oakland, Calif.: Holmes, 1970.

Mirrielees, Edith R. *Stanford: the Story of a University.* New York: Putnam, 1959.

Nash, Gerald. *State Government and Economic Development.* Berkeley: University of California Press, 1964.

Nasaw, David. *Schooled to Order: A Social History of Public Schooling in the United States.* New York: Oxford University Press, 1979.

Oestreicher, Richard Jules. *Solidarity and Fragmentation: Working People and Class Consciousness in Detroit, 1875–1900.* Urbana and Chicago: University of Illinois Press, 1986.

Paul, Rodman W. *California Gold: The Beginnings of Mining in the Far West.* Cambridge, Mass.: Harvard University Press, 1947.

———. *Mining Frontiers of the Far West, 1848–1880.* New York: Holt, Rinehart and Winston, 1963.

Perlman, Selig. *A History of Trade Unionism in the United States.* New York: Macmillan, 1923.

Peterson, Richard H. *The Bonanza Kings.* Lincoln: University of Nebraska Press, 1971.

Purtell, Joseph. *The Tiffany Touch.* New York: Random House, 1972.

Quigley, Hugh. *The Irish Race in California and on the Pacific Coast.* San Francisco: A. Roman, 1878.

Rayback, Joseph G. *A History of American Labor.* New York: Free Press, 1959.

Reddy, William. *The Rise of Market Culture: The Textile Trade and French Society, 1750–1900.* Cambridge, England, and New York: Cambridge University Press, 1984.

Richter, Donald C. *Riotous Victorians.* Athens, Ohio, and London: Ohio University Press, 1981.

Ross, Steven J. *Workers on the Edge: Work, Leisure, and Politics in Industrializing Cincinnati, 1788–1890.* New York: Columbia University Press, 1985.

Rudé, George. *The Crowd in History, 1730–1848.* New York, London, Sydney: John Wiley paperback, 1964.

Sandmeyer, Elmer Clarence. _The Anti-Chinese Movement in California._ Urbana, Chicago, London: University of Illinois Press paperback, 1973.

Saxton, Alexander P. _The Indispensable Enemy: Labor and the Anti-Chinese Movement in California._ Berkeley: University of California Press, 1971.

Schrier, Arnold. _Ireland and the American Emigration, 1850–1900._ New York: Russell & Russell, 1958.

Schultz, Stanley K. _The Culture Factory: Boston Public Schools, 1789–1860._ New York: Oxford University Press, 1973.

Smith, Grant H. _The History of the Comstock Lode, 1850–1920._ Reno: University of Nevada Press, 1943.

Starr, Kevin. _Americans and the California Dream, 1850–1915._ New York: Oxford University Press, 1973.

Swisher, Carl Brent. _Motivation and Political Technique in the California Constitutional Convention, 1878–79._ New York: Da Capo reprint, 1969.

Thernstrom, Stephan. _The Other Bostonians._ Cambridge, Mass.: Harvard University Press, 1973.

Thompson, F. M. L. _English Landed Society in the Nineteenth Century._ London: Routledge & Kegan Paul, 1963.

Tilly, Charles. _The Contentious French._ Cambridge, Mass., and London: Harvard University Press, 1986.

Tilly, Charles, Louise Tilly, and Richard Tilly. _The Rebellious Century, 1830–1930._ Cambridge, Mass.: Harvard University Press, 1975.

Townshend, Charles. _Political Violence in Ireland: Government and Resistance Since 1848._ Oxford: Oxford University Press, 1983.

Veblen, Thorstein. _The Theory of the Leisure Class._ New York: New American Library paperback, 1953.

Ware, Norman J. _The Labor Movement in the United States._ Gloucester, Mass.: Peter Smith, 1959.

Wecter, Dixon. _The Saga of American Society._ New York: Charles Scribner's Sons, 1937.

Weinstein, Allen. _Prelude to Populism: Origins of the Silver Issue, 1867–1878._ New Haven, Conn.: Yale University Press, 1970.

Williams, R. Hal. _The Democratic Party and California Politics, 1880–1906._ Stanford, Calif.: Stanford University Press, 1973.

Wilson, Neill Compton. _400 California Street: the Story of the Bank of California._ San Francisco: Bank of California, 1964.

Woodard, Bruce A. _Diamonds in the Sand._ Boulder, Colo.: Pruett, 1967.

Wright, William. _The Big Bonanza._ New York: Alfred A. Knopf, 1947.

General Histories

Altrocchi, Julia Cooley. _The Spectacular San Franciscans._ New York: E. P. Dutton, 1949.

Angel, Myron. _History of Nevada._ Oakland, Calif.: Thompson & West, 1881.

Atherton, Gertrude. *Golden Gate Country*. New York: Duell, Sloan & Pierce, 1945.

————. *My San Francisco: A Wayward Biography*. Indianapolis and New York: Bobbs-Merrill, 1946.

Bancroft, Hubert Howe. *The History of California*. 7 vols. San Francisco: History Company, 1884–90.

————. *History of Nevada, Colorado, and Wyoming*. San Francisco: History Company, 1890.

Commons, John R. et al. *History of Labour in the United States*. 4 vols. New York: Macmillan, 1918.

Cross, Ira B. *Financing an Empire: Banking in California*. 4 vols. Chicago: S. J. Clarke, 1927.

Davis, Sam P., ed. *The History of Nevada*. 2 vols. Reno, Nev.: Elms, 1913.

Elliott, Russell R. *History of Nevada*. Lincoln: University of Nebraska Press, 1973.

Hittell, John S. *A History of San Francisco, and Incidentally of the State of California*. San Francisco: A. L. Bancroft, 1877.

McGowan, Joseph A. *A History of the Sacramento Valley*. 3 vols. New York: Lewis Historical Publishing, 1961.

McWilliams, Carey. *California: The Great Exception*. New York: Current Books, 1949.

Muscatine, Doris. *Old San Francisco: The Biography of a City*. New York: Putnam, 1975.

Ostrander, Gilman M. *Nevada: The Great Rotten Borough, 1859–1964*. New York: Alfred A. Knopf, 1966.

Soulé, Frank, John H. Gihon, and James Nisbet. *The Annals of San Francisco*. New York: D. Appleton, 1855.

Young, John P. *San Francisco: the Pacific Coast Metropolis*. 2 vols. San Francisco: S. J. Clarke, 1912.

Index

DATE DUE